Making Sense of Cybersecurity

Making Sense of Cybersecurity

THOMAS KRANZ

Foreword by NAZ MARKUTA

MANNING

SHELTER ISLAND

For online information and ordering of this and other Manning books, please visit
www.manning.com. The publisher offers discounts on this book when ordered in quantity.
For more information, please contact

> Special Sales Department
> Manning Publications Co.
> 20 Baldwin Road
> PO Box 761
> Shelter Island, NY 11964
> Email: orders@manning.com

 Manning Publications Co.
20 Baldwin Road
PO Box 761
Shelter Island, NY 11964

Development editor:	Doug Rudder
Technical development editor:	Tanya Wilke
Review editors:	Ivan Martinović, Adriana Sabo
Production editor:	Kathleen Rossland
Copy editor:	Michele Mitchell
Proofreader:	Melody Dolab
Technical proofreader:	Alain Couniot
Typesetter:	Dennis Dalinnik
Cover designer:	Marija Tudor

ISBN: 9781617298004
Printed in the United States of America

For Emms, who made it all possible.

brief contents

contents

foreword

As a cybersecurity researcher, it's my job to try to understand how a specific technology works, try to find ways to break it, and find ways to fix it or prevent attacks from happening. Even before starting my professional career, I was involved in various hacking activities or "hobbies," some of which were not legal and came with consequences.

I first met the author, Tom Kranz, in London during my first face-to-face interview with a consulting company. He eventually became my line manager. Tom has a way of simplifying complex problems into bite-sized chunks, making them easier to digest and implement.

When it comes to technology and cybersecurity, most people don't really think about how things work; they only care that it works. This lack of diligent preparation makes it almost impossible to keep information secure and opens the door for security breaches. *Making Sense of Cybersecurity* guides readers through what it takes to identify real-world threats and create strategies to combat them.

Understanding how attackers think and act, knowing what to protect, and devising defenses against attacks are vital to protecting our data, assets, and businesses. This book provides a great introduction to the fascinating (and entertaining) world of cybersecurity.

—Naz Markuta
Cybersecurity Researcher

preface

I started out in the 80s as a 10-year-old armed with a BBC Micro, a modem, and illicit access to British Telecom's Prestel system. The tools have changed since then, but not much else has.

Technology has always fascinated me since those early days in the home computing revolution. My summer job turned into full-time employment as a PC and network support engineer back in the heady days of Novell Netware and Lotus cc:Mail. Finding out how stuff worked was difficult: you had to pay a lot of money to get technical manuals, and even more money to license the software. Hunting on bulletin board systems (BBSs) and early FTP sites for text files and trading with other knowledge-starved acolytes became a way of life. Stumbling on Phrack and 2600 ezines was a revelation.

I spent most of the late 90s building, protecting, and breaking into SUN Microsystems and Silicon Graphics UNIX systems, getting involved in the fledgling internet and high-end, high-performance computing. I deployed early intrusion detection systems (IDSs) to protect the systems I'd designed and built from people like me, and Marcus J. Ranum (firewall and security guru) scared the hell out of me by calling out of the blue from the US to see what I thought of his Network Flight Recorder product.

I've always gone where the technology was cool, the people fun, and the problems tough. Consequently, I've been involved in some amazing things: a stint at Lucent Labs in the UK was fascinating (getting an email from Dennis Ritchie was like getting a benediction from the Pope), working at various gambling start-ups was hilarious, and I've been able to do cool things like design and build a fault-tolerant system that was used daily by a third of the UK population.

The emergence of PDAs, and then mobile phones, was a real game-changer. War dialing with a Palm III PDA and modem, tucked into the false ceiling of an office, soon led to usable, powerful, portable computing from Nokia's Communicator phones.

The technology has improved in leaps and bounds, even if the innovative giants that got us here are no longer with us. I saved up £100 to buy a 32 MB—yes, that's megabytes—memory expansion I had to hand-solder for my BBC Micro. And my mobile phone now has a 512 GB memory card that's the size of my fingernail.

At the same time, the fundamentals—the basics of what makes everything around us work—have been abstracted and hidden. While computers have become easier to use, they've been deliberately made more difficult to understand. And that's a problem, because the security issues we had almost 40 years ago (weak passwords, badly written software, poorly protected systems) are still present today.

I've enjoyed a long and endlessly entertaining career building interesting things, breaking them, and then trying to protect them from someone else breaking them. That's been distilled down into the book you're now reading, and I hope you have as much fun learning about this as I did.

acknowledgments

Writing a book is a great deal of hard work, and not just for me. An amazing group of people have helped behind the scenes to produce this fabulous tome you now read.

Thanks to Emma, who has been patient and supportive while I've been putting this book together.

Mick Sheppard, Steve Cargill, Jeff Dunham, Naz Markuta, and Orson Mosley have been bad and good influences in equal measures, as good friends should be. Thank you for putting up with my antics over the years; I wouldn't be where I am today without you all.

The team at Manning deserves a special mention: Mike Stephens, for taking on a book that was a bit different; and Deborah Bailey, Heidi Nobles, and Doug Rudder have been tireless, patient, and enormously helpful and supportive editors. I'm glad I was able to give you a few laughs as the book took shape. A special thanks to Naz Markuta for kindly writing the foreword and to Alain Couniot for his thorough (and thoroughly helpful) technical proofreading. Behind them stands the rest of the Manning team, without whom you wouldn't be reading this now; they have all been amazing.

I'd also like to thank the reviewers who took the time to read my manuscript at various stages during its development and who provided invaluable feedback: Alex Saez, Amit Lamba, Andi Schabus, Chad Davis, Craig Smith, Deniz Vehbi, Derek Hampton, Desmond Horsley, Deshuang Tang, Eric Cantuba, Ethien Daniel Salinas Domínguez, Fernando Bernardino, Frankie Thomas-Hockey, George Onofrei, Gustavo Velasco-Hernandez, Henrik Kramselund Jereminsen, Hilde Van Gysel, Hugo Sousa, Iyabo Sindiku, Jean-Baptiste Bang Nteme, Jens Hansen, Josiah Dykstra, Karthikeyarajan

Rajendran, Leonardo Anastasia, Mikael Byström, Milorad Imbra, Najeeb Arif, Neil Croll, Peter Sellars, Pethuru Raj, Pierluigi Riti, Ranjit Sahai, Ravi Prakash Giri, Roman Zhuzha, Ron Cranston, Satej Sahu, Scott Hurst, Stanley Anozie, Sujith Surendranathan, Sune Lomholt, Thomas Fischer, Veena Garapaty, William Mitchell, and Zoheb Ainapore.

Lastly, a big shout out to the groups, personalities, heroes, and villains of the hacking scene, from its formative years in the 80s to the industry-defining juggernaut it has now become. We've lost some things, gained some others, but security will always have its rough edges—and that's the way it should be.

about this book

Making Sense of Cybersecurity was written to demystify cybersecurity for you. It begins by focusing on the attackers: how they think, their motivations, and their most common and popular attacks. The second half deals with the defenders: armed with the knowledge of how the attackers work, you'll learn the best approaches to successful defense and how to recover from the inevitable breach.

Who should read this book

Making Sense of Cybersecurity is for anyone who is interested in learning more about cybersecurity but doesn't necessarily have a security or technology background. While there are a number of excellent books aimed at experienced cybersecurity professionals, this book brings together foundational concepts for the attack, defense, and management of cybersecurity in a clear, easy-to-read style that will benefit project managers, developers, team leads, and managers interested in knowing more about cybersecurity.

How this book is organized: A roadmap

The first two chapters of the book introduce core concepts about cybersecurity, strategies, and vulnerabilities. Then the book is divided into two sections, covering 10 chapters. Part 1 covers how to think like the bad guys, explaining their motivations and methods:

- Chapter 3 discusses the different classifications of hackers in the industry, as well as their motivations and mindsets, with some examples of (in)famous figures from across the spectrum.

- Chapter 4 describes the most common external attacks, from data injection and malware to dodgy Wi-Fi and mobile networks.
- Chapter 5 continues the theme of how attacks work by diving into social engineering.
- Chapter 6 then looks at the other side of the coin: what attackers do once they are inside your organization and how to spot and deal with inside attackers.
- Chapter 7 wraps up part 1 by looking at where attackers go to sell and trade their illicit data hauls: the Dark Web.

Part 2 explains how to think like the good guys and looks at building out successful defenses against the attacks from part 1:

- Chapter 8 dives into a commonly misunderstood but important area of cybersecurity: risk management.
- Chapter 9 discusses how to test your own systems and discover vulnerabilities, covering penetration testing, bug bounty programs, and dedicated hacking teams.
- Chapter 10 builds on chapters 8 and 9 by describing how security operations work, covering the key areas of monitoring, alerting, and incident response.
- Chapter 11 describes how to protect our most valuable asset—and biggest danger—our people.
- Chapter 12 ends the book by looking at what to do after the inevitable hack: how to recover, whom to get help from, and how to improve for the next attack.

While you can dip in and out of chapters based on interest, you'll get the most out of the book by reading part 1 first. Understanding how attackers think and how their most successful and common attacks work is a prerequisite to being able to build out effective defenses. Part 2 can then be tackled in any order, based on the reader's particular needs.

liveBook discussion forum

Purchase of *Making Sense of Cybersecurity* includes free access to liveBook, Manning's online reading platform. Using liveBook's exclusive discussion features, you can attach comments to the book globally or to specific sections or paragraphs. It's easy to make notes for yourself, ask and answer technical questions, and receive help from the author and other users. To access the forum, go to https://livebook.manning.com/book/making-sense-of-cybersecurity/discussion. You can also learn more about Manning's forums and the rules of conduct at https://livebook.manning.com/discussion.

Manning's commitment to our readers is to provide a venue where a meaningful dialogue between individual readers and between readers and the author can take place. It is not a commitment to any specific amount of participation on the part of the author, whose contribution to the forum remains voluntary (and unpaid). We suggest you try asking the author some challenging questions lest his interest stray! The forum and the archives of previous discussions will be accessible from the publisher's website as long as the book is in print.

about the author

TOM KRANZ is a cybersecurity consultant who helps organizations understand and address cybersecurity threats and issues. Tom's career has spanned 30 years as a cybersecurity and IT consultant. After a successful career helping UK government departments and private-sector clients (including Betfair, Accenture, Sainsburys, Fidelity International, and Toyota), Tom now advises and supports organizations on their cybersecurity strategy and challenges.

Tom lives with his partner in Italy, where they rehabilitate their collection of rescue dogs and cats, as well as manage their many opinionated ducks, some angry goats, and a cuddly wild boar.

about the cover illustration

The figure on the cover of *Making Sense of Cybersecurity* is "Bavarois," or "Bavarian," from a collection by Jacques Grasset de Saint-Sauveur, published in 1788. Each illustration is finely drawn and colored by hand.

In those days, it was easy to identify where people lived and what their trade or station in life was just by their dress. Manning celebrates the inventiveness and initiative of the computer business with book covers based on the rich diversity of regional culture centuries ago, brought back to life by pictures from collections such as this one.

Cybersecurity and hackers

Warwick Castle, in England, sits on a cliff overlooking the river Avon, in rural Warwickshire. Built by William the Conqueror in 1068, it's been updated and enlarged over the centuries.

Castles have a simple job: to serve as obvious, strong defenses, protecting valuable assets. Giant stone purses, castles also naturally became centers of commerce, meeting places for merchants and decision makers—places of power and wealth.

The problem is that a castle is not subtle; a castle is a giant marker saying, "Here's where the good stuff is!" The defenders have to be constantly vigilant, and attacks can come from anywhere and at any time. You can't just move your castle to a new location after it's been attacked a few times.

The defenders have to be successful every single time. One failure on their part means the castle falls. Attackers, on the other hand, can try as many times as possible to get in; they just need to be successful once.

This constant vigilance defines cybersecurity. Our businesses are online around the clock, with valuable assets (data) used for commerce, communication, and decision making.

Warwick Castle changed radically over the years in response to new methods of attack. As attackers tried digging under the walls, lighting the castle on fire, chucking big rocks at it, and blasting it with cannons, the castle was changed and updated to continue protecting its occupants and their assets.

This determined adaptability is key to developing a cybersecurity strategy. We work out who attacks us and how, and then change our defenses to keep us secure.

There is no such thing as perfect security; there is only better security. Warwick Castle survived because the occupants were constantly refining it to provide better security. This book will teach the mindset and techniques we need to build our own Warwick Castles, helping us defend against the new types of attackers we face.

1.1 Cybersecurity: How it has evolved

In the 80s, a film called *WarGames* first brought hacking to the attention of the general public. Back then, many systems didn't have passwords and could be directly accessed via the phone line using a modem. In the UK, Robert Schifreen and Stephen Gold demonstrated how easy it was to break into a national system called Prestel, leading to the introduction of the 1990 Computer Misuse Act.

In the United States, in the middle of increasing Cold War hysteria, *WarGames* prompted authorities to sit up and take notice. Hackers were headlines, laws were passed, systems were locked down, and hackers started going to jail. Bruce Sterling's book *The Hacker Crackdown* is an excellent and entertaining account of those exciting times.

We've moved on from *WarGames* and the threat of a hacker starting nuclear war. Stealing money and information remains as popular as it was back then, but now attackers can control cars and interfere with and damage industrial systems, and rogue tweets can tank the stock market.

As computers and technology have become more complex and embedded in more aspects of our lives, the threats from poor cybersecurity have changed as well.

The one constant truth is that everyone will be hacked at some point. There is no such thing as perfect security, and it is impossible to be completely secure. How many of these incidents have you read about, or experienced yourself?

- Bogus charges on our credit cards
- Accidentally getting a virus on our computer from downloaded software or music
- Having to freeze an account and get a new card from the bank after our card details were stolen in a big data breach

But how much worse can hacks get?

Let's look at an example that had a real financial impact. How about crashing the stock market with false information? Back in 2013, Syrian hackers managed to gain control of the Associated Press's Twitter account. The hackers tweeted that the US president, Barack Obama, had been injured in an explosion at the White House—shocking news that was seen by the AP account's 2 million followers, and retweeted over 1,500 times. The markets reacted immediately, with the Dow crashing 150 points, wiping out $136 billion in equity market value. The impact was short lived, however; it took less than 10 minutes for a retraction and confirmation that it was a hoax. Once the tweet was confirmed as bogus, the Dow recovered back to its original position.

How about something really fun, such as remotely taking control of a car? Back in 2015, researchers Charlie Miller and Chris Valasek did exactly this with a Jeep Cherokee. They found a vulnerability in the Jeep's entertainment software and were able to come up with a way to remotely take control of the car's various computers and systems. Famously, they brought the car to a complete halt on the highway, with *Wired* journalist Andy Greenberg inside, frantically flooring the accelerator pedal to try and keep speed up. Fiat Chrysler Automobiles (FCA, the owner of Jeep at the time) quickly developed a patch and issued a recall notice.

The following year, at the Black Hat security conference in Las Vegas, Miller and Valasek showed how they could now control the steering and brakes as well. This time they needed a laptop that was physically in the car and connected; but now, with the tiny size of computers, it would be possible to hide a miniature computer in a compromised car and remotely control it.

These examples seem like they've come straight out of an outrageous Hollywood hacking film like *Swordfish*, but they're just examples of people trying to get computers to do something unexpected. No matter how good our security is, we will all struggle in the face of a determined, hostile nation's hacking teams.

What good cybersecurity can do, though, is give you a better chance to defend against the easy, common attacks, to make it more difficult for hackers to get in, to make it easier to spot them once they're in, and to make it easier for you to recover.

1.2 Why should you care about cybersecurity?

Today, everyone—*everyone*—will get hacked. Defense is hard, as the various inhabitants of Warwick Castle found over the centuries. Larger, more grandiose castles fell, but Warwick survived.

As technology becomes more deeply embedded in our lives, it becomes both more complex and more hidden. We carry around mobile phones with the computing power and complexity of supercomputers from less than 20 years ago. The batteries we use in our laptops have processors in them and run their own software.

Our cars are complex networks of computers, with most of the major functions—engine management, braking, even putting the power down on the road—controlled by computers (even my old Fiat Panda 4x4 has a few computers hidden away). Technology controls and manages all aspects of our personal and professional lives: our employment history, our finances, our communications, our governments.

Like the defenders of Warwick Castle, we cannot defend ourselves and the things we value unless we understand how the attackers work. How can our technology be abused? Where is it unsafe? Is that relevant to me personally? Will it affect my job, my project, my company?

Nothing is perfectly secure, but armed with this knowledge, we can provide ourselves with better security to better protect ourselves.

1.3   Who is the ideal reader for this book?

You don't have to be involved in cybersecurity, have any security knowledge, or even work in IT. You've read about security breaches, hacking, and cybersecurity in the mainstream press. You've read—and seen—that bad people are doing scary things with technology.

How much of that is hype, made up for the headlines and the article clicks? Can hackers really do all that? How can they be stopped? What if it happens to me?

You want to understand the real-world threats to you and your work and what you can do to protect yourself, your code, your project, and your business.

Team leaders, project managers, executives, and developers—if you work with or are affected by IT and computers—then cybersecurity, understanding how and why hackers work, is going to be important to you.

1.4   How does hacking—and defending—work?

Obviously, the detailed work of cybersecurity can be technical and complex; cybersecurity is a very wide field, and we have entire teams of experts working together to manage our defenses. We'll talk about the specifics throughout this book so that you'll have a working understanding of what these teams are working on and why. But to understand how attackers and defenders think, the best way to approach cybersecurity is to use a process called the OODA loop.

The OODA (Observe, Orient, Decide, Act) loop was developed by a clever chap named John Boyd in the US Airforce. He was tasked with working out why US Airforce pilots were losing dogfights, despite having superior technology and better training, and this is what he came up with (figure 1.1).

The OODA loop is a powerful tool to help us. We don't have to be dogfighting with enemy jets; we can be defending against a hack attack, and the process remains the same.

I was working for a large financial services organization when we came under attack. Thousands of computers around the world were sending requests to the web servers, asking for random pages from a trading website. Normally, the organization would see a few thousand requests per minute—and their infrastructure was built to cope with that load. What I was seeing, though, was hundreds of thousands of requests

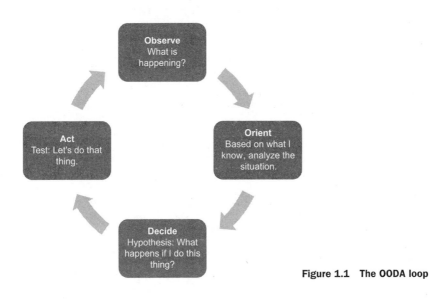

Figure 1.1   The OODA loop

a minute. Their website kept crashing under the load, and no website, no trading. This was costing them money.

Once I had an idea of what was happening, I had a crisis meeting with the heads of the various IT teams. We needed to work out how to respond in order to stop, or at least slow down, the attack.

This is where the OODA loop came in handy. Here's the thought process used (figure 1.2).

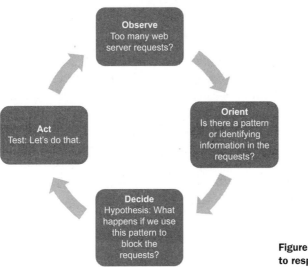

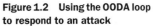

Figure 1.2   Using the OODA loop
to respond to an attack

Breaking it down into more detail:

- *Observe*—The volume of random web server requests is overwhelming the web servers and they are crashing.
- *Orient*—Is there a pattern to the requests? Do the requests themselves have any common identifying information?
- *Decide*—Can we configure our firewalls to spot these requests and then block them?
- *Act*—Let's set a timeframe for analysis of the attacks (in this case, an hour), and if that's successful, then another timeframe for changing the firewall configuration.

Using the OODA loop in this way gives us a quick and easy way to understand what is happening, respond, and then reevaluate.

In this case, the requests were all being logged on the web servers. I found that each request contained a specific string of text left there by the automated tool that attackers were using to launch the attack. The network team then reconfigured the firewalls to block any request that contained that text pattern.

This took less than 45 minutes, and once the firewalls were updated, the attacks were stopped successfully. This gave the teams breathing space to restart the crashed web servers and fix other bits of infrastructure that had crashed as well. Now that we knew what to look for, I was able to share that information with the hosting company that provided our connectivity. They were able to block all of those malicious requests from entering any of their networks and reported back that after a few hours, the attackers had given up and turned off the attack.

Good, effective cybersecurity is all about using the OODA loop and its feedback to improve our defenses in a relevant, proportional way.

1.5   *What will you learn in this book?*

Hacking is a mindset, a way of looking at things and wondering "What happens if I do this?" Like technology, hacking is neither bad nor good; the techniques we use for breaking into a system are the same ones we need to know in order to protect that system.

Robert Morris was a student at Cornell University in 1988. He wanted to write a program that would check other computers on the network for a handful of known security flaws in common services. This sort of program was called a worm—it would infect one system, then springboard from there to another, and another. Morris wrote the worm so that it would check to see if a system was already infected, but he was worried about mistakes, so he made one of his own—a big one. Randomly, the worm would infect a system, regardless of whether a copy was already running.

Morris's worm was hugely successful in mapping out how many systems had the security flaws—too successful. The worm rampaged across the internet, infecting tens of thousands of key computers. Worse still, because of Morris's programming error, multiple copies of the worm kept re-infecting these computers, slowing them to a crawl.

The internet was much smaller back then, and having to shut down large chunks of it for days while systems were patched and disinfected caused a huge disruption. Morris was swiftly arrested, and after appeal received 400 hours of community service and a $10,050 fine. The Government Accountability Office in the United States estimated the cost of cleaning up to run into millions of dollars.

The icing on the cake? Morris's dad was chief scientist at the National Computer Security Center, a division of the National Security Agency (NSA), the secretive US spy agency.

I'm going to show you how hackers think by using the most common, effective, and easy attacks that I see happening time and again, simple security flaws that are easily fixed—like the ones Morris exploited with his worm. Once we know how and why the attackers work, we can start to put in place relevant, proportional defenses, leveraging models like the OODA loop to make sure what we're doing is actually working.

What you'll learn is not just how to defend yourself against these common attacks, but also to build on that understanding to start thinking like a hacker. What if you were Robert Morris? How would you try to check the security of hundreds of computers on the network? Once you start thinking like a hacker, you can anticipate and defend against their attacks. That hacker mindset is the key skill that will help you improve your security everywhere. As the well-known security guru Yoda said, "Named must be your fear, before banish it you can."

1.6 What we won't cover

Cybersecurity is a broad and deep topic that covers everything from programming and hardware to behavioral analysis. There are a couple of common security topics that we deliberately won't cover, though.

1.6.1 Denial-of-service attacks

Denial of service (DoS) and distributed denial of service (DDoS) attacks are types of attacks that overwhelm a server with requests until it is unable to respond. A DoS attack uses a handful of machines to overwhelm a server. A DDoS attack uses many thousands of compromised computers in the attack.

Think of how busy your favorite coffee shop gets. Imagine what happens if I ask 50, 100, or even 200 people to show up and try to order coffee. You wouldn't be able to even get in, let alone order a decent espresso. This is what a DoS attack is.

Although they used to be popular, with most people migrating their services to the cloud, DoS attacks are becoming less successful. Internet service providers (ISPs) and cloud service providers (CSPs) have also invested heavily in technology that mitigates the effects of a DoS attack.

Thanks to this, we're seeing far fewer DoS attacks, and their relevance and impact is waning. As these attacks are dealt with by cloud providers and ISPs, there's not much we can do about them, so we'll pass over DoS attacks.

1.6.2 *Encryption*

Encryption is the process of taking data, converting it to meaningless numbers and letters to secure it, and then converting this back to meaningful data.

We hear a lot about encryption for online banking and instant messaging. Let's quickly look at how encryption is used for a banking app in your phone in figure 1.3.

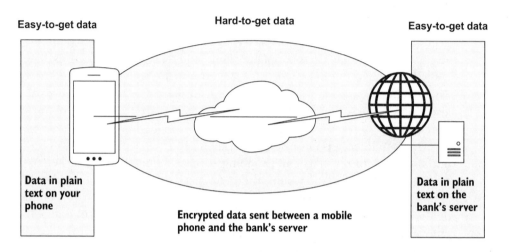

Figure 1.3   How encryption is used to protect transmitted data in a mobile banking application. Note that, at some point, the sensitive data at both ends must be unencrypted.

Your data—your bank details, account balance, and so on—is in clear text on your phone. Then, your banking app encrypts the data to transfer it to the bank's application servers. Once there, the data is decrypted—turned back into plain text.

Encryption is a well-understood and mature technology. For decades, it's been good enough to defeat attempts to break it by state actors and well-funded adversaries, and it's constantly being refined and improved in the face of these attacks.

As an attacker, it's much easier and quicker for me to try and attack your phone or the bank's servers than it is to try and attack the encryption mechanism. The data is in plain text on your phone and on the server, and that's much easier to try and grab.

There is already a host of excellent books out there that specialize in understanding encryption and cryptographic attacks, but that is an advanced topic with an extra-heavy serving of complex mathematics. This book is focused on the most common attacks, so we'll skip encryption. But later on, in chapter 5, we'll look at encryption's close cousin—hashing—as a way of protecting and securing passwords and credentials.

If you're interested in learning more about encryption and the complex mathematics behind it, I can highly recommend reading *Cryptography Engineering* by Bruce Schneier et al. (Wiley, 2010) and *Applied Cryptography*, also by Bruce Schneier (Wiley, 2015).

1.7   *What tools do you need to get started?*

You need a computer, an internet connection, and a curious mind. It doesn't get much easier than that.

Later on in the book, I'll show you how to download and install tools to access the Dark Web, and we'll take a look at some nifty, inexpensive hardware to protect against USB attacks. Let's get started!

Summary

- Threats from poor cybersecurity have increased as computers and technology have become more complex and integrated into our lives.
- Good cybersecurity can provide a better chance of defending against common attacks, make it more difficult for hackers to succeed, make it easier to identify when they're in, and help you recover from an attack.
- The OODA loop provides a powerful method to defend against attacks.
- Effective cybersecurity entails using the OODA loop and the feedback gained from it to enhance our defenses in a relevant, proportional, and sustainable way.

Cybersecurity: Everyone's problem

2

This chapter covers

- Developing a list of organizational assets that hackers might target
- Building a profile of potential attackers based on your assets
- Evaluating your existing defenses
- Using the three pillars of a successful cybersecurity strategy (relevant, proportional, and sustainable)
- Using CVE details and CVSS to understand and prioritize newly discovered security issues

Everyone will get hacked. No matter how great your defenses are or how well prepared you are, it's a matter of *when*, not *if*. It happens to us all. Companies can spend millions of dollars on security tools and technologies and still end up in the news for a massive data breach. The important thing, then, is to be prepared for the hack and be able to respond and recover quickly. I want to help you achieve this through better security, and this chapter is all about understanding and building the fundamental skills and concepts you'll need.

10

In chapter 1, we walked through some real-world impacts of a security breach. Now we'll look at what underpins a successful cybersecurity strategy and what its objectives should be. Building on that, we'll learn how to communicate, measure, and patch vulnerabilities, which will then feed into sustaining a culture of security in your organization. Finally, we'll finish up by working through an exercise to see how prepared you are and how to start building your own security strategy.

By the end of this chapter, you'll be able to use these skills to assess your security, as well as the security of your project, team, or even entire company.

2.1 Keeping it simple

There's a lot of fluff out there, and entire companies are devoted to not only selling a security framework, but then selling you consultancy to understand and use it, the classic "steal your watch to tell the time" consultant approach. I worked with a client who was undertaking a billion-dollar modernization project, where a team of consultants was trying to sell the program leadership on a strategy revolving around equations to measure risks. They weren't making much progress. I left behind algebra at school, and I can't think of anyone who'd want to revisit it when dealing with hacking and digital transformation.

We can cut through the noise, though, and boil everything down to the three factors of cybersecurity (see figure 2.1).

Figure 2.1   Three factors of cybersecurity. These three questions—and their answers—are the cornerstone of any successful cybersecurity strategy.

These three factors are the simplest and fastest way to understand your current situation:

- *What assets do you have?* What valuables do you have that you want to protect? Customer data? Source code? Confidential business data?
- *Who would want to attack you?* This builds on the first question—who would want to steal your assets? Why would they want to take them, and what would they do with them?
- *What defenses do you have?* Now that we have a good idea of what we want to protect and from whom, we need to look at what things we already have in place to protect them. Are we using antivirus software? Do we have firewalls to filter malicious data? Do we have a dedicated security team protecting our IT? Are we using unique passwords on our different accounts?

Each of the three factors builds on the previous one. As we work our way around the loop, answering each question, we build up a picture of what we need to protect and where the gaps are in that protection.

Let's walk through two large-scale data breaches from the last few years and see how we can apply these three factors to model and understand the two very different responses to these attacks.

2.2   *Impacts of a security breach*

Having a sensible security strategy makes the difference between being devastated by a hack or moving on from just another business disruption. In 2017, Equifax (the credit scoring and reporting company) came clean about a data breach they had suffered some months earlier.

The data that was stolen was pretty comprehensive: 146 million names, birth dates, and social security numbers; 99 million addresses; 209,000 payment card details; 38,000 drivers' licenses; and 3,200 passports—a field day for identity thieves, from a company that sells, among other things, identity theft protection.

The root cause was a vulnerability in the Apache Struts software framework that some of Equifax's applications used. The vulnerability—and its patch—were disclosed in March 2017. Equifax failed to fix the problem and was breached in July of that year. Although they first noticed it and announced the breach in September 2017, they didn't know the full extent of the data that had been taken until much later.

Equifax's problem wasn't just with a software vulnerability in Apache Struts; what also helped the hackers was an insecure network design, inadequate encryption of personally identifiable information, and an ineffective ability to detect the data breach. Not only did this make it easier for the hackers to get in, it also meant that Equifax took almost a year—with outside help—to discover the full impact of the breach. They literally didn't know what the hackers had taken.

The fallout for Equifax was severe. For months after the announcement, their systems kept crashing due to the volume of people trying to log on to check and freeze their credit files.

The US Federal Trade Commission (FTC) agreed to a settlement in 2019 with Equifax after a raft of lawsuits against the company. Equifax ultimately ended up paying $300 million to a fund for victim compensation, $175 million to the US states and territories in the FTC agreement, and $100 million to the Consumer Financial Protection Bureau (CFPB).

In December 2018, Quora—the "question and answer" website—suffered a data breach. Almost 100 million user accounts had their information taken, which included users' names, email addresses, encrypted passwords, questions they had asked, and answers they had written.

The breach happened on a Friday, and on Monday, Quora issued a statement to the press and all users detailing the full extent of the breach. They confirmed password information was secure, as it had been encrypted, but enforced a site-wide password reset for users just to be safe.

The insecure database server that was the cause of the breach had been patched and secured by the time of Monday's announcement. By May 2019, Quora was valued at $2 billion as a company and was finalizing a $60 million investment round.

Two huge headline-making hacks, with similar amounts of data, and two very different outcomes. The Equifax saga is still dragging on, and they have had to pay $575 million in financial penalties, while Quora continues to gain users and revenue. Why the disparity? Let's revisit our three factors of cybersecurity (see figure 2.2).

We can use this model to compare Equifax and Quora, without giving away too many details of their internal systems and processes (see table 2.1).

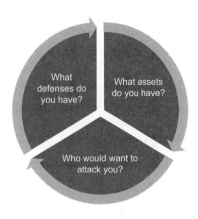

Figure 2.2   Three factors of cybersecurity

Table 2.1   Applying the three factors to Equifax and Quora

	Equifax	Quora
What assets do you have?	User data User financial data No clear idea what was stored where, or how it was accessed	User data Clearly understood where it was held and how it could be accessed
Who would want to attack you?	Identity thieves Criminal gangs	Identity thieves
What defenses do you have?	Monitoring (not configured correctly or regularly tested) Segregated networks (not configured correctly or regularly tested) A patch management policy and testing tool set that wasn't used	Tested, effective monitoring Segregated networks and systems Patch management and testing policy that was used and regularly reviewed

Equifax had thought about how to protect their assets—their data and systems—many years ago. Things had changed and had been updated since then, but Equifax didn't review them or revisit their assumptions and processes. They didn't regularly test and review their tools and processes and didn't find out that they didn't work until after the data breach.

Quora had thought about how to protect their assets, their data and systems. They also regularly tested and reviewed their tools and processes.

During the time it took Equifax to find out the full details of the breach, their systems were intermittently unavailable, and Equifax couldn't tell if those system outages were due to extreme load or further hacks until many months later.

Quora took a weekend to understand the full details of their breach, and the impact was limited because unlike Equifax, Quora had built an effective cybersecurity strategy based on a good understanding of what they had and what they needed to protect. In the next section, I'll show you how you can do that too.

2.3   *Objectives of a cybersecurity strategy*

Cybersecurity strategies define an organization's approach to security and how to improve it. Too often, they focus on technology solutions, because it seems easier to buy a solution to a problem rather than investigate the core, root causes. Understanding what your business has that is valuable to others and who might want to attack you to steal that information is often overlooked.

Our cybersecurity strategy tells everyone, "This is what we're doing to make things more secure"; it defines a direction of travel toward your goal of *better security* (see figure 2.3). Your policies—for example, how you should patch vulnerable systems—are driven by your strategy and help you get to your goal of better security.

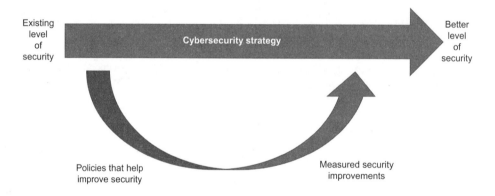

Figure 2.3   How a cybersecurity strategy helps to improve your security. The strategy helps you generate policies that address specific security issues and improve your level of security.

Cybersecurity people love their acronyms, which is part of why the whole field can seem complex and difficult to understand. Two of the main acronyms the security industry uses when talking about strategy are as follows:

- *PPT: people, process, and technology*—This is the ideal order in which a company should tackle their cybersecurity issues. First, train people or hire more. Second, look at (and fix) processes. Third, and finally, invest in suitable technology.
- *The CIA triad*—This refers to the three main objectives of cybersecurity: to ensure the **c**onfidentiality, **i**ntegrity, and **a**vailability of data and systems.

These are both great approaches, and they absolutely have a place in every organization. The problem with them both is that they assume you have complete knowledge of who would attack you, what they would steal, and how they could attack you. Both should be used to improve and expand on your cybersecurity strategy, but they don't help if you're starting completely from scratch.

We're going to look at the core concepts we need to build a strategy from the beginning, ensuring we build a security strategy that is

- Relevant
- Proportional
- Sustainable

Combining these core concepts with the three factors of cybersecurity will enable us to build a security strategy that is focused on the specific risks we are facing. This is called a *risk-based strategy* and is the most effective way to create a security strategy that will have a positive impact (see figure 2.4).

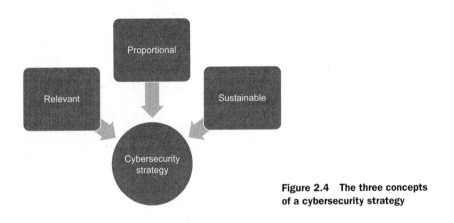

Figure 2.4   The three concepts of a cybersecurity strategy

Let's look these three concepts in more detail:

- *Relevant*—Any strategy needs to be relevant to your organization, your needs, and the threats you face. If you're a 200-person software house, trying to use a strategy designed for a global bank will fail. There is no one-size-fits-all.
- *Proportional*—The defenses you build and the technologies you use to protect your organization need to be proportional to the size of your organization and the threat you face. A 200-person software house will have a hard time spending tens of millions on a security system designed to defeat a hostile nation's spies. Equally, the NSA won't be using freeware antivirus software on their laptops!
- *Sustainable*—Sustainability is the key factor for ensuring that your strategy actually gets implemented. If you're planning to plug in solutions that need four times your existing head count to manage and that cost your entire budget, your organization won't be able to sustain them.

2.3.1 Applying what we've learned so far

Let's look at a fairly typical scenario for a medium-sized business. We have two main systems: an e-commerce website and an HR payroll system.

The HR payroll system has financial details of all our company's employees. It's an old system that has a number of known vulnerabilities, but it needs internet access, so we've put it behind a firewall to protect it from incoming malicious data. Only the HR team can access this system.

We also have a new e-commerce website that allows customers to buy models of Warwick Castle from us. This is completely separate from the HR system and has been developed from the ground up by a team using secure coding principles. The system is very secure, but as extra protection, it's also behind a firewall to stop malicious incoming data. The development team has admin access to the system.

EXERCISE 1: CONSIDERING THE THREE FACTORS OF CYBERSECURITY

Let's work through the three factors of the cybersecurity model (figure 2.5), listing our answers to each factor:

- *What assets do we have?* Think about what is valuable to the company. What would an attacker want to steal?
- *Who would want to attack us?* Based on the type of assets we have, who would want to steal them? If someone was going to commit fraud, for example, what would they need?
- *What defenses do we have?* Are there any technologies the company has that protect their systems? What is the company using to block any malicious attacks?

Figure 2.5   Our three factors of cybersecurity model

The key in each of these steps is to carefully think about what data each system holds and would find that data valuable. There are no right or wrong answers; everyone will have a slightly different view. Working through this exercise helps you explore how to map out these factors in a way that makes sense to you. You can compare your answers to mine.

ANSWERS

- What assets do we have?
  - *HR payroll system*—Old, lots of vulnerabilities
  - *E-commerce website*—New, securely developed
- Who would want to attack us?
  - *Disgruntled ex-employees*—Low threat
  - *Financial fraudsters*—Medium threat

- *Identity thieves*—Medium threat
- *Financial fraudsters*—Medium threat
- *Criminal organizations*—High threat
- What defenses do we have?
  - *A firewall*—Limited admin access (the HR team)
  - *A firewall*—Limited admin access (the development team)

Now that we have a good understanding of where we are today, we can look at building a security strategy.

RELEVANT

The HR system has lots of vulnerabilities and holds sensitive financial data. The e-commerce site has been built securely and isn't at risk from attackers.

It makes sense to focus on protecting the HR system. We should probably look at either fixing the vulnerabilities or upgrading/replacing it with a newer system that is more secure.

We should also probably look at some sort of monitoring to see who is accessing the system and what data they are accessing. We can then build in some alerts in case someone outside the HR team tries to access it, and then expand the monitoring to include the firewall as well. Once that's in place and working properly, we can expand it to cover the e-commerce site and its firewall.

PROPORTIONAL

We don't know if any of our systems are under attack at the moment. We know financial fraudsters, identity thieves, and criminal gangs pose the greatest threat; they are the groups most likely to attack us.

At this stage, we don't need to buy a lot of expensive firewalls or identity and access management (IAM) software. Monitoring will help us understand if we're right about the sort of attackers we face, as well as how often (if at all) people are trying to get in.

We should, however, invest in some training for our two groups with admin access: the HR team and the development team. At this stage, the training just needs to be something basic:

- Don't share your logins.
- Don't allow other people access to the systems.
- Limit access to an important system to protect its data.
- Make sure the teams safeguard the assets; they are the ones with admin access, the guardians of these systems.

After this, we could also look at some simple vulnerability scanning software. We assume we know all the bugs in our two systems, but are we right? Regularly scanning them for vulnerabilities—either software bugs or misconfiguration—will ensure we continue to have a good idea about which systems need the most protection.

SUSTAINABLE

We need to regularly review our monitoring to check that our team's training is effective and that our initial ideas about who would want to attack us are still correct.

Is the level of monitoring getting too time-consuming to manage? If so, we will need to look at some automation to remove any false positives or incorrect alerts, and it's probably a good idea at that stage to start hiring some dedicated security staff to look after it.

If the e-commerce site is doing well, we should look at subscribing to a cyber threat intelligence feed. This will give us up-to-date information on existing and emerging threats; criminal gangs and identity thieves might be using new tools and techniques or targeting specific industries.

Putting all of this together allows us to build a roadmap—an easy-to-understand way of showing how we are going to improve our security. This is useful because it allows anyone to understand what is happening, to protect our organization, and to measure our progress. The roadmap also gives us an easy-to-understand timeline; we've used our model to identify the most pressing security issues, and our plan clearly shows that we will be addressing those first (see figure 2.6).

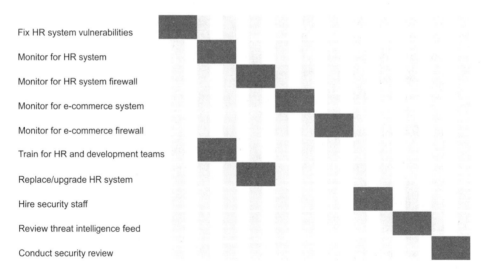

Figure 2.6   Our cybersecurity roadmap

Once we've completed the work we've identified, we can carry out a review to help feed all of this data back into our model. Monitoring and alerts now can be added to our list of defenses. Have any new systems or applications been added to the company? Do we have any new assets to protect? Are there new attackers who would target us?

By regularly reviewing our model, we can refine it and make it more sophisticated, without making it so complex as to be useless. This will never give us perfect security, but it will keep on giving us better security over time, keeping us ahead of the attackers.

2.4   Supporting our strategy: Building a patching policy

Once we know who would want to attack us and why, what assets we have, and if we have any existing defenses, we can then look at the first steps we can take to improve our security. Developing security policies gives us a way of fixing things, but also of measuring if they are broken. Going back to our overview of what a strategy is, we can see that we need policies to help us improve our overall level of security. The most common and effective security policy is one that deals with applying security patches (see figure 2.7).

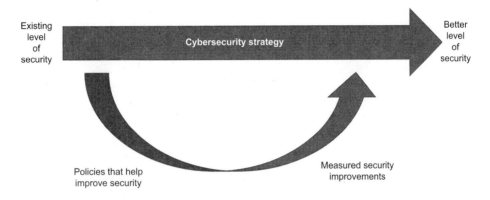

Figure 2.7   How security policies support our strategy and help us improve overall security

The easiest way to keep computers and software secure is to keep them patched. Hackers and vendors find new bugs all the time, and vendors regularly release patches to improve the security of software and hardware, so it's clear that a strategy for patching our systems should be a key part of delivering better security via our cybersecurity strategy.

The trick is working out which patches affect you and how important they are. With so many systems and software products in use today, patching can quickly become overwhelming. Where are the actual patches? How do you install them? What other systems could be affected?

All organizations these days have an internet firewall, often from Cisco. Back at the start of 2018, a flaw was found that allowed attackers to remotely execute code on Cisco's firewalls, their ASA line of products. Cisco contacted their customers with the information on the problem and the patches, and also put the details on their security site; the computing press was also full of articles about the problem.

But how do we know that we are all talking and reading about the same problem? How can we understand how the attack works and how serious it is?

That's why the industry came up with the Common Vulnerabilities and Exposures (CVE) system and the Common Vulnerability Scoring System (CVSS) score.

2.4.1   *CVEs are used to coordinate all information around a specific bug, and a CVSS score is used to rate how serious it is*

Let's look at how this helps us. In our problematic firewall case, Cisco was allocated the CVE of CVE-2018-0101. The National Vulnerability Database is run by NIST in the US and is where CVEs are published and stored. We can head over there to look up the Cisco CVE (http://mng.bz/yvEJ).

Instantly you can see how easy the CVE format is to read (see figures 2.8–2.11). We're shown the following:

- A high-level description of the problem
- The CVSS score to show how severe the problem is
- Links to third-party security advisories and even exploited code
- A list of the affected hardware and software versions

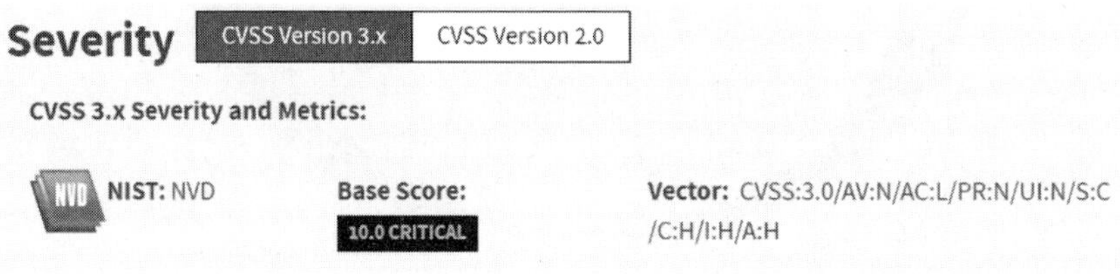

Severity CVSS Version 3.x   CVSS Version 2.0

CVSS 3.x Severity and Metrics:

NVD   **NIST:** NVD   **Base Score:**   **Vector:** CVSS:3.0/AV:N/AC:L/PR:N/UI:N/S:C
                            10.0 CRITICAL   /C:H/I:H/A:H

Figure 2.8   The CVE starts with the CVSS and associated criticality rating of the vulnerability, along with a summary of the attack vectors.

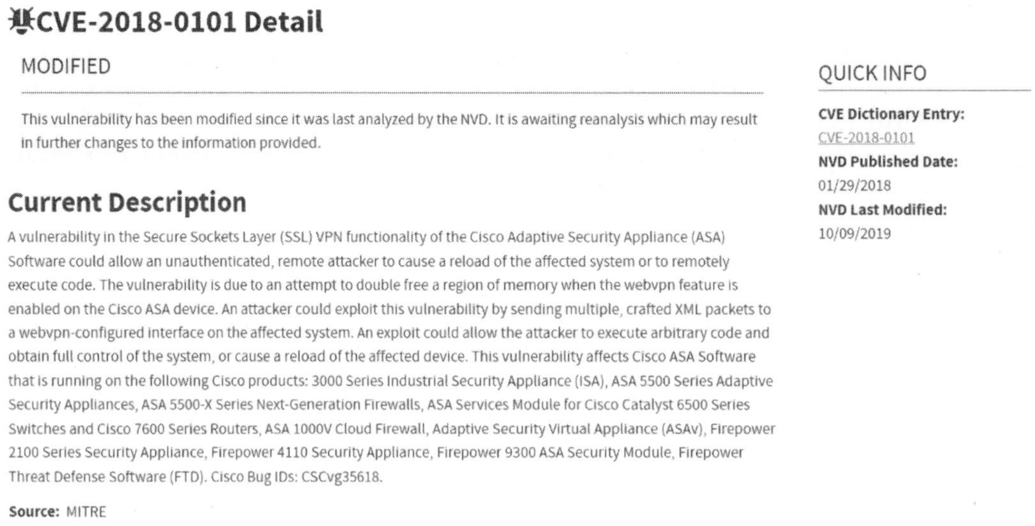

🦠CVE-2018-0101 Detail

MODIFIED
———

This vulnerability has been modified since it was last analyzed by the NVD. It is awaiting reanalysis which may result in further changes to the information provided.

Current Description

A vulnerability in the Secure Sockets Layer (SSL) VPN functionality of the Cisco Adaptive Security Appliance (ASA) Software could allow an unauthenticated, remote attacker to cause a reload of the affected system or to remotely execute code. The vulnerability is due to an attempt to double free a region of memory when the webvpn feature is enabled on the Cisco ASA device. An attacker could exploit this vulnerability by sending multiple, crafted XML packets to a webvpn-configured interface on the affected system. An exploit could allow the attacker to execute arbitrary code and obtain full control of the system, or cause a reload of the affected device. This vulnerability affects Cisco ASA Software that is running on the following Cisco products: 3000 Series Industrial Security Appliance (ISA), ASA 5500 Series Adaptive Security Appliances, ASA 5500-X Series Next-Generation Firewalls, ASA Services Module for Cisco Catalyst 6500 Series Switches and Cisco 7600 Series Routers, ASA 1000V Cloud Firewall, Adaptive Security Virtual Appliance (ASAv), Firepower 2100 Series Security Appliance, Firepower 4110 Security Appliance, Firepower 9300 ASA Security Module, Firepower Threat Defense Software (FTD). Cisco Bug IDs: CSCvg35618.

Source: MITRE

QUICK INFO

CVE Dictionary Entry:
CVE-2018-0101
NVD Published Date:
01/29/2018
NVD Last Modified:
10/09/2019

Figure 2.9   The next section of the CVE has a detailed description of the vulnerability, along with a note on any updates and modifications.

References to Advisories, Solutions, and Tools

By selecting these links, you will be leaving NIST webspace. We have provided these links to other web sites because they may have information that would be of interest to you. No inferences should be drawn on account of other sites being referenced, or not, from this page. There may be other web sites that are more appropriate for your purpose. NIST does not necessarily endorse the views expressed, or concur with the facts presented on these sites. Further, NIST does not endorse any commercial products that may be mentioned on these sites. Please address comments about this page to nvd@nist.gov.

Hyperlink	Resource
http://www.securityfocus.com/bid/102845	Third Party Advisory VDB Entry
http://www.securitytracker.com/id/1040292	Third Party Advisory VDB Entry
https://icanthackit.wordpress.com/2018/01/30/thoughts-on-the-handling-cve-2018-0101-cisco-bug-cscvg35618/	Third Party Advisory
https://pastebin.com/YrBcG2Ln	Exploit Third Party Advisory
https://tools.cisco.com/security/center/content/CiscoSecurityAdvisory/cisco-sa-20180129-asa1	Vendor Advisory
https://www.exploit-db.com/exploits/43986/	Exploit Third Party Advisory VDB Entry

Figure 2.10   The CVE then has links to third parties that have provided more detailed research into the vulnerability, any vendor security advisories, and links to any known exploit code.

Known Affected Software Configurations Switch to CPE 2.2

Configuration 1 (hide)

	Up to	
cpe:2.3:a:cisco:adaptive_security_appliance_software:*:*:*:*:*:*:*:* Show Matching CPE(s) ▾	(excluding) 9.1.7.23	
	From	Up to
cpe:2.3:a:cisco:adaptive_security_appliance_software:*:*:*:*:*:*:*:* Show Matching CPE(s) ▾	(including) 9.2.0	(excluding) 9.2.4.27
	From	Up to
cpe:2.3:a:cisco:adaptive_security_appliance_software:*:*:*:*:*:*:*:* Show Matching CPE(s) ▾	(including) 9.3.0	(excluding) 9.4.4.16
	From	Up to
cpe:2.3:a:cisco:adaptive_security_appliance_software:*:*:*:*:*:*:*:* Show Matching CPE(s) ▾	(including) 9.5.0	(excluding) 9.6.4.3

Figure 2.11   Lastly, the CVE has a list of affected hardware and software.

The CVSS score is worked out with some fairly complex calculations that dig into the type of vulnerability, how easy it is to exploit, whether you can do so remotely, and so on.

The good news is that we don't need to know any of that. A CVSS score goes from 1 to 10, where 1 is a minor annoyance and 10 is "OMG, patch it now or your world will end."

We can see straight away that the issue only affects Cisco's ASA firewall appliances and only those running specific versions of software. We can also see that the CVE has the highest, most critical CVSS score: 10. This is a bad one.

From this, we can see how to check whether we are vulnerable, and if we are, we need to apply the patches from Cisco immediately. We've also got some links to advisories from other organizations that contain further detail about the vulnerability, as well as links to some actual exploited code that will allow us to test whether our firewalls really are vulnerable and to check that they are fixed after we have patched them:

- CVEs give us an easy-to-understand and consistent way to communicate vulnerabilities.
- CVSS scores allow us to understand how severe these vulnerabilities are.

Together, this gives us all the information we need to work out if, when, and how we need to patch our infrastructure.

2.4.2   *Building a patching policy*

We can use our three concepts of cybersecurity strategy to develop a patching policy that works for us (figure 2.12).

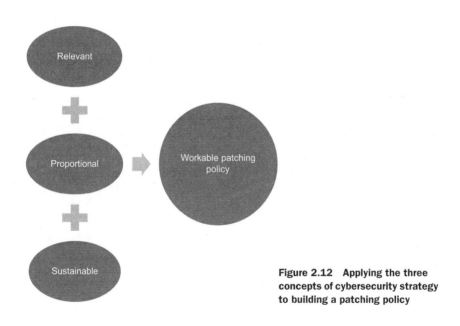

Figure 2.12   Applying the three concepts of cybersecurity strategy to building a patching policy

Applying patches to our systems is *relevant* for us, but applying all patches straightaway is neither *proportional* nor *sustainable*. Patching is a time-consuming and disruptive business. But we can use the CVSS score to come up with a patch policy that is both *proportional* and *sustainable*. The CVSS score lets us group vulnerabilities into three main severity ratings (see figure 2.13).

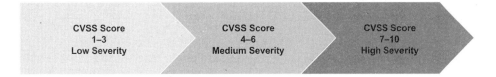

Figure 2.13 **Assigning severity to CVSS scores**

We don't need anything more complex; that wouldn't be *proportional* at this stage. We can start with the following approach:

- CVSS scores of 7+ should be patched immediately.
- CVSS scores of 4–6 should be patched within 30 days.
- CVSS scores of 3 and below should be patched within 180 days.

The next stage is to test it. Let's see how that works for us with CVE-2018-0101.

EXERCISE: PATCH FOR CVE-2018-0101

Let's revisit our two systems: the HR payroll and the e-commerce site. The HR payroll system has financial details of all our company's employees. It's an old system that has a number of known vulnerabilities, but it needs internet access, so we've put it behind a Cisco ASA firewall to protect it. It seemed like a smart move at the time, but now we have CVE-2018-0101 to consider.

We also have our brand-new e-commerce website that allows customers to buy models of Warwick Castle. This is completely separate from the HR system and has been developed from the ground up by a team using secure coding principles. The system is very secure, but as extra protection (defense in depth!), it's also behind a Cisco ASA firewall.

The HR payroll system can be taken offline at any time, because it's only really needed once a month to process payroll for everyone. The e-commerce website is our business's income, and it's very busy from 7:00 a.m. until 9:00 p.m. If we take it offline during that time, the business will suffer a loss of revenue; plus, it will look bad for our customers!

Figure 2.14 **Three factors of cybersecurity**

We can return to our security model of the three factors of cybersecurity to assess our response to CVE-2018-0101 (see figure 2.14):

- *What assets do you have?*
  - *HR payroll system*—Old, lots of vulnerabilities
  - *E-commerce website*—New, securely developed

- *Who would want to attack you?*
  - *Disgruntled ex-employees*—Low threat
  - *Financial fraudsters*—Medium threat
  - *Identity thieves*—Medium threat
  - *Financial fraudsters*—Medium threat
  - *Criminal organizations*—High threat
- *What defenses do you have?*
  - *A Cisco ASA firewall*—Vulnerable
  - *A Cisco ASA firewall*—Vulnerable

So, what should we do? Our patching policy says that this vulnerability has a high CVSS score, and so must be patched immediately.

A *proportional* and *sustainable* way forward, then, would be to immediately take the HR payroll system offline so we can patch the firewall. We can wait until after 9:00 p.m. for the e-commerce traffic to drop off, and then take that system offline overnight to patch its firewall. This addresses the vulnerability, but in a way that enables the business to continue making revenue, while protecting our assets.

2.5   *A culture of security*

A financial services client I worked with wanted to build a "culture of security" within the company. They handled sensitive financial data, executed millions of dollars in transactions per day, and handled financial data for some of the largest global corporations.

They recognized—quite rightly—that security was everyone's problem and every employee had a role to play in keeping the company and their client's data secure.

The problem was that they kept having leaks of data. They were under constant attack, and fraud was a big problem. Financial services regulation is tough, and they were worried about fines and loss of confidence from their clients.

Another problem was that their approach to training their staff and building that culture of security was based on forcing everyone to watch a half-hour training Power-Point deck once a year. I'm sure you've come across "mandatory security training" before. Personally, I love it; it's a great chance to zone out with a coffee while blindly clicking Next on a PowerPoint deck. It does nothing to build awareness of security issues, but it's a great break from doing real work.

The client was right, though: security involves everyone. A culture of security in an organization is where everyone—from junior staff to the leadership team—is aware of the security issues their organization faces.

This doesn't start with the nitty-gritty of how to protect yourself, your team, and your company from attacks. It starts with a cybersecurity strategy that can be understood—and used—by everyone in your organization.

Cybersecurity isn't a technology problem; it's a people problem. Let's revisit the three concepts again and see how we use them to build policies and strategies that then create a culture of security in our organization (see figure 2.15).

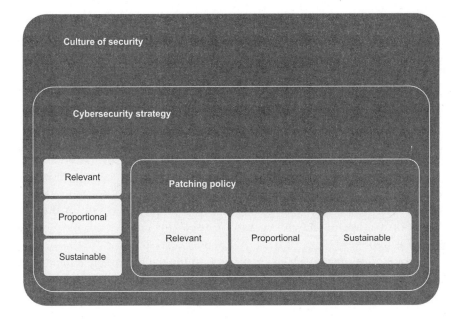

Figure 2.15 How our three concepts support our policies and strategy to build a culture of security

The three concepts depend on each other to form a workable strategy. A workable strategy, supported by workable policies, will build a culture of security within your organization.

A strategy that is complex or technical isn't relevant to people in the organization. It's acronym soup that's only understood by your security team. No one will follow the policies or pay attention to security requirements if they feel the strategy isn't relevant to them and their job.

A proportional strategy addresses the threats you face within the budget and manpower you have. Armed guards outside your company's toilets and by the entrance probably make sense if you're the Government Communications Headquarters (the UK spy agency; GCHQ) but are clearly disproportional if you run a coffee shop.

A strategy that impacts people's working habits isn't sustainable. I worked with a client who wanted people to have 30-character passwords that had to be changed weekly for a key system. That wasn't sustainable. Worse, it bred a culture of distrust of the security team. If I had to start my week by coming up with a unique password that's 30 characters long, I'd start to question the sanity of who thought that policy up, too.

Our supporting policies also have to be relevant, proportional, and sustainable. A patching policy that demands every system be immediately shut down the moment a security patch is released would damage our business. How does this all pan out in the real world?

HB Gary Federal was a security contractor for the US government, selling cybersecurity services to various federal agencies. In 2010, the hacker collective Anonymous was causing a commotion, attacking major corporations like Mastercard and Visa, and pushing a new style of "hactivism" in support of WikiLeaks.

HB Gary's CEO, Aaron Barr, claimed that he had exploited social media to infiltrate Anonymous and was going to sell their identities to clients. The lead developer for the tool at HB Gary told the rest of the team that not only was this not true, but that they were making themselves targets by making these claims. Barr carried on regardless, directly taunting key leaders in Anonymous by threatening to unmask them.

The response was swift and devastating. HB Gary used a custom content management system for their website, which was full of security vulnerabilities. The team at HB Gary—including Barr—used weak, easily guessable passwords. They also used these same weak passwords across multiple systems, none of which were patched for major security flaws. Barr was also the administrator for their email and document management systems, and he used the same, weak password on those systems as well.

A group of Anonymous hackers broke into the content management system, stole the passwords, used those to get into the email and document management systems as Barr, and gutted the company. They stole everything—emails, documents, client lists, financial details, software and projects HB Gary was working on for government clients—and then posted the lot on the internet. The team at HB Gary was completely unaware anything bad had happened until Anonymous told them where they had put the leaked data.

Everyone involved was fired, and HB Gary Federal was shut down, with parent company HB Gary eventually asset-stripped by ManTech International a year later.

HB Gary was a cybersecurity specialist. Their government clients paid them—a lot—to help them with tools, strategy, and defense. They had no internal security strategy of their own, and they didn't even follow basic best practice. All that was exploited to destroy their company were the very things they were telling their clients not to do.

HB Gary's security practices weren't *relevant*: they didn't improve their processes and security tools in the face of the massive and obvious threat that Anonymous posed. Neither were they *proportional*: they were dealing with sensitive government client data and didn't take the most basic steps to secure it. And, clearly, none of this was *sustainable*, as Anonymous so clearly demonstrated.

On the other end of the scale, we have Home Depot. In September 2014, a reporter wrote that he had seen credit card numbers linked to Home Deport purchases being sold online, which seemed like evidence of a breach.

A week later Home Depot announced that they had indeed suffered a data breach, via hackers who had installed malware on their point-of-sale terminals. It only took Home Depot another week to discover the extent of the hack: 56 million credit card numbers stolen.

Their CEO, Frank Blake, had announced that he was stepping down, and had appointed his successor. However, he stayed on to take personal responsibility for the breach and to oversee Home Depot's response to the crisis, spending significant time in the security operations room with the team carrying out the investigation.

Home Depot moved quickly, not only to confirm the size and scope of the breach, but also to implement systems to help their customers, which included renting a dedicated call center that was capable of handling 50,000 calls a day, and within two weeks, installing new encryption systems to protect customer data and foil similar attacks.

In an interview with the *Wall Street Journal*, Blake took responsibility for the security failings of the company. He said, "Our security systems could have been better; data security just wasn't high enough in our mission statement" (http://mng.bz/XZJY).

Home Depot had a security strategy that was relevant, proportional, and sustainable. The leadership team knew that the cyber team would investigate and address the vulnerabilities and empowered them to get on with that difficult task, while the CEO took personal responsibility and dealt with the PR and client fallout.

While the breach had a financial impact on Home Depot, it was much, much less than it could have been. They ended up paying out $19.5 million to compensate the more than 50 million consumers affected. By quickly being able to warn consumers, understand the impact of the stolen data, and put in systems to protect both the company and their customers from fraud, the financial penalty was much less than Equifax suffered a few years later.

This is what a true culture of security looks like.

2.6 How ready are you?

Now it is time to bring it all together and give you a chance to build your own initial strategy. Think about your team and your project—even your entire organization.

Grab a pen and a notepad and start working through the following questions. First, we'll work through the three factors of cybersecurity (figure 2.16):

- *What assets do you have?* This could be data—personal, financial, technical. It could be source code. It could be a computer system or other infrastructure, either on premises or in the cloud. Write down your list of assets.
- *Who would want to attack you?* Apart from thinking about any obvious Ernst Stavro Blofelds (James Bond's nemesis) in your life, who would want your assets? Does your profile or job make you a target to specific groups? How dangerous are these attackers? How much of a threat do they pose to you and your assets? Write down your list of attackers.
- *What defenses do you have?* This could be something as simple as a password manager or a USB key required to access your computer. Or it could be more complex: firewalls for your servers, antivirus software on your laptop, even encrypted storage. Write down your list of defenses.

Now you should have a good list to work with. The next stage is to look at the three concepts of cybersecurity strategy (figure 2.17).

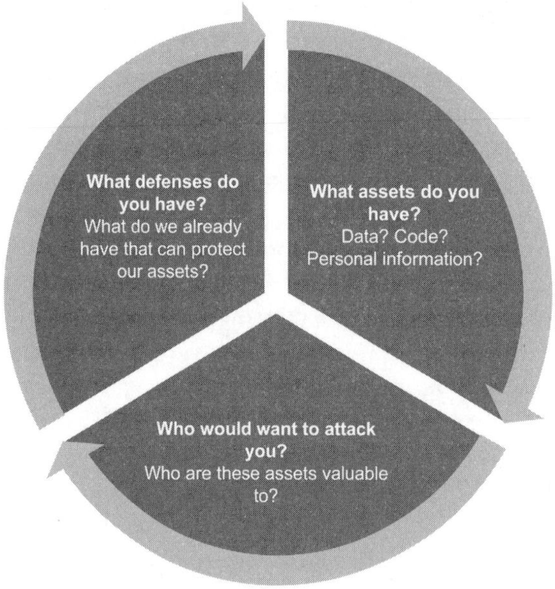

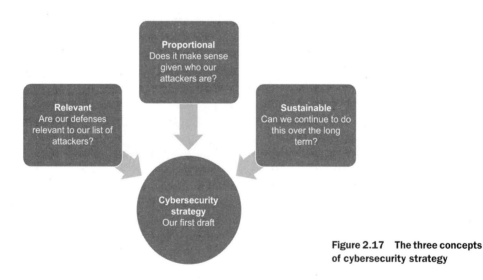

Figure 2.16   The three factors of cybersecurity

Figure 2.17   The three concepts of cybersecurity strategy

Let's apply these three concepts to our list and build out our draft strategy:

- *Relevant*—Let's look at two things:
  - Which of your existing defenses are relevant to your attackers or your assets?
  - What improvements to your defenses can be made to protect your assets from your attackers?

- *Proportional*—Add some weightings. Does the amount of time, money, and effort justify the increase in security? Armed guards for your laptop are a nice idea but probably should only be brought in once you've gotten antivirus software, access control, and a firewall in place.

  Think about short, medium, and longer-term improvements to your defenses.

- *Sustainable*—If you really do need those armed guards protecting your laptop, how long can you afford to pay them? Will they end up getting in the way of you actually using your laptop?

  Think about how people use and access your systems and data. If you put defenses in that change or disrupt that access, you're going to change people's routine—and that's the biggest source of failure for any strategy.

- *Review*—Now review what you've got. Go back to the start—what assets do you have?—and work through the questions again. Have any of your answers or views changed now that you have a better picture?

  You should review the entire set of answers on a regular basis—at least once a month. New attacks come out all the time, and improvements in technology often bring about some big changes in our approach to security.

A static strategy is a failed strategy. Regularly review your assumptions, answers, and ideas to make sure they are still accurate and relevant.

Everyone, at some point, will get hacked. What we've covered so far will prepare you for this and help you to not just make it harder for an attacker to succeed, but also help you to notice and recover from the attack. In the next chapter, we'll look at the hackers themselves and understand who they are, what motivates them, and how they work.

Summary

- A cybersecurity strategy defines a direction of travel—a series of improvements—to achieve better security for our organization. This is supported by policies that help identify and address security issues.
- There are three core factors of cybersecurity:
  - What assets do you have?
  - Who would want to attack you?
  - What defenses do you have?
- The core factors can be used to build up a profile of our existing security, allowing us to understand what we need to protect, who will try to steal it, and what defenses (and gaps) there are in the security protecting our assets.
- We also looked at the three concepts of a cybersecurity strategy:
  - Relevant
  - Proportional
  - Sustainable

- The three concepts of cybersecurity strategy are used to ensure that we have a balanced, sensible, and workable approach to security that suits our own specific needs. Companies that fail to apply all of these concepts suffer worse data breaches and are less able to recover successfully from them.

- The security industry gives us details about security vulnerabilities (via CVEs) and a scoring mechanism to judge how severe they are (using CVSS scores). We can use this information, along with our three concepts, to build policies that support and improve our organization's security.

- Tying together our strategy and supporting policies while remembering the three principles helps us build a culture of security in our organization. This not only makes it more difficult for attackers to get in, but also helps us recover faster from any attacks.

Part 1

Cybersecurity is an immense and complex field, yet it has become one of the most critical and important areas of information technology (IT). In 2020, data showed that the average cost of a data breach for a US company was $8.19 million USD. But the fun doesn't stop there; the resulting financial damages cost, on average, an extra 11.45. million USD per security incident. Globally, the total cost of cybercrime to the economy is currently $400 billion USD per year—and rising.

Before we can successfully defend our organization from attack, we need to understand the fundamentals of security—and nothing is more important (or fundamental) than thinking like an attacker and understanding how their most common attacks work.

Part 1 of this book will get us thinking like the bad guys—understanding their motivations, how they operate, and how their most common (and successful) attacks work.

Chapter 3 introduces different types of hackers and their motivation; chapter 4 builds on this by getting into the details of the most common attacks, including often-overlooked physical attacks. Chapter 5 looks at a firm favorite with attackers: social engineering.

Chapter 6 then looks at the other side of the coin: what attackers do once they are inside your organization and how to spot and deal with inside attackers. Finally, chapter 7 wraps up part 1 by looking at where attackers go to sell and trade their illicit data hauls: the Dark Web.

Understanding hackers

3

This chapter covers

- Exploring the different types of hackers
- Approaching problem solving in a new way with the hacker mindset
- Applying the OODA loop to efficiently discover and exploit vulnerabilities

In this chapter, we will look at the different types of hackers, how they think, some of their most common attacks, and what separates the bad from the good. Hacking itself is neither good or bad; it's a way of working out how something works and then getting it to do something different. This mindset can be applied to everything, not just software and computers but processes, machinery—even companies themselves.

Hackers are a varied bunch, with a wide range of skills, backing, and motivation. Having a high-level working knowledge of the different types of hackers is the first step to understanding the attackers you may face and how sophisticated and tenacious their attacks will be.

3.1   *Who are the hackers?*

There are three main categories of hackers that have emerged over the years (see figure 3.1). Although not exhaustive, this list provides us with an easy way to understand their motivations and how they are likely to operate. When talking about hackers and hacking, you'll often hear these terms used to describe someone's actions or motivations:

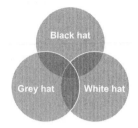

- *Black hats*—The attackers, criminal gangs, or individuals who break the law via hacking for personal gain and profit (or just to cause chaos).

Figure 3.1   **The overlap between black, grey, and white hat hackers**

- *White hats*—The defenders, security researchers, and security teams protecting individuals and companies.
- *Grey hats*—The in between. They break the law, but often for altruistic reasons.

The terms *black hat* and *white hat* popped up on message boards in the 1980s and are thought to have come from classic US cowboy films, where the good guys and bad guys respectively wore white and black cowboy hats.

Each of the categories has its own motivation and way of operating. Let's look at each group in detail.

3.1.1   *Black hat*

Black hat hackers is the name we give to the traditional *bad guys*, the stereotypical illegal hackers in popular culture. Usually criminals, part of a criminal gang, or working for a hostile nation state, black hat hackers are often highly skilled and well resourced. Their goals are data theft, the compromise of organizations, and destructive hacking, while making a nice living from their crimes.

Many hackers start out as black hats, breaking into systems without permission. When caught, some will repent and become white hats; many more will double down and concentrate on their criminal careers. We'll look at some examples in depth later on.

3.1.2   *Grey hat*

Grey hat hackers fit into the grey area between black and white. Frequently breaking laws and carrying out criminal hacks, they also publish and share information on security vulnerabilities. They are often involved in *hacktivism* and are comfortable with illegally breaking into companies and governments to expose social injustice and corruption.

Their insights and research into how criminal hacks are carried out are invaluable to law enforcement and IT teams tasked with defending networks and systems. However, this information is often obtained from their own exploits in breaking the law.

> **What is hacktivism?**
> Hacktivism (a combination of hacking and activism) is using hacking as a form of civil disobedience to promote political or social change. The phrase was first coined by the hacker Omega, of the group Cult of the Dead Cow, in 1996.

3.1.3   White hat

White hat hackers work on the legal side of the fence to improve security and protect organizations and data. They will often work with law enforcement to track down and expose black hats.

White hat hackers carry out what's called *ethical hacking*, testing security with permission and sharing their findings so security can be improved.

In the early 90s, this approach of using hacking techniques to test and improve the security of systems was popularized by computer security researchers and programmers Dan Farmer and Wietse Venema. Their tool, Security Administrator Tool for Analyzing Networks (SATAN), caused a great deal of controversy when it was launched in 1992, with many saying it would encourage illicit hacking of networks and systems.

SATAN was one of the most successful and well-publicized scanning tools, fueling the debate over making powerful hacking tools available to everyone. Despite drawing the ire of the US Department of Justice, SATAN was in popular use for a decade, spawning similar tools like Nmap and Nessus.

These tools have proved invaluable for allowing white hat hackers to probe and test the security of networks and systems for their employers and clients. They have been used equally by black and grey hat hackers to scan and attack vulnerable organizations. People who run these tools without understanding how they work are called *script kiddies*—a derogative term used by hackers to label anyone who relies on ready-made programs and scripts to attack a system.

3.2   Where do they come from?

One truism for all types of hackers is that the stereotypes are often far from the reality. Forget the usual stereotype of a hacker in a hoodie, tucked up in their parents' basement with screensavers from *The Matrix* playing all around them.

To really understand how hackers think and operate, we need to look at their backgrounds. Understanding what motivates the different groups and what they try to do is the best way to start building defenses against them. Let's look at the reality, the history and experiences, of notable hackers from each of the three categories.

3.2.1   Black hat hacker: Alberto Gonzalez

Albert Gonzalez (not the former attorney general of the US) started his career at age 14 when he hacked into NASA. While attending school in Florida, he continued to break into systems and carry out petty computer crime before moving to New Jersey.

It was here that Gonzalez led a group of hackers called ShadowCrew, who traded in stolen credit card numbers as well as other personal information, including counterfeit passports, drivers' licenses, social security cards, and birth certificates. This activity earned the group over $4.3 million.

Gonzalez was arrested by the Secret Service as part of Operation Firewall. He managed to avoid any jail time by becoming an informant, passing details of the rest of the ShadowCrew team and their activities to the Secret Service.

While working as an informant for the Secret Service, Gonzalez continued to hack, considering himself untouchable thanks to his cooperation with the authorities. He masterminded the theft of over 45 million credit and debit card details from TJX, as well as carrying out attacks against other companies, including Office Max and Barnes & Noble. He also masterminded the Heartland Payment Systems hack, which resulted in the theft of over 130 million card numbers.

When Gonzalez was finally arrested, authorities seized over $1.6 million in cash. He is currently serving a 20-year sentence, which he is appealing, claiming that he was aiding the Secret Service.

3.2.2   *Grey hat hacker: Sabu and the Anonymous collective*

Starting with Operation Chanology (a series of pranks and protests against the Church of Scientology), the Anonymous collective started to publicize a new form of protest: hacktivism. Publicly supporting and driving pranks, hacking, and protests against everything from strict copyright enforcement to oppressive regimes in the Middle East, groups within Anonymous expanded to attacks against global organizations like Mastercard, VISA, and Sony.

Anonymous itself is a strange group—by design. A loose collective of different subgroups and cliques, the actions of different Anonymous groups cover the entire range, from black hat to white hat.

A small group of Anonymous hackers formed a group called LulzSec and were responsible for the devastating attack against US government contractor HB Gary (you'll remember what happened to them from our discussion of a culture of security in chapter 2). One of these hackers, Sabu, had been secretly arrested and pressured into working as an FBI informant; his testimony and evidence later led to the arrests and convictions of some of the hackers who had helped in the operation against HB Gary, including Topiary, Kayla, and tFLOW.

Groups within the Anonymous collective have caused significant disruption and financial loss since they first became active in 2003. However, the group's hacktivism has also achieved some amazing things. For example, they were pivotal in the Arab Spring uprisings, attacking censorship technology used by oppressive regimes, as well as deploying technology solutions that allowed protestors to organize and communicate. Sabu was active in these campaigns, organizing and leading groups within the collective, and was also involved in later campaigns to take down and expose revenge pornography and child exploitation websites, leaking the operators' details to law enforcement. This typifies the grey hat hacker mindset: somewhere between right and wrong, achieving positive outcomes from openly criminal actions, aligned to personal values that are at sometimes at odds with those of society.

Self-taught, at the time of his involvement with Anonymous, Sabu was unemployed. Since completing his sentence, he works as a security researcher and white hat hacker, working to protect organizations from the sort of attacks he and his colleagues used to carry out.

3.2.3 *White hat hacker: Mudge*

A great example of a white hat hacker—and of an excellent career in hacking—is Peiter Zatko, also known as Mudge. With a background in music, he joined the hacker group the L0pht.

One of the earliest and most famous hacking collectives, the L0pht started out as a shared space for hackers to tinker, play with hardware, and research computer software and hardware vulnerabilities.

The group's members eventually quit their various day jobs and formed L0pht Heavy Industries, the first real hacker think tank, with the goal of improving computer security. L0pht Heavy Industries later merged with security research startup @stake, which was later acquired by security company Symantec.

Mudge discovered and shared a number of security advisories and tools and was an early proponent of the concept of full disclosure: sharing full details of a security vulnerability as early as possible, allowing victims to protect themselves and forcing vendors to provide fixes.

As a member of the L0pht, he presented to a US Senate committee about internet vulnerabilities, and he was one of the first hackers to reach out to build relationships with government and industry bodies and organizations.

He worked at a number of security firms before becoming project manager of a DARPA project focused on directing research in cybersecurity. He continued to conduct research, publish vulnerabilities, and give conference talks, and currently he is part of a project called #CyberUL, a testing organization for computer security.

Mudge is a great example of the white hat hacker: working to discover new vulnerabilities and building new tools, openly sharing his findings to help improve cyber security, and working with disparate groups (from government to private sector) to increase cybersecurity capabilities and understanding.

3.2.4 *The hacker mindset*

The one thing that all hackers have in common is their approach to problem solving. We can map this out as a series of questions hackers ask themselves when faced with a new target. The hacker mindset is a completely different way of looking at new technologies, systems, applications, or hardware.

Where developers will typically think "How can I fix this?" or "How can I improve this?" hackers instead are asking "How can I break this?" or "What else can I make this do?" Figure 3.2 shows the flow of the hacker's mindset.

Figure 3.2   The hacker mindset

We can compare the hacker mindset to a typical developer thought process when facing a problem. You'll see that the hacker and the developer approach things from completely different ways: hackers want to find problems; developers want to fix them. Figure 3.3 shows how a typical developer's thought process flows.

Figure 3.3   How developers typically approach problem solving

Hackers approach things by trying to understand the solution and then trying to break it (or make it misbehave). Developers approach things by trying to understand a problem and then working out how to fix it. These approaches are the complete opposite, which is why it's so important to understand how hackers think and operate. Once we're inside their heads, we can look at our software and hardware in the same way a malicious hacker does.

3.3   *What are hackers capable of?*

With the different types of hackers come different motivations and behaviors. Luckily, when Gary Gygax invented *Dungeons and Dragons* (*D&D*), he gave us a great way to measure and understand people's behaviors and personalities: alignment. Alignment uses two main ways of defining personality and behavior: lawful versus chaotic and good versus evil.

The third edition of *D&D* rules give us the following definitions:

- *Lawful alignment* implies trustworthiness, obedience to authority, and reliability. On the downside, lawfulness can include close-mindedness, reactionary adherence to tradition, judgment, and lack of adaptability.
- *Chaotic alignment* implies freedom, adaptability, and flexibility. On the downside, chaos can include recklessness, resentment toward legitimate authority, arbitrary actions, and irresponsibility—pretty spot on for hackers.
- *Neutral alignment* fits in the middle, implying a normal respect for authority, with neither a compulsion to obey nor a compulsion to rebel.

We can then map these against the three traits of good, evil, and neutrality:

- Good implies altruism, respect for life, and a concern for the dignity of others.
- Evil implies harming, oppressing, and destroying others.
- Neutral falls into the middle of the two, carrying out acts of good and evil, with neutral people committed to others by personal relationships.

This gives us nine different alignment types (see table 3.1).

Table 3.1   Mapping out the nine different alignment personality types

	Lawful	**Neutral**	**Chaotic**
Good	Lawful-Good The crusader	Neutral-Good The benefactor	Chaotic-Good The rebel
Neutral	Lawful-Neutral The judge	Neutral The undecided	Chaotic-Neutral The free spirit
Evil	Lawful-Evil The dominator	Neutral-Evil The malefactor	Chaotic-Evil The destroyer

This gives us a pretty comprehensive way to define behavior and personality. You can use table 3.1 to start thinking about your colleagues and coworkers in *D&D* alignment terms. Clearly, chaotic alignment types map very nicely to our different types of hackers.

We'll look at some specific hacker techniques—such as social engineering—in chapter 5. For the moment, now that we've got some context, let's look at how the different groups operate.

3.3.1   *The bad guys: Black hats*

Not just your classic criminals, black hat hackers can work on their own, for criminal gangs, or for hostile state actors. Exploiting victims for personal gain (or on behalf of their employers), black hat hackers are skilled and experienced and are hacking for profit. Many criminal hacking gangs run sophisticated operations, with "employees" getting health coverage and pensions. Larger operations provide resellers, offering online training, and even support contracts for their hacking tools. Some malware even comes with warranties and money-back guarantees, as well as 24/7 support via forums and online chat channels.

An investigation by Check Point in 2016 into the Cerber malware found a thriving franchise system. The "malware as a service" approach provides customers with an easy-to-use dashboard to track infections and payments. Online support is available from both forums and premium phone numbers. The malware is tagged to ensure that a vulnerable system can't be infected more than once to ensure franchisees don't encroach on each other's territory. All of this activity takes place on the Dark Web, a hidden parallel internet that we'll explore in detail in chapter 7.

Alberto Gonzalez is a typical black hat hacker, comfortable with repeatedly breaking the law and showing no remorse for his victims. From the *Dungeons and Dragons* role-playing games, black hat hackers are your classic chaotic evil.

3.3.2 *The middle ground: Grey hats*

We can get an even better understanding of black hat hackers by comparing them to the other two types: grey hat and white hat hackers.

Grey hat hackers are often found supporting more aggressive forms of hacktivism. The Anonymous collective provides good examples of this: deploying mass DDoS attacks against corporations and carrying out targeted attacks against individuals supporting oppressive regimes or unpopular government activities.

Grey hat hackers skirt that grey area of the law. Is their activity illegal? Sometimes. Is their activity social disobedience? Sometimes. Is their activity beneficial? Sometimes. Maybe.

A good example is Operation Darknet, carried out by Anonymous in October 2011. Breaking the law, groups of Anonymous hackers attacked child exploitation websites and forums across the internet. They brought the sites down, hacked personal data on the subscribers and administrators, and then leaked the personal information to law enforcement agencies across the globe. Numerous arrests were made and a large number of websites and forums were permanently shut down.

Sabu is the classic grey hat hacker, breaking the law with sophisticated hacks while also carrying out acts of social disobedience and hacktivism to expose illegal activities and social injustice. Using our *D&D* alignment, grey hat hackers are chaotic neutral.

3.3.3 *The good guys: White hats*

Finally, giving us the starkest comparison to the black hat hackers, we can look at the white hats. White hat hackers are found working on the legal side of the law, carrying out research and defense.

Defense needs little explanation: good cybersecurity practitioners, from analysts to engineers and architects, will be good hackers. Having a solid understanding of technology and development is key to knowing the best way to protect companies and their assets.

Research is the other key area where you will see a lot of activity from white hat hackers, not only finding new vulnerabilities and bugs, but also analyzing malware, working out how black hat hackers have penetrated a company, and even tracing and dismantling control and communication systems used by criminals. White hat researchers will share their research and results openly, giving us some of the best insights and information on how the black hats are working and the steps they used to cause major breaches.

In 2013, cybersecurity firm Mandiant released a paper called "APT1: Exposing One of China's Cyber Espionage Units," in which they exposed a group of state-sponsored Chinese hackers they dubbed "APT1." Mandiant exposed their activities going back as far as 2006, identifying not just their victims, but also the tools and techniques used in their attacks.

Mandiant's research was deeply comprehensive, uncovering that the group had four large networks in Shanghai and was one of 20 such groups operating under the People's Liberation Army General Staff Department. Mandiant tracked attacks aimed at stealing trade secrets and confidential information from Lockheed Martin, Telvent, and other companies in the aeronautics, engineering, and manufacturing industries in the US.

In 2014, this information led to the US Department of Justice issuing an indictment against five members of the group, with charges of theft of confidential business information and intellectual property from US commercial firms, and of planting malware on their computers.

Hackers like Mudge and organizations like Mandiant highlight the positives of hacking, with important, high-profile research that has made computing safer for everyone. White hats fit into the classic chaotic-good alignment from *D&D*.

3.4 Working through a real-life problem: How do hackers think?

Let's walk through a real-life scenario from a client I worked with to understand how hackers approach an application they want to break. I was working with a global financial services client who managed billions of dollars in assets. They wanted me to test their security by breaking into their website. Let's go through the process together.

3.4.1 Breaking a financial services website

This financial services client had a simple web application that allowed clients to log in over the internet and see what investments they had in their ISAs (individual savings accounts—a UK tax-efficient investment scheme; see figure 3.4).

The application was fairly straightforward:

1 A web server served a simple login page to the user.
2 Once the user logged in, the web server retrieved their data from the database server.
3 The web server then presented this data back to the user.

My job was simple: I'd been given a dummy username, password, and user record. Armed with these, I had to discover any flaws or problems in the application.

Think about what you would do with this knowledge. How could you attack this system? How could you break it or make it misbehave? Could you retrieve any sensitive data? What would a black hat do? Let's work through the process together.

First, we have a pretty good idea how this application works. It's simple and straightforward, with limited functionality. The "good stuff"—all that sensitive user data about investments—is tucked away on the database server. So, clearly, we want to work out some way of getting to that data.

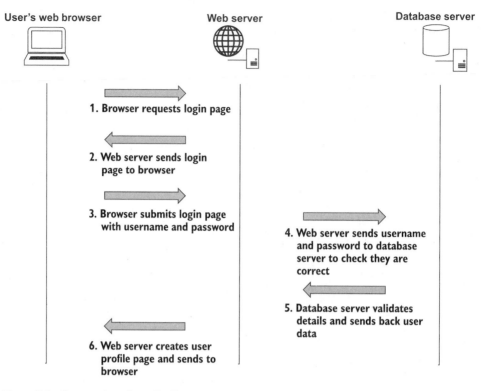

User's web browser   **Web server**   **Database server**

1. Browser requests login page

2. Web server sends login page to browser

3. Browser submits login page with username and password

4. Web server sends username and password to database server to check they are correct

5. Database server validates details and sends back user data

6. Web server creates user profile page and sends to browser

Figure 3.4   Our sample web application

We know that the web server talks to the database server (see figure 3.5). We also know that we can give the web server some data (our username and password), which is then passed to the database server for processing.

Relational databases (like Oracle and MySQL) use a special programming language called Structured Query Language (SQL). For the database server to understand the web server, the web server must convert our username and password login sequence into SQL before sending it to the database server.

So, could we insert something other than a username and password? How would the web server react? What would the database server do? One option we have is to try injecting the database server language—SQL—directly into the username field of our web page.

This is called an *SQL injection attack* (SQLi), and we'll cover it in much greater detail in chapter 4. But by learning a bit about SQLi now, we can understand how a hacker thinks through attacking a website to steal customer data.

Normally, the SQL statement processed by the database server scans through the lists of usernames and passwords it has until it finds one that matches (see figure 3.6). It then returns a positive result (TRUE) to the web server. If our username or password

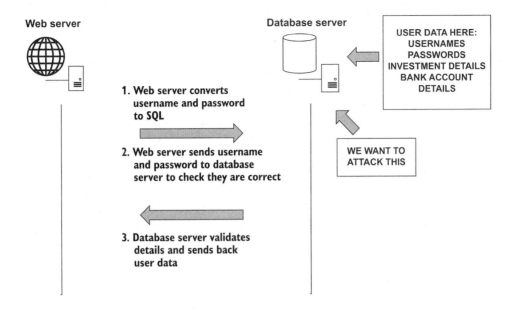

Figure 3.5   Conversation between web server and database server

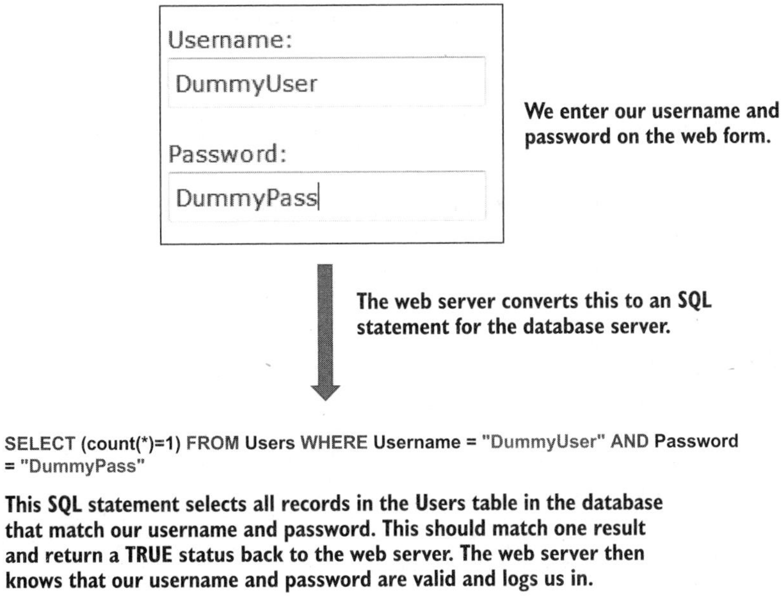

We enter our username and password on the web form.

The web server converts this to an SQL statement for the database server.

SELECT (count(*)=1) FROM Users WHERE Username = "DummyUser" AND Password = "DummyPass"

This SQL statement selects all records in the Users table in the database that match our username and password. This should match one result and return a TRUE status back to the web server. The web server then knows that our username and password are valid and logs us in.

Figure 3.6   How the web server converts our username and password into SQL for the database server to process

was incorrect, the database server wouldn't find it and would return a negative result (FALSE) to the web server—in which case, we wouldn't get logged in.

If the web server converts our username and password into SQL for processing by the database server, what will happen if we use some SQL in the username field of our login form?

SQL is a pretty straightforward language, and it's easy to learn the basics. What we want to try to do is change our SELECT statement so that we can retrieve some other data from the database server (see figure 3.7). What we're doing is injecting some valid SQL directly into the username and password fields. This is a simple formula that always evaluates to a positive (TRUE) result, which means that we can use this to say that every entry in the Users table is a valid match.

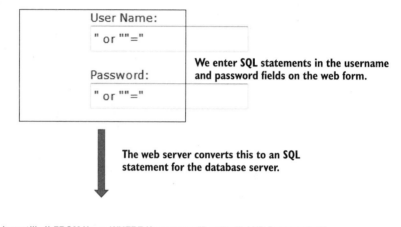

SELECT (count(*)=1) FROM Users WHERE Username ="" or ""="" AND Password ="" or ""=""

This is the SQL statement that is generated and passed to the database server.

Figure 3.7   Injecting SQL statements into the web server's login form

Essentially what we're sending to the database server is a command to retrieve all records from the table that stores the usernames and passwords. This has the handy result of getting the database server to spill its guts and pass back to the web server a list of *all* usernames and passwords. The web server doesn't know how to deal with this, so it will usually show an error with a plain-text list of the data, similar to figure 3.8.

This error message shows us we are able to inject our own SQL commands into the web form, and the web server will happily send those to the database server for processing.

Now that we know there is a data injection vulnerability here, we could explore more complex queries to retrieve other users' data from other tables in the database server, including their passwords and payment card data. Again, we'll explore this in

```
Unexpected Error at line 43;

Dummyuser,dummypass,Admin,adminpass,Bob,bobspass,Joe,joespass,Test,testpass;
```

Figure 3.8 Successful SQL injection will break a web page, but the fruitful results usually look similar to this.

more detail in chapter 4, but now you can already see that with relatively little effort, we can subvert a poorly designed application to steal user data.

SQLi attacks are very simple to defend against; we'll cover the different defenses in detail in chapter 4. Unfortunately, many companies out there still have poorly written applications like this exposed to the internet.

As for my work with this client, what did I end up doing? Using SQL injection, I was able to retrieve not just other users' login details, but also details about their investments, addresses, and even bank accounts—all data that was held in the database server.

3.4.2 Combining the hacker mindset with the OODA loop

We've already talked about the hacker mindset: understanding how hackers approach a situation and how it differs from the approach of a developer. As a reminder, the process is presented again in figure 3.9.

Figure 3.9   The hacker mindset

Thinking back to chapter 1, where we first touched on the OODA loop as a way to approach cybersecurity issues, we can now see how this applies with the hacker mindset to give us a really powerful model: an iterative loop that allows us to quickly work out how to find and exploit a security flaw (see figure 3.10).

Here, we've mapped the different steps in the hacker mindset directly into the OODA loop. Using the OODA loop in this way allows us to iterate across the many different ways we can think of to break something, to force an application or piece of hardware to work in unexpected ways. This iterative approach to hacking allows us to quickly test and discard different approaches to hacking something while simultaneously learning more about our target.

We can apply both these frameworks to our hacking exercise (see figure 3.11).

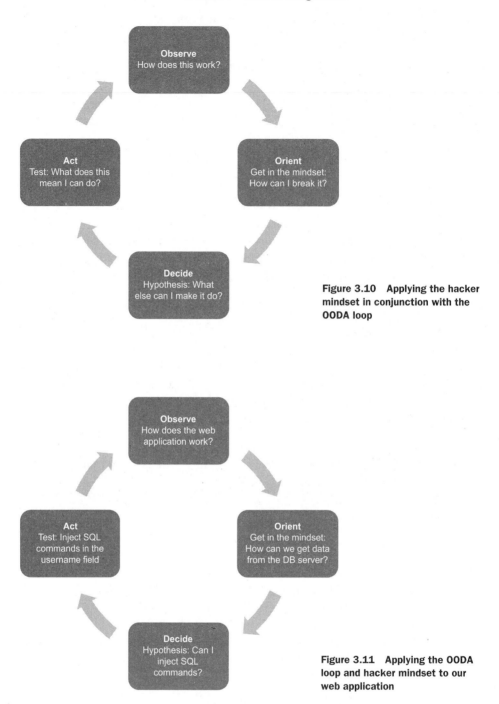

Figure 3.10   **Applying the hacker mindset in conjunction with the OODA loop**

Figure 3.11   **Applying the OODA loop and hacker mindset to our web application**

For each way we can think of to break the system, we can use the OODA loop to iterate through trying different methods and seeing where we end up.

Thinking this way will feel odd at first; it's the polar opposite of what we would normally do in IT. Instead of thinking about how to fix things and solve problems, we're spending our time trying to work out how something works so that we can break it. Practice applying the hacker mindset and asking those questions for each bit of software or technology you use; it's a useful habit. The hacker mindset is a powerful tool to help you learn more about systems, processes, and technologies.

Now that we're thinking like hackers, chapter 4 will go into the details of their most common and successful types of attacks, and how we can protect against them.

Summary

- There are three main categorizations of hackers: black hats, grey hats, and white hats:
  - Black hats are the stereotypical hacking "bad guys."
  - The white hats are the "good guys" defending against the black hats.
  - The grey hats sit somewhere in between, with flexible morals and motivations.

  With an understanding of these three categories, we can start to understand and think like our attackers.
- The hacker mindset is a very different approach to problem solving and is the complete opposite of how developers would normally approach a problem. The hacker mindset has four stages for analyzing an application, system, or environment:
  - How does this work?
  - How can I break it?
  - What else can I make it do?
  - What does this mean I can do?
- We worked through an example where we could use the hacker mindset to approach breaking into a financial services website.
- The OODA loop gives us a useful model for approaching security issues. The four steps within the OODA loop are observe, orient, decide, and act, and we can combine this model with the hacker mindset to create a powerful model for understanding security issues.

External attacks

4

This chapter covers

- Leveraging the hacker mindset and the OODA loop models to plan out our own theoretical attacks against home and company networks
- Exploring how data injection attacks work
- Using knowledge of the different types of malware to create defensive strategies
- Exploring Wi-Fi and mobile phone networks and how data can be intercepted and spoofed

Now that we've looked at how to think like a hacker and what mental models we can use, we get to the really fun stuff: exploring how the most common external attacks work. As part of helping you anticipate external attacks, this chapter will have several exercises to teach you how to think and plan an attack yourself. We'll also look at the different types of malware, as well as dig into the security problems with Wi-Fi and mobile phone networks.

By the chapter's end, you will be able to think like an attacker—to understand how and why some of the most common attacks work. By understanding how to use malware and attacks using security problems with Wi-Fi and mobile networks to steal users' credentials and data, you'll be better able to defend against these attacks.

4.1 How do hackers get in?

Chapter 3 showed the differences between the different types of hackers. Now we're going to focus on just the bad guys—the black hats—and how some of their most common attacks work. We'll start by looking at how an attacker thinks about someone else's network and how they try to get in. We'll make use of our models (the OODA loop and the hacker mindset), so let's quickly revisit them.

The OODA loop (figure 4.1) gives us a way of quickly working out what is happening, analyzing what is happening, deciding what we could do, and then acting on it.

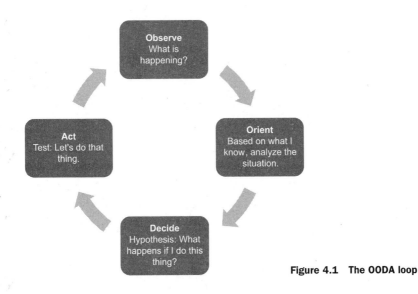

Figure 4.1 **The OODA loop**

The hacker mindset (figure 4.2) is our mental model on how we approach a working system—how we break it—where our goal is the opposite of a developer: we want to create problems (or find existing ones) and then exploit them rather than fix them.

Figure 4.2 **The hacker mindset**

Both of these are key to understanding how a hacker will view our network, applications, and computers. Let's look at two common examples of infrastructure—a typical home setup to connect to the internet and a simplified corporate network—and see how hackers view them as targets and opportunities.

4.1.1   *Home setup*

For most of us, our ISP provides a broadband router, which plugs into our phone line. The broadband router is a device that routes data between our home and our ISP's network over the phone line, normally using a networking technology called ADSL. When our data reaches the ISP's network, the ISP then sends it on—for example, to their email server, to one of Google's search website servers, or to download a book from Manning's web server. We connect our home computer (a PC or laptop) to our broadband router either with a network cable or by using Wi-Fi (see figure 4.3).

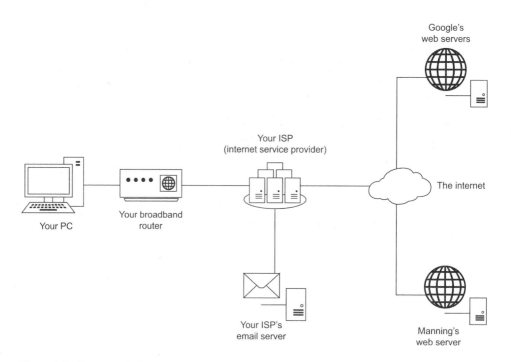

Figure 4.3   Our example home network

This is a nice, simple scenario to start with; there aren't many network devices or complex technologies involved. One of the reasons that internet usage has exploded is how simple and easy it is to get online now, as opposed to the hassle we used to have with dial-up modems, special software, and limited download speeds.

Now that we know how to view our internet connection as an end user, how would a hacker view it? Look at the diagram again and rate each of the components (our PC, broadband router, ISP's email server, etc.) in terms of how difficult they would be to attack and whether someone would try and attack them. Rate each of them with the scale in table 4.1.

Table 4.1 The scale we can use to measure attack difficulty and likelihood

How difficult is it to attack?	How likely is it to be attacked?
High	High
Medium	Medium
Low	Low

Once you've scored each component on the diagram, let's look at how an average skilled hacker might view this (figure 4.4).

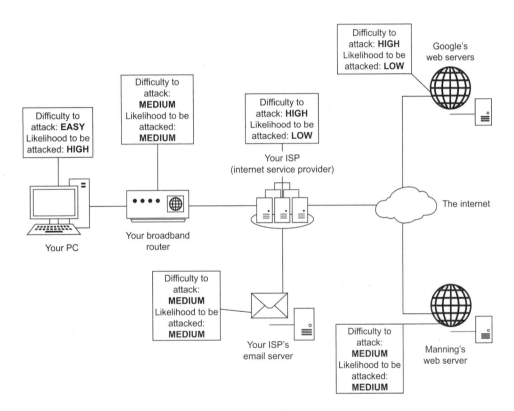

Figure 4.4 How an attacker might view our example infrastructure

How easy something is to attack is always dependent on the capabilities of your attacker. If we were under attack from, for example, the US National Security Agency (NSA), all of these items would be easy for them to attack (and we'd have far more serious problems). Someone with little security knowledge who has downloaded some attack tools from the internet would find all of these components difficult to attack.

EXERCISE

Let's use our two models to plan out how we would attack the home network to get access to the user's data. There is no right way here (or in any hacking); there's just "This is what worked for me." Keep that in mind while working through the exercise!

We've already worked out which components on this network are the easiest to attack. We can start to use the OODA loop to build our plan:

- *Orient*—Where is the user's data? What happens to the user's data while they are working?
- *Observe*—Is the user's data stored on, or passing through, any devices that are easier to attack? Would that make it easier to get to the data?
- *Decide*—What sort of attack will we try, and on which component? Why?
- *Act*—Launch our attack.

Here's where we use our hacker mindset to further dig into the problem:

- How does this work?
- How can I break it?
- What else can I make it do?
- What does this mean I can do?

SOLUTION

Bearing in mind what I said earlier, there are two things to remember:

- There is no right or wrong solution; there's only what worked for you to get to your goal.
- It doesn't matter if you can't get to the user data; you just loop through the process again and try something else.

This is what attackers do, and what hacking is all about: iteratively looping through these processes until we get what we want. My suggested solution is hinted at in our diagram showing the vulnerability of each component on the network; plus, I'm incredibly lazy.

Consumer broadband routers are manufactured by the thousands at a very low cost. This means security is almost always a last resort, and if these devices do have any security, it's going to be pretty basic. The majority of these broadband routers will leave the factory with a default username and password. To make things even more fun, many ISPs will have installed a default admin username and password that they can use to remotely administer the devices when needed.

Naturally, this information never stays hidden. Sites like http://mng.bz/o2dr have been around for years and have gradually collected up all the various usernames and passwords used across the different routers.

My approach would be to try to see if the administration interface for the broadband router is reachable, and then try the different default usernames and passwords to get access. Once you can control the router, you have access to all the data being transmitted and received by the user.

Another approach would be to attack the user's laptop. We could try and get some malware installed to steal the data or give us remote access to steal it ourselves. Our PCs run lots of software, the majority of which has bugs and security issues. There are lots of different ways to exploit these.

In a training session I ran, an enterprising CFO came up with the plan to break into the user's home and just steal the laptop—with all the data on it. (To be clear, this is a shockingly bad idea, even if it does solve the problem of how to get the data. We will, however, get into physical security in chapter 5, where we'll look at some much more subtle methods attackers use.)

Again, there's no right approach, no one right way to achieve your goal. What is important is going through the thought process and understanding how attackers think. Once we think like an attacker, we can not only spot the security flaws for ourselves, we can address them as well.

4.1.2 *Corporate network*

When you go to work in the office and get connected, things get a lot more involved. Corporate networks tend to be larger and more complicated, as companies provide more digital services internally and externally. Companies also have important customer and financial data to protect, so they tend to have more security technology to protect their network.

Let's look at a fairly standard—and basic—company network in figure 4.5. Notice that there's still a router to transmit traffic to and from the internet. We have a few extra bits as well: a firewall and some extra networks.

The firewall is in place not only to stop malicious data and attacks from getting onto the internal networks, but also to stop data and attacks going out. Companies will often split their data between two networks (here we have desktops and servers) to keep the network data separate. This helps stop, say, a problem on the desktop network from affecting the operation of the company's servers.

We can instantly see two things:

- It's a lot more complicated. We have multiple networks, multiple internal company servers, and some security devices.
- Fundamentally, it's just a bigger version of our home network. We have our PC, which connects to a router, which routes our data to and from an ISP.

How do you think a hacker would view this network? Again, look at the diagram and rate each of the components (the company PCs, the application server, the firewall, etc.) in terms of how difficult they would be to attack and whether someone would try to attack them (table 4.2).

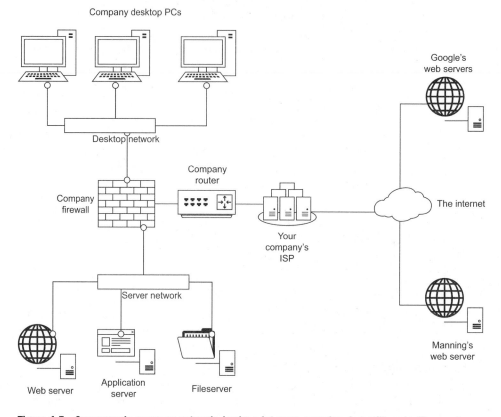

Figure 4.5   Our example company network. Looks a lot more complex, but still works like our home network.

Table 4.2   The scale we can use to measure attack difficulty and likelihood

How difficult is it to attack?	How likely is it to be attacked?
High	High
Medium	Medium
Low	Low

Once you've scored each component on the diagram, let's look at how a hacker might view this (figure 4.6).

We can see that, similar to our home network, the PCs are the most vulnerable and most likely to be attacked. Again, because of the range of different software that they run, there are lots of bugs and security problems an attacker can exploit. We can also see that the company's various servers, although probably slightly more difficult to attack, will still be prime targets for attackers. The servers will probably be running

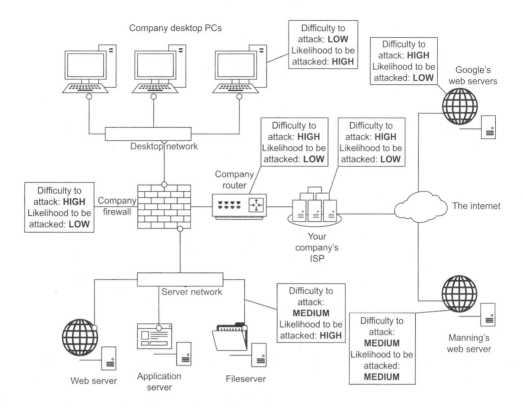

Figure 4.6   How a hacker might view our example company infrastructure

older, complex software, which is difficult to fix. Turning off those servers to fix them also stops people from working and costs the company money; many companies will put that off for as long as possible.

You might be thinking that a company that's invested lots of money in IT systems would also invest lots of money in protecting them and keeping the software up to date. Unfortunately, that's rarely the case. A survey in 2016 found that 80% of companies that had a data breach or had failed an audit could have addressed this by patching it in time (http://mng.bz/nNBg). A 2018 survey found that the average time for a company to patch a discovered vulnerability was 67 days (http://mng.bz/v62J). And another report in 2018 found that 37% of all organizations don't even scan their systems for vulnerabilities (http://mng.bz/44ya).

Company routers and firewalls tend to be better secured and configured. Although serious security flaws can be found, the manufacturers are much better at fixing them and supplying patches and updates.

Let's now try to use our models to think about how—and where—we could attack the company network. Use the same scoring, work through the OODA loop and hacker mindset models to plan out a possible attack. Again, there's no right solution for this; use the models to think about how you would use your current skills and knowledge to formulate an attack.

EXERCISE

Let's use our two models to plan out how we would attack the home network to get access to the user's data. There is no right way here (or in any hacking); there's just "This is what worked for me." Keep that in mind while working through the exercise!

We've already worked out which components on this network are the easiest to attack. We can start to use the OODA loop to build our plan:

- *Orient*—Where is the user's data? What happens to the user's data while they are working?
- *Observe*—Is the user's data stored on, or passing through, any devices that are easier to attack? Would that make it easier to get to the data?
- *Decide*—What sort of attack will we try, and on which component? Why?
- *Act*—Launch our attack.

Here's where we use our hacker mindset to further dig into the problem:

- How does this work?
- How can I break it?
- What else can I make it do?
- What does this mean I can do?

4.2   *Data injection attacks*

Any time an application asks us for input, it opens up the possibility for us to throw in some malicious data. Data injection attacks are a common and popular route for attackers to gain access to systems and to steal data; they are easy to exploit, and they don't require much effort from the attacker.

There are lots of ways to attack an application or bit of infrastructure by injecting bad or malicious data. We're going to look at the two most common—and most successful—approaches that are still used by attackers today: SQLi and cross-site scripting (XSS).

First, let's do a very high-level recap of how a website is built. Web applications are written using three main types of coding:

- *HTML*—A mark-up language that tells a browser how to lay out and display the text and graphics on the page
- *Cascading style sheets (CSS)*—A way of enforcing the look and layout of the HTML elements
- *JavaScript*—A scripting language that provides the interactive elements of a page (collapsing menus, user input forms, etc.)

At the simplest level, a website has two parts:

- *The web server*—Holds all the code and website content (images, text, etc.) and deals with requests from web browser clients
- *A database server*—Stores all the data for the site (usernames, passwords, payment details, addresses, etc.)

4.2.1   SQLi

We touched on a data injection attack with SQLi briefly in chapter 3. Let's look again at our simple financial services web application and how data is sent between the user's web browser and the application's servers.

Quick reminder: the relational databases (like Oracle and MySQL) that websites use have a special data manipulation language called Structured Query Language (SQL). For the database server to understand the web server, the web server converts the data and commands into SQL before sending it to the database server.

The financial services client has a simple web application that allows clients to log in over the internet and see what investments they have in their ISAs (figure 4.7).

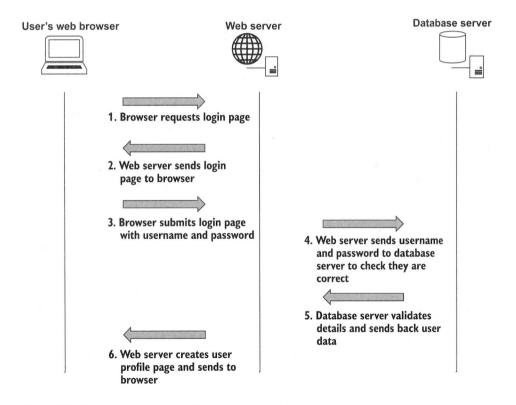

Figure 4.7   Our sample web application

The application itself is fairly straightforward:

- A web server serves a simple login page to the user.
- Once the user logs in, the web server retrieves their data from the database server.
- The web server then presents this data back to the user.

SQLi attacks are all about injecting SQL commands into a vulnerable web application to try to get the web server to send our malicious SQL to the database server (figure 4.8). The database server then executes our command and should display back lots of sensitive data for us.

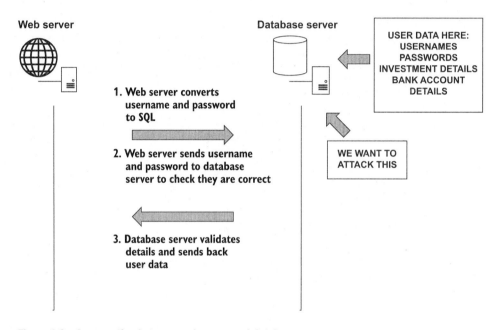

Web server

1. **Web server converts username and password to SQL**

2. **Web server sends username and password to database server to check they are correct**

3. **Database server validates details and sends back user data**

Database server

USER DATA HERE:
USERNAMES
PASSWORDS
INVESTMENT DETAILS
BANK ACCOUNT
DETAILS

WE WANT TO
ATTACK THIS

Figure 4.8   Conversation between web server and database server

We covered the actual SQL code used to carry out this attack in chapter 3. To summarize, anywhere we can enter data that ends up at the database server is somewhere we can try an SQLi attack. Poorly written applications don't check that the data that's entered (like a username) is valid, and so can be used to inject extra SQL statements.

In our financial services example, the SQL statement processed by the database server scans through the lists of usernames and passwords it has until it finds one that matches. It then returns a positive result (TRUE) to the web server (if the record exists). If our username or password was incorrect, the database server won't find them and will return a negative result (FALSE) to the web server—in which case we wouldn't get logged in.

What we're trying to do here is trick the database server by giving it no username, but an SQL statement saying "or else assume this value is true." The database server won't find the username (we didn't give it one!) but the "assume this value is true" part means it will then select *every single username*.

Once we've established that SQLi is possible, the gloves are really off. We can send all sorts of interesting and complex SQL queries to the database server. In a real-world scenario, the database server would hold multiple databases, each containing multiple tables of data. If we could launch a SQLi attack, we could craft the more complex SQL queries that the developers and database administrators (DBAs) would use to retrieve data across those multiple databases and tables.

When we hear about major breaches—tens of millions of credit card details being stolen or hundreds of thousands of social security numbers—the attacks have used SQLi to pull that data out of a backend database somewhere.

If you want to find out more about SQL, I recommend *SQL in Motion*, by Ben Brumm, available from Manning (https://www.manning.com/livevideo/sql-in-motion).

DEFENSES

Defending against SQLi attacks is very easy: check all data being input by a user and strip or reject any characters used by SQL. Things like ", =, and ; characters should never appear in fields on a web form that ask for plain-text data, such as usernames, passwords, or addresses. There are a wide range of tools available—many built into web developer languages and development environments—which can spot and warn about input data that hasn't been sanitized. There's also a wide range of scanning software that can check your existing web applications for SQLi flaws.

A prepared statement (or parameterized statement) is a method to pre-compile SQL code, separating it from any data. This means any SQLi attack will fail because the code that's being executed can't be modified by adding extra statements to it. Prepared statements also offer the ability to sanitize data and carry out sanity checks on the data, like making sure a username actually matches the format of stored usernames.

SQLi remains one of the most common—and most devastating—coding flaws that allow attackers to steal huge amounts of confidential data. Protecting against it is an easy fix, and there's really no excuse for seeing so many breaches that involve SQLi.

4.2.2 *Cross-site scripting*

Cross-site scripting is a shockingly common flaw that is one of the most widespread attacks. XSS occurs when a web application takes data from a user and then dynamically includes that data in a web page without properly checking the data. Common examples include these:

- Search boxes
- Username and password forms
- Online web forums, where you can post a message or include graphics

In all situations, a web application is taking data from the user—and an attacker can embed a malicious script, which then gets executed by the unwitting end user.

Rather than having to log in for every single page we load from a website, after we first log in, the web server will send our browser a small string of digits called a *session cookie*. For every request our web browser sends to the server afterward, the session cookie is included. This shows the web server that we are logged in, which is much easier than sending our username and password each time we load a page.

However, if an attacker can steal our session cookie from our browser, they can send it with their requests to the web server, which will then assume the attacker is logged in with our credentials, allowing them access to our data. XXS is an effective and simple attack that can be used to steal user credentials like the session cookie— the two most common being *reflected* XSS and *persistent* XSS.

Reflected XSS is where an attacker tricks a user into clicking on a link to a valid website, but the link includes the malicious JavaScript code as well. The user's browser sends the request to the vulnerable website, and the malicious JavaScript is then reflected back to the user's browser, where it gets executed (see figure 4.9).

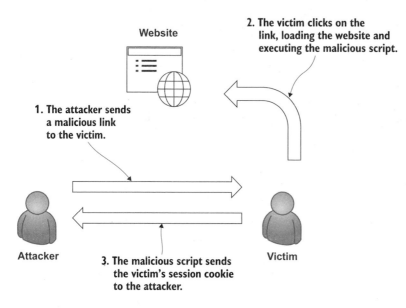

Figure 4.9   How a reflected XSS attack is used to steal a victim's session cookie

Persistent XSS is commonly found in web applications like discussion forums, where users are able to configure their own custom usernames, which get displayed on each post. This information is stored in a database, making it persistent. An attacker can enter malicious JavaScript as their custom username: this way, whenever a user views the attacker's profile page, the malicious code is automatically executed.

Any website that permanently stores user-entered data, which is to be displayed to other users, could be vulnerable to persistent XSS. This is a powerful attack; every time a user views my profile page, for example, I could be stealing their session cookies.

Reflected XSS is used to target a single user at a time. Persistent XSS is used to target lots and lots of users at the same time (see figure 4.10).

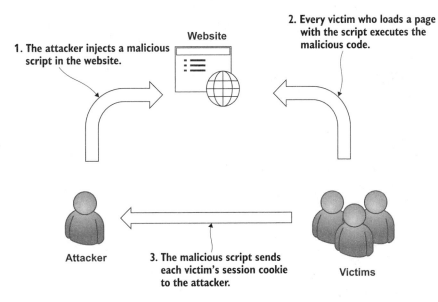

Figure 4.10   How a persistent XSS attack is used to steal lots of victims' session cookies

EXERCISE

The process behind a XXS attack is very simple, and testing for the vulnerability is even easier. All we need to do is paste some JavaScript code into a web form and then click Submit. We don't need to do anything malicious; all we need is our simple Java-Script code that pops up a message on the screen.

Developers can craft some complex JavaScript, but at its core, it's a simple language. As with HTML, we enclose our JavaScript with some opening and closing tags:

```
<script>
    ......
</script>
```

When we're testing for XSS, we want to do something basic, like pop up a message box. For this, we use the alert function:

```
alert("OUR_MESSAGE_GOES_HERE")
```

When we plug this into the opening and closing tags, our simple XSS script structure looks like this:

```
<script>
    alert("OUR_MESSAGE_GOES_HERE")
</script>
```

If you want to go further into the power of JavaScript (malicious embedded images, for example, are very powerful), I highly recommend the Manning book *Get Programming with JavaScript*, by John R. Larsen (http://mng.bz/Qv1w).

Here's our basic bit of code, presented so it's easy to copy and paste; its job is to do nothing more than pop up a box on the screen with the message "XSS Worked!":

```
<script>alert("XSS Worked!")</script>
```

Running off to random websites—especially our employers'—and trying out even a benign test for XSS would be a bit rude. Luckily, there are a range of websites and tools out there that are built to allow people to test these things. In this case, we'll use a site built by some engineers at Google called XSS Game. The site can be found at https://xss-game.appspot.com/ and presents a series of simulated websites, each of which are vulnerable to increasingly complex XSS attacks.

For this exercise we just want level 1, which requires injecting the above JavaScript into a webform, to get our pop-up message.

Read the instructions, and then try it for yourself. Once you complete level 1, you can either stop or continue through the levels. Although knowledge of HTML and JavaScript is needed to complete the rest of the levels, it's a very good way to test your understanding of XSS and secure web coding.

DEFENSES

Defending against XSS is actually pretty simple. A website user never needs to enter code into a form or application, so all user-provided input should be checked to see if it contains code or coding characters, and these should be stripped or rejected back to the user with an error. *Validating input* (also called *sanitizing input*) in this way ensures that our web application is only getting the input data we expect. We also need to make sure our web application properly encodes all data sent back to the user's browser to ensure that we're not sending nasty scripts or data back to the user.

There are numerous tools and scanners available to check a web application for XSS flaws, and there are also a large number of secure coding tools, which developers can use when writing code, that ensure XSS flaws never happen in the first place. Unfortunately, these aren't in widespread use, making XSS still one of the most common—and effective—web application attacks.

Lots of security vendors and far too many security professionals will talk about stopping and fixing XSS and SQLi attacks with a web application firewall (WAF). A WAF works in the same way as a normal firewall, except instead of stopping malicious traffic at the network level, the WAF stops malicious requests at the application level.

While there is a place for WAFs as an extra layer of defense, they are rarely fully effective. The majority of software is badly written and doesn't interact well with other software components. This means that a WAF will block valid requests because they look like malicious ones. This then breaks the actual web application and results in the WAF being turned off.

A WAF needs to be trained and configured over time to understand what it should block and what it should allow. A global asset management company I worked with, which had a complex global infrastructure, was unable to turn on all of their WAFs' abilities even after two years of configuration. A WAF can be configured to block some of the simplest and most obvious XSS and SQLi attacks, but the simplest and most cost-effective thing to do is to address the problem at the root cause: *within the application*. Fix the software first, and then look at expensive security solutions to add extra layers of defense and protection.

4.3   Malware: Viruses, Trojans, and ransomware

Malware is the term given to the arsenal of malicious software that forms a key part of any attacker's tool kit. Malware is the vector of many attacks; the attacker's goal is to get the malware onto our computer, where it can wreak various amounts of havoc.

Let's look at the different types of malware and see what they can do.

4.3.1   Viruses

For as long as there have been computers, there have been viruses. A computer virus is a malicious program that mimics its real-world namesake: infect a host, display some symptoms, and then get transmitted to the next host. There's a huge variety of viruses out there, and they all have some common traits:

- *Self-replicating*—A computer virus is designed so that it can copy itself from machine to machine, either over the network or via removable media like USB (or floppy discs, if you're old like me). Some of the most effective, like the ILOVEYOU virus, spread by attaching themselves to all your outgoing emails.
- *Destructive*—The early viruses merely stopped your work or slowed down your computer. As the malware became more sophisticated, however, it also became more dangerous. Some would accidently delete data required to boot your computer, but some viruses deliberately tried to erase (for example) all Word documents on your computer or overwrite key operating system files, causing your machine to crash. These effects are always delayed after the initial infection to give the virus a chance to spread.
- *Funny*—These viruses started out as a way to play a programmatical joke on people. The Techno virus would blast out a couple minutes of techno music once every 10 times that your computer started. Cookie Monster was unleashed on students at MIT and would flash "cookie" on your screen. If you didn't immediately type "cookie" in return, the virus would display more requests, more frequently, as well as the message "Cookie, cookie, give me a cookie." This would

carry on for several minutes—interrupting all work that you or your computer was trying to do—until the message "I didn't want a cookie anyway" appeared, at which point the virus would go dormant again for a random amount of time.

Viruses are pretty amazing bits of code. They hide in special areas of your computer's storage and memory. They can insert copies of themselves into your data and your normal programs so that more copies are run all the time. Some of them can actually modify their own code each time they run to try to avoid detection from antivirus software.

4.3.2   *Trojans*

Trojans get their name from the famous trick at Troy. Rather than being self-replicating, Trojans are spread by *social engineering*: the act of psychological manipulation to trick a user into doing something for an attacker. We'll cover social engineering in a lot more detail in chapter 5, but in the meantime, think about the most recent deluge of spam in your email inbox. How many emails have you seen that claim to be from

- An insurance company, with a payout for an accident you had?
- HR, with a surprise bonus?
- The taxman, unbelievably offering you a refund?
- A courier company who can't deliver an order?

All these emails have something in common: they have an attachment for you to open to find out more information. They're also all examples of social engineering, and all of those attachments contain a Trojan.

Unlike a virus, a Trojan isn't normally destructive. The most common *payloads* (actions the malware takes after infection) open a *backdoor* (a remote connection) to your computer and make you vulnerable to data theft.

Beast is a Trojan that infects Windows computers and was a successful backdoor Trojan. Also called a *remote administration tool* (RAT), backdoor Trojans run a second application as their malicious payload, which allows a remote operator to take over administrative control of your machine. Once the attacker had control, they could steal copies of your data, run further malicious code, or chain your infected computer with hundreds (or even thousands) of others to form a distribute network of robot attackers: a *botnet*.

The Zeus banking Trojan infects a user's machine, and then lies dormant until the user accesses an online banking website—at which point it will copy the user's credentials and then send them over the internet to an operator. Zeus is a complex and very dangerous bit of code that's still in widespread use today, some 13 years after it was first discovered by security researchers. Zeus uses stealth techniques to hide itself from antivirus software, making it very difficult to remove.

Because Zeus is so effective at spreading itself and so good at evading detection, the actual Trojan code is used to deliver all sorts of other types of malware as well, most notably ransomware.

4.3.3   *Ransomware*

Ransomware is the final type of malware we'll look at, and it's particularly nasty. Combining the worst attributes of viruses and Trojans, ransomware is both self-replicating and spread by social engineering and will hide itself inside normal data and applications.

Once your machine is infected, ransomware will either take copies of your data and threaten to publish it or will encrypt your data (or your entire hard drive), denying you access to it. In both cases, you are greeted with an unpleasant message popping up on your screen, and you'll be unable to use your machine (or get your data back) until you pay the operators a ransom.

Cryptolocker was one of the most successful bits of ransomware spread by our Trojan friend Zeus. Cryptolocker looked for a specific list of data files to encrypt and then demanded a ransom paid via Bitcoin (an almost anonymous online currency) or prepaid cash cards. When Cryptolocker first appeared in 2013, this ransom worked out to around $2,500 per infected machine. Cryptolocker was so successful that the US Department of Justice got involved, which resulted in the Zeus botnet used to spread the ransomware being shut down a year later—after the developer pocketed an estimate $3 million in extorted ransoms.

Another famous piece of ransomware was WannaCry, which appeared in 2017 and quickly spread to over 203,000 computers in over 50 countries. Like Cryptolocker, WannaCry encrypted data files and demanded a ransom payable via Bitcoin. WannaCry infected a huge range of high-profile organizations, including FedEx, Deutsche Bahn, Honda, Renault, and the Russian Interior Ministry. WannaCry also infected computers across the UK's National Health Service (NHS), resulting in 16 hospitals having to almost completely close, cancelling operations and turning away patients.

WannaCry was particularly controversial because it spread by using a tool called EternalBlue, which exploited a vulnerability in Windows. EternalBlue had been developed by the NSA to deliver their own custom malware to target computers. The NSA hadn't told Microsoft about the Windows flaw to ensure no patch was developed to fix it, so that the NSA could continue to attack computers. A hacking group called the Shadow Brokers managed to compromise an NSA server and steal EternalBlue (along with other malware developed by the NSA), which they then leaked to the internet after first auctioning off other NSA code.

4.3.4   *Protection*

There is an eternally escalating arms race between the developers of malware and the companies building operating systems, applications, and antimalware software. Most operating systems now have built-in abilities to try to defend against malware:

- Software must be digitally signed by an approved certificate from an approved developer.
- Software can only be installed from the vendor's app store.

- The operating system warns the user (and asks for confirmation) each time they try to carry out a "restricted" action.
- The computer will only allow limited, approved operating systems (or even specific operating system versions) to be booted on the machine.

While this is all a great improvement from the wild "anything goes" days of general-purpose computing, it does cause problems for end users. Manufacturers will only provide a limited number of operating system updates to our phone, after which it becomes unsupported and largely useless for use with approved apps. Tablets will only run one operating system, tying us into the services of the manufacturer.

These protections improve security a bit but are still easy to bypass with modern, sophisticated malware, which is where antimalware (previously just antivirus) programs come in. Some sort of antimalware software is now essential for your devices, whether that's a computer or a phone. Software initially developed as antivirus has developed in sophistication alongside the malware it's designed to defend against.

The most common antivirus companies (Symantec, Kaspersky, McAfee) all now have antimalware software suites for computers and phones, which can scan your email and protect your web browsing, as well as scan for infections. Other companies, like Bitdefender and Malwarebytes, offer powerful, free, antimalware software, with paid upgrades to provide further security. All of these also include a software firewall that will limit and control the data that is sent and received by your device. This can help stop attackers launching attacks against your machine and also stop malware from communicating or copying our data.

Clearly, there's no one-size-fits-all approach to defending from malware. However, by combining several different approaches to defense, we can give ourselves the best possible protection. Consider these the four golden rules of malware security:

- Keep our operating system patched and up to date.
- Keep our applications patched and up to date.
- Install antimalware software and a software firewall, and keep them up to date.
- Don't click on email attachments (unless we are absolutely, positively certain they are attached files we were expecting).

4.4   *Dodgy Wi-Fi*

When we connect to a Wi-Fi network—especially one in public, like a coffee shop or airport—we are implicitly trusting that network. We assume that the network is well run, with no malware or attackers on it, and that the services we connect to are all legitimate. Free Wi-Fi is a service they're providing to us, the customer—of course it's safe! Essentially, we treat it as if it were the same as our home network.

This is a huge mistake. We face two big problems with a public Wi-Fi network:

- *We don't know who else is using it.* There could be malicious attackers connected who will attack our computer when we connect.

- *We don't know anything about the network.* Are we really connecting to the public Wi-Fi at Heathrow Airport, terminal 5? Or are we connecting to a network *pretending* to be the public Wi-Fi?

Before we dig into how these attacks work, let's look at how a Wi-Fi network works and how it differs from our home and office networks. As you can see from figure 4.11, there is a Wi-Fi network access point (sometimes called a *base station*), which is constantly broadcasting the ID of its Wi-Fi network (called an *SSID*). Our laptop (or tablet or mobile phone) listens to these broadcasts and presents us with a list of Wi-Fi networks within range. We select the one we want and then authenticate with the Wi-Fi network access point, which then gives us access and routes our data out to the internet.

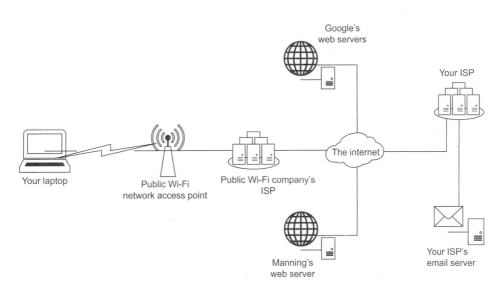

Figure 4.11   An example of how a public Wi-Fi network allows us to connect over the internet to websites and our email server

As we can see, there's an awful lot of trust going on here. We're trusting

- That the Wi-Fi network access point is actually the real one for the network
- That there are no attackers connected to the network
- That the Wi-Fi network access point isn't analyzing and storing our data as it routes it to the internet

EXERCISE

Now that we know how a public Wi-Fi network works and how much trust we're placing in its operators, what are some of the attacks you can think of? Write down three attacks that could take place and why you think they'd be dangerous.

So, what dangers does a malicious Wi-Fi network pose? We face two real issues:

- An attacker is running a fake Wi-Fi network access point.
- An attacker is connected to the same public Wi-Fi.

When the attacker is running a fake Wi-Fi network access point, they rely on unsuspecting users to connect to their fake access point; the attacker then routes all traffic through to the real network access point. In other words, they are *spoofing* the Wi-Fi network. This means that the attacker can view and analyze all of the unprotected data going from our machine to the internet, allowing them to grab usernames, passwords, confidential documents, and so on.

Running a fake Wi-Fi network access point like this to intercept a user's data traffic is called a *man-in-the-middle* (MITM) attack. These are devastating because they give the attacker access to all of the data we send and receive, while also being undetectable. Figure 4.12 illustrates how a MITM attack works.

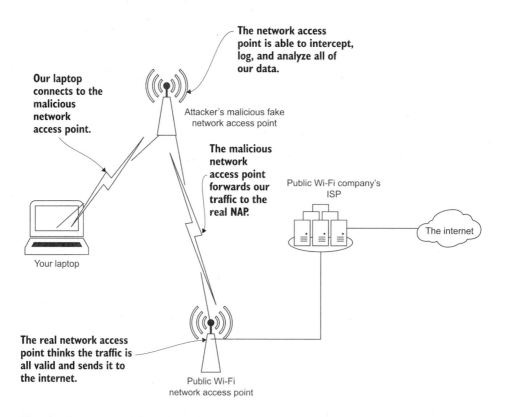

The network access point is able to intercept, log, and analyze all of our data.

Our laptop connects to the malicious network access point.

Attacker's malicious fake network access point

The malicious network access point forwards our traffic to the real NAP.

Public Wi-Fi company's ISP

The internet

Your laptop

The real network access point thinks the traffic is all valid and sends it to the internet.

Public Wi-Fi network access point

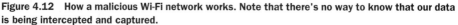

Figure 4.12   How a malicious Wi-Fi network works. Note that there's no way to know that our data is being intercepted and captured.

Setting up a malicious Wi-Fi hotspot is very easy; you just need to configure a device to

- Broadcast the same network name (SSID) as the legitimate Wi-Fi
- Forward all traffic to/from the legitimate Wi-Fi network access point
- Log all the interesting traffic that passes through your device

This is very simple; in fact, my mobile phone has a couple of neat little apps on it for just this purpose, which I use a lot when testing the bring-your-own-device (BYOD) Wi-Fi networks for clients. No one is going to notice someone playing with their phone or that they have a small box next to their laptop that looks like a battery pack.

4.4.1 Defenses

In the section on malware, we looked at two of the most effective solutions that can protect us from an attacker on the same network:

- Antimalware software (including a software firewall)
- Keeping our operating system and applications patched and up to date

We have another powerful but easy-to-use security tool to protect us from fake Wi-Fi network access points: a virtual private network (VPN). A VPN creates a secure, encrypted virtual network between our computer (or phone) and a trusted server (see figure 4.13). All our data is sent over this secured, encrypted link, which is *tunneled* over the hostile public networks. The VPN server then sends out our requests to, for example, our email server. The VPN server receives any replies and sends them back

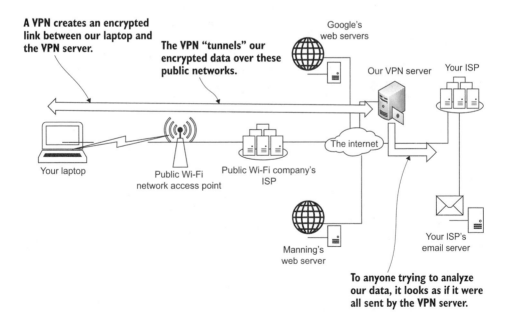

Figure 4.13 How a VPN works. All data and communications between our laptop and the VPN server are encrypted.

to our laptop over the encrypted VPN tunnel. If anyone is trying to spy on us, our data and communications are hidden inside the encrypted VPN tunnel.

More importantly, this allows us to treat the public Wi-Fi network as a *hostile* network—one that we don't trust. The Wi-Fi becomes literally just a conduit to the internet: once connected, we immediately start our VPN, and then all our traffic and data is sent over the VPN's secure connection. Many antimalware software suites will also include a VPN, but there are many other cheap solutions available that are easy to use. Even if there is nothing malicious about the Wi-Fi network, using a VPN maintains our privacy and keeps our data safe; it's a great habit to always be using one.

For a corporate Wi-Fi network, we have another option: authentication to the network with certificates. Our company will install certificates on our laptop or mobile device. When we connect to the company's Wi-Fi (we need the password to do so), the Wi-Fi network will check our device's certificate, and our device will compare the network's certificate. If either of these certificates has been modified, this check will fail, and we can't connect (see figure 4.14).

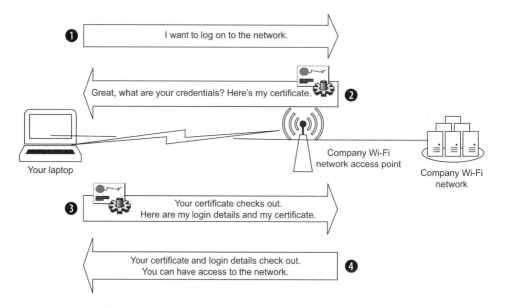

Figure 4.14   Using certificates to authenticate to a company Wi-Fi network

4.5   *Mobile phones, SMS, and 5G*

Mobile phones pose a large security problem. Many people still think of their mobile phone as a smaller, portable version of a desk phone: it's there to make calls. But our mobiles are actually portable, powerful computers, running complex applications, and they have a constant connection to the internet. Most mobile phones have more memory than a cheap laptop and multicore processors that run as fast as a desktop machine. My current mobile phone, for example, has more processing power and memory than a Silicon Graphics supercomputer I installed and operated in the early 2000s.

These mobile computers have all the same problems with malware—and the same solutions—as laptops and desktops. The extra layer of security complexity comes with how a mobile phone communicates with the actual mobile network.

Let's look at a simple diagram that shows how your phone connects to your mobile phone provider's network (figure 4.15). We can immediately see how similar a mobile phone network is to a Wi-Fi network. Much like a Wi-Fi network, each cell tower in a mobile network broadcasts a constant signal—"Connect to me"—over an area, which is called a *cell* (which is why some people call mobile phones *cell phones*). Our mobile connects to the nearest tower and then exchanges some data: the ID of the mobile phone (called the IMEI), the ID of the network, what sort of speed they will operate at, and how much bandwidth the cell tower will give to the mobile phone.

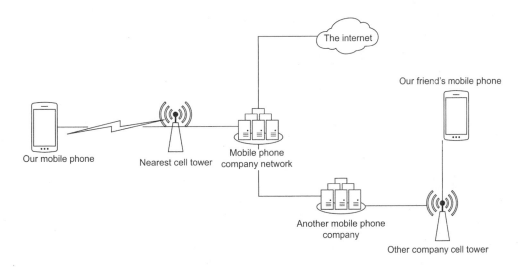

Figure 4.15   A simple view of how a mobile phone network works, showing data connections to the internet and voice/SMS connections to another user's mobile phone

When we're in another country or the nearest cell tower belongs to a different mobile network provider, the connection is slightly more complex (figure 4.16). This situation is called *roaming*—and if you're unlucky, you'll be caught by the harsh charges other networks charge to route your data and calls. The connection takes place, as previously explained, but the cell tower then talks over the network to a cell tower or network device that belongs to your mobile service provider, who then authenticates your device and access.

We'll use these two basic examples of how our phones connect to mobile networks as we look in more detail at the security problems with mobile phones.

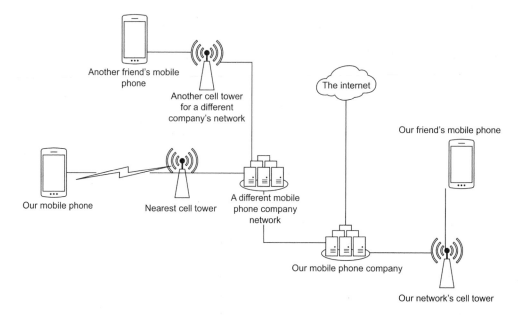

Figure 4.16 How our phone connects to a different mobile provider's network. Note that data is still sent out via our "home" mobile network, but voice/SMS is sent within our roaming network when needed.

4.5.1   *Malware*

We have the same problems with malware on a mobile phone as we do on our desktops and laptops, which makes sense when we think of our phones as powerful, portable, always networked computers. Viruses first started appearing on Nokia's Symbian handsets back in the early 2000s when Nokia had a 90% share of the mobile phone market.

Complex Trojans still manage to evade the security scans and software controls of Google and Apple's app stores, and unless you know what you're doing, downloading apps from third-party websites can be even more risky. Just as with PCs, the phone vendors are building protection mechanisms into the operating system, and there's a range of antimalware software available that can be installed.

5G, the next-generation mobile communication protocol, brings much greater bandwidth to our mobiles. The downside is that this enables malware to copy and upload larger amounts of our sensitive data before being detected. Again, like with PCs, mobile phones have firewall apps (e.g., NetGuard and Blokada) that can be installed to block outgoing traffic. As an added bonus, these will also block requests to advertising and tracking websites, enhancing privacy, reducing the amount of data we use, and helping to improve the speed of apps and web browsing.

4.5.2 IMEI cloning

Each modern phone has a unique identifier—a "network identity"—called an international mobile equipment identity (IMEI; see figure 4.17). Each time our mobile phone connects to a cell tower, it broadcasts the IMEI, a sort of "Hey, network, it's me!"

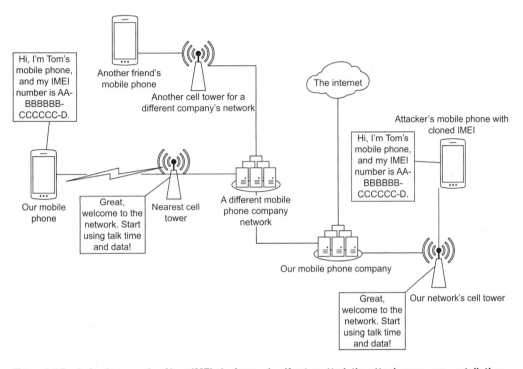

Figure 4.17 **A simple example of how IMEI cloning works. If not spotted, the attacker can use our talk time and data and can send out SMS spam and malware.**

This IMEI is broadcast not just from your phone to the nearest tower, but from that tower to other towers. All of this happens *in the clear;* in other words, this data isn't encrypted. This means that an enterprising attacker can set up relatively cheap equipment to scan for an IMEI and then clone it by programming the same number into their phone.

IMEI cloning has been going on since digital GSM mobile phones were first developed and is a way for an attacker to steal your data and talk time. Devices to clone and reprogram IMEIs are very cheap and common; this is an easy attack to carry out. Network providers have developed large, complex fraud-detection systems to tackle the problem of cloning. These systems are constantly monitoring where and how often an IMEI is being picked up by their network.

If I'm using my IMEI in Milan, and then suddenly the network notices that minutes later my IMEI has popped up in New York, the provider knows that this is fraud, and the IMEI is locked out of the network. In many countries in Europe, IMEI cloning is illegal, with jail time if caught. By law, network providers have to lock an IMEI if asked and have to authenticate a user with an ID to unlock the IMEI.

4.5.3   *SMS spoofing*

Along with IMEI cloning, another cheap and easy attack is intercepting and spoofing SMS (short messaging service) messages—what most people call texts. Again, the equipment to do this is cheap and freely available, and the problem comes down to how the networks send SMS messages.

Calls and texts use a special protocol called SS7 (Signaling System No. 7; I know, it sounds like a beauty product). Regardless of the data protocol (2G, HSDPA, 5G, etc.), all phone networks support and provide SS7; it's the scaffolding across all networks that allows us to call and text someone on the other side of the world.

To make it easy for every network provider to handle and pass on calls and text messages, SS7 has very weak encryption and no authentication. SS7 was developed when there were only a handful of state-controlled mobile network providers, so trust between networks wasn't an issue. Because of this, it's possible to craft SS7 messages to a network that diverts incoming texts to our malicious phone or device, and then forward spoofed texts to the end user. We can also set up fake cell towers and intercept all user data that way. This is another example of a MITM attack, just like with our dodgy Wi-Fi network.

Additionally, an attacker can use SS7 commands to track a specific user by tracing their mobile phone number as it is broadcast between cell towers. With the density of cell towers in a city, it is possible to track someone down to where they are on a street. None of this requires expensive or bulky equipment; we can do this for less than the price of a decent laptop and carry all the gear needed in a small backpack.

Back in 2014, at the Chaos Communications Congress in Berlin, researchers Tobias Engel and Karsten Nohl presented two different talks that showed how easy it was to track mobile phone users, intercept SMS messages, and even send commands with SS7 to force a user's phone to dial premium paid numbers in the background (http://mng.bz/XZQG).

SS7 used to be a closed system and thus was difficult for researchers to play with. Since the protocol has been opened up for third parties to provide extra services, we've been able to really dig into how it all works.

Let's revisit our diagram that shows how our mobile phone communicates when we're not connected to our home network (figure 4.18).

Now let's look at the two different ways we can cause problems with SS7. Figure 4.19 shows that we can plant a fake cell tower on the network by being closer to the user and by broadcasting with more power, which causes the user's phone to automatically connect to it. This is how Stingray interception devices, used by law enforcement (and criminals), work. You'll notice that this works a lot like the malicious Wi-Fi network access point.

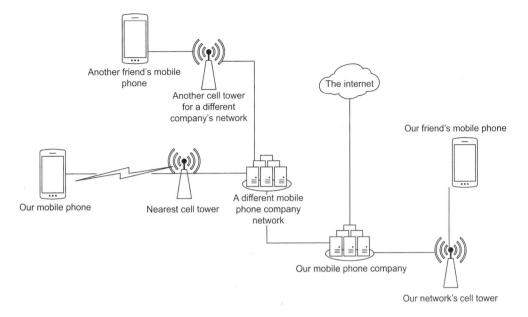

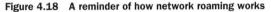

Figure 4.18   A reminder of how network roaming works

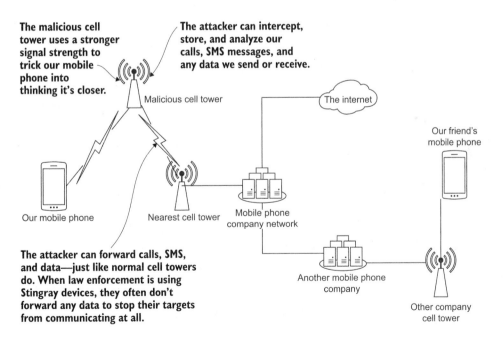

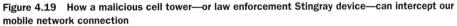

Figure 4.19   How a malicious cell tower—or law enforcement Stingray device—can intercept our mobile network connection

By taking advantage of the constant messages sent between our mobile phone and cell towers outside our home network (which is legitimate traffic), we can also trick our home network into thinking that our mobile has moved somewhere else. This enables us to intercept and spoof SMS messages.

A mobile phone network contains more than just cell towers. There are also special components that are used to track a phone's location (to make the most efficient use of the cell tower bandwidth) that register and authenticate a user on the network and that decide where and how to route calls and data. An SMS spoofing/interception attack utilizes three of these devices:

- *The Mobile-Services Switching Center (MSC)*—This is the interface between the radio network (the cell towers) and the physical network of servers and services. As the name implies, the MSC's job is to switch (direct) mobile services like SMS, voice, and data between the two networks.
- *The Home Location Register (HLR)*—This is a database that contains the details of every mobile phone that is authorized to use the network. There are multiple HLRs on a network, but a user can only be registered on one of them. The HLR is used by the MSC to understand where to route the services to so that our phone can use them.
- *The Short Message Service Gateway (SMSC)*—This is the gateway between the radio network (the cell towers) and the central Short Message Service Center, which is what processes all SMS messages.

When our phone connects to a network, as well as broadcasts our IMEI, as part of the network authentication process, our mobile number is sent to the network as well. Although it looks like just a phone number to us, mobile providers call it the Mobile Station International Subscriber Directory Number (MSISDN). We also have a unique identifier on every single SIM card, which is called an International Mobile Subscriber Identity (IMSI). Together, these two numbers are used to tell the network where we are so that the MSC can properly route calls and SMS messages to us (see figure 4.20).

So far, so good—if a bit acronym-heavy. Let's summarize the steps in bullet points to make it easy to see where the problem is:

- We register our IMSI and MSISDN with our nearest HLR.
- The HRL tells the MSC where we are located.
- The MSC routes all SMS traffic through our nearest SMS-C.
- The SMS-C is able to send SMS messages to our closest cell tower.

Think back to our malicious Wi-Fi hotspot example or our IMEI cloning example. Can you spot the step where an attacker can intercept—and spoof—our SMS messages?

The problem lies with registering with the HLR. The same cheap, easy-to-set-up, and easy-to-deploy equipment that can sniff IMEIs being broadcast to the network can

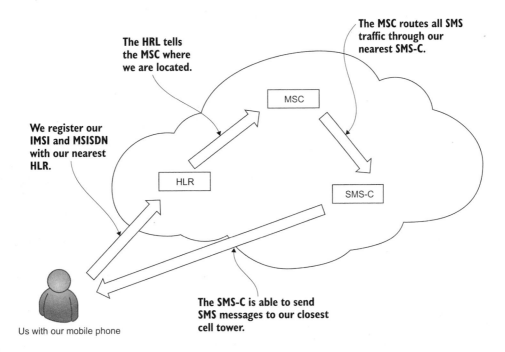

We register our
IMSI and MSISDN
with our nearest
HLR.

The HRL tells
the MSC where
we are located.

The MSC routes all SMS
traffic through our
nearest SMS-C.

The SMS-C is able to send
SMS messages to our closest
cell tower.

Us with our mobile phone

Figure 4.20 A simplified view of the normal sequence of events when we register with the mobile network and SMS messages get routed to our phone

also catch IMSI and MSISDN numbers. These numbers are all constantly being broadcast, updating the numerous HLRs on the network as we move around.

How can an attacker intercept our SMS messages? Exactly the same technique allows the attacker to spoof SMS messages, making them appear to be from us. All a hacker has to do is register our IMSI and MSISDN numbers, and then the MSC will route our SMS messages to the attacker. Let's look at how that could be used in an attack (see figure 4.21).

There's a lot going on in this diagram, so let's list the steps as well to make the sequence of events clear:

1 The attacker uses a fake MSC to register our IMSI and MSISDN with an HLR.
2 The HRL tells the MSC that "we" are in a new location.
3 We try to log in to our online banking, which uses SMS authentication.
4 Our bank sends us an SMS message to authenticate our login.
5 The MSC sends the SMS message to the SMS-C.
6 The SMS-C asks the HLR where we are located. The HLR tells the SMS-C the attacker's location.
7 Our SMS authentication message ends up with the attacker.

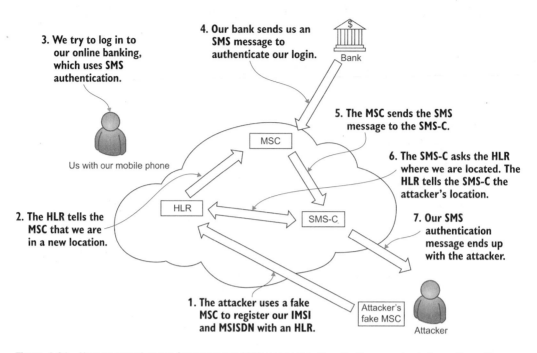

3. We try to log in to our online banking, which uses SMS authentication.

Us with our mobile phone

4. Our bank sends us an SMS message to authenticate our login.

Bank

MSC

5. The MSC sends the SMS message to the SMS-C.

6. The SMS-C asks the HLR where we are located. The HLR tells the SMS-C the attacker's location.

HLR

SMS-C

2. The HLR tells the MSC that we are in a new location.

7. Our SMS authentication message ends up with the attacker.

1. The attacker uses a fake MSC to register our IMSI and MSISDN with an HLR.

Attacker's fake MSC

Attacker

Figure 4.21   How an attacker can intercept our SMS messages. Exactly the same technique allows the attacker to spoof SMS messages, making them appear to be from us.

Again, this is a very powerful attack, and all of the equipment needed is readily available and costs less than a new Apple laptop. Think of all the online services that use SMS as a secondary authentication method, alongside a username and password:

- Online banking (obviously)
- Facebook
- Twitter
- Google
- Cryptocurrency exchanges (Bitcoin)
- And many more

Also, as SMS messages (and phone calls) from the attacker appear to be coming from us, it allows an attacker to request things like a mobile number or password change on an account. This attack has been used to take over celebrities' Twitter accounts and to steal hundreds of thousands of dollars' worth of Bitcoin from online exchanges. A *Forbes* article told the sorry tale of a Bitcoin pioneer who had millions of dollars in Bitcoin transferred out of his account by attackers using these same SMS intercept and spoofing attacks.

As SMS messages are so easy to spoof, try to avoid using SMS authentication as the *sole* means to secure things like your banking or online services accounts. Almost all online services now support more secure—and easier-to-use—solutions to securing those accounts, and we'll cover them in great detail in chapter 10, where we'll talk about multi-factor authentication (MFA).

4.5.4 Problems with 5G

No, 5G doesn't give you COVID-19, and despite the best efforts of conspiracy theorists, 5G cell towers also don't beam out mind-control rays. I'm also going to ignore the ongoing argument about Huawei and their role in providing 5G technology to network providers: all governments use the communication networks to spy on each other; there are no surprises or shocking revelations there.

However, there are some security issues with the 5G protocol itself, and they are related to how the previous mobile communication protocols were developed. 5G is the fifth generation of mobile communication protocols that have been developed globally by industry-working groups, the two main ones being the Global System for Mobile Communications Association (GSMA) and the 3rd Generation Partnership Project (3GPP). Figure 4.22 shows what the evolution of these protocols looks like, the technologies each uses, and the data transfer rates they are capable of.

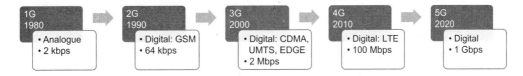

Figure 4.22   How the various mobile technologies have evolved. Note the rapidly increasing data transfer rates.

As a communications protocol, 5G has to be backward compatible with all the previous protocols; otherwise, you won't be able to, well, communicate. The mishmash of broadcast frequencies and protocols in the US is, frankly, pretty broken, but across the rest of the world, 2G is still used a lot because it is able to travel longer distances and can cope much better with obstacles blocking the signal. As the bandwidth made available by each protocol increases, the distance the signal travels gets shorter, and a greater number of cell towers are needed. However, each generation of protocol makes more-efficient use of the broadcast frequency (the *spectrum*), so each cell tower can give more bandwidth to more users (see figure 4.23).

As we can see from figures 4.22 and 4.23, 5G provides the most bandwidth, but its signal travels the shortest distance and so needs more cell towers to provide coverage; 2G, on the other hand, is the opposite: not much bandwidth, but great signal transmission and penetration. All this means that 2G remains very popular globally—not just for mobile phones, but for all sorts of devices that need to communicate wirelessly over long distances.

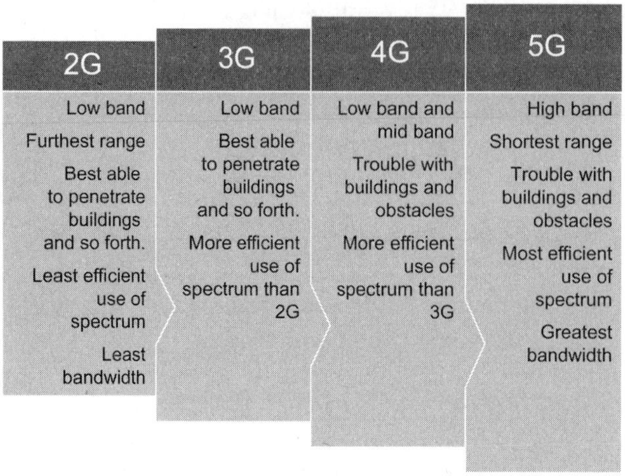

2G	3G	4G	5G
Low band	Low band	Low band and mid band	High band
Furthest range	Best able to penetrate buildings and so forth.	Trouble with buildings and obstacles	Shortest range
Best able to penetrate buildings and so forth.	More efficient use of spectrum than 2G	More efficient use of spectrum than 3G	Trouble with buildings and obstacles
Least efficient use of spectrum			Most efficient use of spectrum
Least bandwidth			Greatest bandwidth

Figure 4.23   Comparing the different mobile protocols

This is why backward compatibility is so important: we still need to make voice calls and send SMS messages to the hundreds of millions of older phones and devices out there.

Because of this backward compatibility, the full 5G communications protocol still includes all the old communication and authentication methods that make 2G, SMS, and voice calls work, like our friend SS7. This means that the same attacks to clone IMEI numbers and intercept and spoof SMS messages still work on 5G. Making the problem worse, the increase in bandwidth that each new protocol generation gave us created a boom in the number of smart devices that communicate wirelessly.

QUICK EXERCISE

Out of the following list of devices, which do you think communicate wirelessly over the mobile network?

- Smart electricity/gas meter
- Electric car charging point
- Traffic light cameras
- CCTV cameras
- Wind turbines
- Aircraft jet engines
- A new Tesla, BMW, or Mercedes

If you guessed "all of the above," you are correct. They all have some version of mobile communication built into them.

A few years ago, my friend was showing off the text-to-speech capability of his new BMW. He'd enabled the option so that you could send an SMS to the car, and it would read out the message for you while you were driving. Amazing tech!

So, I waited until he was out driving with his wife, and then spoofed an SMS message to his car, pretending to be his pregnant mistress. Apparently, they didn't see the funny side, but I laughed for days. Top marks for BMW technology from me.

This huge increase in devices is making it ever more difficult for the companies running the mobile phone networks to spot and stop fraud like duplicate IMEIs. We're in an arms race between manufacturers, service providers, and attackers; with the speed and coverage increase that 5G brings, this is a problem that will only get worse.

We also have the problem of *botnets*—malicious networks of compromised machines. As a portable computer, a mobile phone has a decent amount of security either built in or available to install. Smart meters, wind turbines, and CCTV cameras don't really have that level of security available, because the manufacturer wants to keep the price down for mass production. This means that a lot of these devices are very vulnerable to security attacks we thought had been solved decades ago.

For example, CCTV cameras often have no passwords on their admin accounts; if they do have a password, it will be the same one across thousands of that model. Botnet operators have been busy installing malware across devices like these, providing them with a huge network of devices they can launch attacks from.

Back in 2016, for example, security company Sucuri uncovered (and stopped) an attack that was launched from a botnet of 25,000 compromised CCTV cameras. This was a simple distributed DDoS attack that was aimed at clogging up a vendor's website, but botnets like this have been used to launch more sophisticated attacks, such as fraudulently registering clicks on a website advertisement, generating income for the attackers from the publishing network.

Unlike a PC, we can't just install some patches across a network of charging stations or CCTV cameras. It's too time consuming (and therefore expensive) for the operators. In many cases, the manufacturers don't provide security patches or updates at all. With the increase in the number of devices and the bandwidth they have available to them that comes with 5G, we're going to see this becoming more and more of an issue.

4.5.5 *Keeping safe*

Individually, there's little we can do about the poor level of security on the increasing number of connected, smart devices—the Internet of Things (IoT). However, we do have control over our own mobile phones, our personal portable supercomputers.

Ultimately, you should treat security on your mobile phone the same way you would treat security on your laptop:

- Keep your operating system and applications updated.
- Don't install applications from unofficial sources.
- Install some antimalware software and a firewall, and keep them up to date.
- Remember the four golden rules of malware protection.

Summary

- We can combine the hacker mindset and the OODA loop models to plan out our own theoretical attacks. An attacker can use these models to loop (iterate) through several different types of attacks until they get what they want.

- The two most common—and easiest to protect against—data injection attacks are SQLi and XSS.
- The four golden rules of malware protection are as follows:
  - Keep our operating system patched and up to date.
  - Keep our applications patched and up to date.
  - Install antimalware software and a software firewall, and keep them up to date.
  - Don't click on email attachments (unless we are absolutely, positively certain they are attached files we were expecting).
- Wi-Fi and mobile phone communications are very similar, which leads to MIMT and spoofing attacks.
- Attackers can spoof a Wi-Fi network by running a fake Wi-Fi network access point and relying on users to connect through the fake access point. The attacker can analyze the data activity via the internet connection and identify key information (e.g., usernames, passwords, confidential documents).
- Attackers can intercept and spoof SMS messages to trick our mobile provider's network into thinking our phone has moved elsewhere and reroute the information to the attacker's location.
- By understanding how to use malware and attacks via security problems with Wi-Fi and mobile networks to steal user's credentials and data, we'll be better able to defend against these attacks.
- Understanding how invisible hacks like MITM attacks—spoofing Wi-Fi and mobile communications—work is incredibly powerful; being able to silently steal data, credentials, and authentication messages was once the province of nations' spy agencies.
- No matter how many protection technologies we deploy, people are always the weakest link in the security.

Tricking our way in: Social engineering

Social engineering is the psychological manipulation of someone, with the goal of getting them to do what we want. In this chapter, we will explore how attackers use various types of social engineering to plant malware and steal credentials. We'll also learn how to stop them.

You'll need to have read chapter 4 to get the most out of this chapter; social engineering builds on the common attacks we covered there. As we explore social engineering, the focus will be on our personal behavior—how social engineering affects and exploits us—to extend this new understanding (and best practices to combat it) to our employees and colleagues.

5.1   *The weakest link: People*

A lot of people who work in security come from an IT, technology-focused background, which makes sense, because you need to have a really broad understanding of IT to do well in security. The downside, of course, is that this means people tend to lean toward technology solutions first.

Back in chapter 2, I mentioned something called PPT—people, processes, and technology—and that this is the order in which established security functions tackle their cybersecurity strategies. Here's a recap:

1 First, train our people—or hire more.
2 Second, look at (and fix) our processes.
3 Third, and finally, once we've done all of this, invest in suitable technology.

There's a reason established security functions should tackle things in this order: because this is the priority that attackers will use to try and breach a company's defenses. No matter how great our security technologies are, our people—and the processes they follow—are always the weakest link in our security.

At the time of writing, Twitter is reeling from a social engineering attack of its staff, one which gave attackers full control over hundreds of high-profile Twitter accounts. The likes of Apple, Barack Obama, Elon Musk, and Jeff Bezos were all merrily sharing cryptocurrency scams from their accounts. To understand why social engineering can be so powerful, let's revisit our hacker mindset model (figure 5.1).

Figure 5.1   The hacker mindset

We've previously looked at applying this to some technology, like a web application. But this is such a powerful model because it can be applied elsewhere—to people and to the processes they follow. Let's look at how we can apply the hacker mindset to a simple process: calling and asking for a user's password to be reset. The process is straightforward (figure 5.2):

1 We call a support team or help desk.
2 We confirm our ID or login name.
3 The helpdesk resets the password for us.

Figure 5.2   A typical example of the steps to reset an account password

We can see how this straightforward process maps to the hacker mindset—and how using the hacker mindset in this way gets us to ask questions about what else we could do and exploring how this process could be exploitable (figure 5.3).

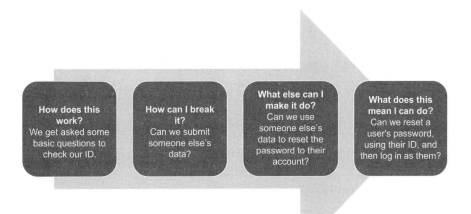

Figure 5.3 Applying the hacker mindset to a process to reset a user's password

From our hacker mindset model, it's also clear what information we need to gather to start trying to exploit this process; in this case, we need to somehow get a user ID. How would you approach getting the information needed to get a helpdesk to reset another user's password for you?

- How could we get the helpdesk phone number?
- How could we get someone's user ID or login account name?
- What other information could we gather to make our request seem more plausible?
- How could we make sure we get the new password?

Now that you've had a chance to think through how you would tackle this, I'll share the steps I used when working for a financial services firm to get access to a user's account:

- *How could we get the helpdesk phone number?* I did two things:
  - Searched on the company's websites to find their helpdesk phone number
  - Loitered in and around reception, pretending to be waiting for someone for a meeting, quietly taking pictures with my smartphone of people's laptops, ID badges, and posters/notices on the walls
- *How could we get someone's user ID or login account name?* Again, loitering in areas where employees meet, work, or grab coffee or food is very useful. People wear

their ID badges clipped to their belts, or on lanyards around their necks, and they don't hide them or remove them when they leave their office. As an added bonus, most ID cards will have the person's name on them.

Their laptops will have ID stickers on them, or if you look over their shoulder, you can see people using an email client or logging in, showing their user ID.

Surreptitiously taking pictures with your smartphone while pretending to type, or pretending to update a report while writing the details down, are great ways to record this information. People rarely question someone with a clipboard with the company's logo on it.

- *What other information could we gather to make our request seem more plausible?* I always look through a company's web pages to see if they have a section that lists out some of their key employees. A web search will also turn up a wealth of information. Data that I found on this engagement included the following:
  - Employees posting to online help forums.
  - This netted me names of people, as well as projects, internal systems, emails, and team names.
  - Details on LinkedIn, including people's names, their job titles, and even what their current projects are.
  - People will share even more details on non-work-related websites; Twitter and Facebook proved a great source of more people's names, positions, and projects.

On top of this, I called the company's switchboard: "Hi, I'm <valid employee name>, working in <valid company department>. I'm trying to find <a different employee's> extension. In case I can't get hold of them, I don't suppose you have their manager's details, do you?" This approach proves surprisingly effective, especially if you can establish your details as an employee.

- *How could we make sure we get the new password?* When I phoned the helpdesk, I made sure I had a plausible story with three key points:
  - *Urgency*—I was working on a specific project for a senior employee. I could provide the details from the data I gathered in the previous step. I needed to provide the report today; otherwise, I'd be in trouble with this senior employee.
  - *Plausibility*—I claimed I had been asked by several senior employees to deliver a report. Again, I could provide information on which departments they worked in, which project the report was related to, and even name some of the key computer systems that were involved. I could also give a valid user ID as well as confirm the name of the employee's account I was trying to steal, along with their department and which building they worked in.
  - *Cooperation*—I explained to the helpdesk that I was working on the train on the way in to the office and that my connection to the company network

was not very reliable. Having established that my request was urgent and plausible, I then pleaded to their good nature to help me out: "Please read out my new password to me so I don't have to wait for an email to come through." I'd given them more information than they would normally need to reset a password; I'd been very helpful by making their job of authenticating me that much easier. Appealing to their good nature and asking them to do something extra to help me out is then much easier.

The end result was that "my" new password was read out to me by the helpful person on the helpdesk, and I then had access to a customer reporting system, full of juicy and confidential client financial data. This is social engineering.

Possibly the most famous example of social engineering is Kevin Mitnick, who started off in 1982 by hacking the North American Defense Command (NORAD)—said by many to be the inspiration behind the film *WarGames*. Mitnick carried out a string of attacks against Digital Equipment Corporation (DEC), Motorola, Fujitsu, NEC, Sun Microsystems, Pacific Bell, IBM, Nokia, and other telecoms and technology companies. He copied proprietary software and source code from these companies and taunted his FBI pursuers, as well as *New York Times* journalist John Markoff and security researcher Tsutomu Shimomura (whose home computer Mitnick hacked). His arrest generated huge controversy: he was held without trial for over four and a half years, while the various victims of his attacks claimed over $80 million in damages for stolen proprietary code. Mitnick was so successful at breaking into companies that eight months of his pre-trial jail time was spent in solitary confinement, as law enforcement officials convinced a judge that he had the ability to "start a nuclear war by whistling into a pay phone."

Mitnick's success came down to social engineering. He convinced support staff to hand over or reset passwords and access codes, which allowed him access to secured systems. Mitnick claims he didn't use hacking tools or software flaws to exploit passwords, and instead relied on convincing company staff that he was a valid user who needed access.

Dealing with social engineering attacks is very difficult. We are wired to be naturally helpful to people, and challenging someone feels rude and inappropriate. Let's look at some common scenarios social engineers have used.

Think about how you would respond to the following situations:

- You have just opened a secured building access door with your key card. You see someone coming toward you with their hands full of files and a laptop; they ask you to hold the door for them. What do you do?
- Someone is at reception for your office, in line to go through the security barrier. They are on the phone, and it's clear they are being chewed out by their boss. Their hands are full of paperwork—lots of graphs and reports on your company's letter head. They give you a pleading look, motioning toward the

barrier and making a helpless shrug to show that their hands are full, all while they are still being shouted at on the phone. What do you do?

- A user calls you late in the afternoon. They are distraught; they have a major project for the chief financial officer that needs to be submitted tomorrow, but their account has been locked. They are able to name the CFO, give you their account login, and tell you which systems they need access to. What do you do?

As you can see, challenging what seem to be valid requests for help is hard—especially when it's such a small act, like holding a door open for someone in need. All of these scenarios have been used by social engineers to break into multinational corporations, gaining access to sensitive corporate data.

One of the most effective ways to protect against these sorts of attacks is to leverage a concept from the military sector: operations security (OpSec). OpSec is a process that identifies critical information, determines if this information could be useful to our adversaries, and then applies specific measures to reduce (or eliminate) the ability of our adversaries to exploit that information. OpSec, like all the best models, is a feedback loop that can be followed to constantly observe and improve our security. As we can see (figure 5.4), OpSec is composed of five stages:

1 Identify information
   a What information is there that can be used by an attacker?
   b This maps to the "What are our assets?" stage of the three concepts of cybersecurity.
2 Analyze threats
   a What attackers are there?
   b This maps to the "Who would want to attack us?" stage of the three concepts of cybersecurity.
3 Analyze
   a What vulnerabilities do we have that an attacker (from the previous step) could exploit to steal our information (from the first step)?
4 Assess
   a What is the risk, the likelihood of the vulnerabilities (from the previous step) actually happening? How bad would it be? What would the result be?
5 Apply
   a Taking everything from the previous steps, what security measures can we apply to stop all this from happening?
   b This is where the three concepts of a cybersecurity strategy—that our solution be relevant, proportional, and sustainable—should be applied.

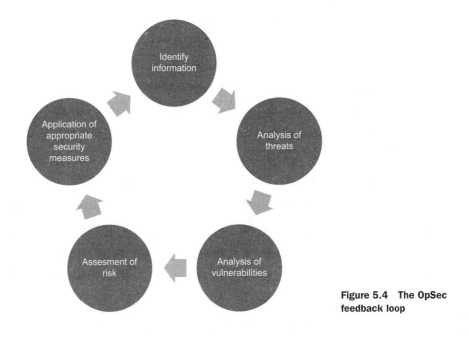

Figure 5.4   The OpSec feedback loop

If you're familiar with the phrase "loose lips sink ships" from World War II propaganda, that's a classic example of OpSec. Let's look at how we can apply this to our first example of social engineering:

- You just opened a secured building access door with your key card. You see someone coming toward you with their hands full of files and a laptop; they ask you to hold the door for them. What do you do?

There is no right or wrong answer—this is a model that allows us to assess how much of a problem we are facing and what we think is a proportional response to protect against it:

- *Identify information*—What is the information that the attacker (the person trying to enter the building) can use to enter the building? What can they observe? What's the situation that they can exploit that will enable them to get through the door and into the building?
- *Analysis of threats*—What could the attacker do with this information? How can the attacker use the information from the previous step to get into the building? Think of the threat as "What are the strengths of the attacker?"
- *Analysis of vulnerabilities*—What can the attacker exploit? What are the problems or weaknesses about the door entry system that would make it easier for an attacker to get through the door? Think of the vulnerability as "What is the weakness of my organization?"
- *Assessment of risk*—How serious is the threat, how big is the vulnerability, and how much impact will a successful attack have? Using all this information, how

likely is the attacker to get through the door and into the building? What bad things could the attacker do once they are inside?

- *Application of appropriate security measures*—How do we stop all of this from happening? Remembering our three concepts of a cybersecurity strategy—that it should be relevant, proportional, and sustainable—what defenses and security measures could be applied to make entry to the building more secure for employees and less easy to exploit for attackers? Armed guards and trained attack dogs sound cool, but are they appropriate and in line with our three concepts?

Compare your answers to mine, and think about how our different perspectives and experiences impact how we view the situation:

- *Identify information*—I have a building access key card in my hand. It's clear I have authorized access to a restricted area, and the door is currently open.
- *Analysis of threats*—The person may be a valid employee. Or, they might be an attacker trying to get access to a restricted area. I don't really know at this stage, but the fact that there is a secure door shows that there is something of value in the restricted area; on balance, it's quite likely that someone will try and push their way in.
- *Analysis of vulnerabilities*—I've already opened the door. I'm highly likely to be helpful in the face of (what appears to be) a struggling colleague.
- *Assessment of risk*—There's a high likelihood here that an unauthorized person will get access to a restricted area. Physical access is always the most powerful route to stealing sensitive data—the impact of this will be high.
- *Application of appropriate security measures*—Well, I have two choices:
  - I can ask them to show some ID.
  - I can just shrug and shut the door on them.

Put in context like this, shutting the door on the person isn't rude; it's a reasonable and responsible response to address a threat and maintain the security of the organization—even if it may not feel like it the first time you do it. In chapter 2, we talked about building a culture of security. A culture of security is more than merely being aware of security threats; it's also about not having a culture of blame. Employees need to feel that they can challenge—and be supported in challenging—suspicious behavior. Rather than following "the rules" like an automaton, this is about ensuring the organization is secure and protected.

For a final example of how effective social engineering is, I encourage you to watch the 1992 film *Sneakers*. With an all-star cast, including Robert Redford, Dan Aykroyd, and Sidney Poitier, it's one of the most accurate Hollywood films dealing with hacking and has some perfect examples of social engineering.

Of course, technology has moved on since the film was made; I'd be surprised if any of it were of use unless we were using tape-based answering machines in our offices. But the core ideas behind social engineering remain as powerful then as they are now. Some common things to watch out for are these:

- Someone becoming agitated and forceful when asked to be let in through a security door or barrier.
- Someone who claims to have forgotten their building pass and that they need to be let in for an important meeting.
- Anyone who asks to borrow your mobile phone for any reason.
- Someone sitting next to you on a train or in an airport who keeps shifting position to try and read your laptop screen or documents.
- False alerts from burglar or fire alarms; always investigate these fully.

5.2   Malicious USB

The Universal Serial Bus (USB) is a great invention for managing computer peripherals. As someone who spent far too many years fiddling with hardware switches to control serial port settings, and then having a portable golf cart of different serial port adapters, USB has been a real gift—even if no one has ever managed to plug a USB cable in the right way the first time.

USB devices—particularly memory sticks and chargers—are so common now that we don't think twice about using them. This makes them ideal attack routes. Let's look at a couple of the most common attacks.

5.2.1   USB devices with malware

USB memory sticks are a boon for penetration testers and criminals. They are everywhere, and we've become so used to treating them as disposable devices that we plug them in without a second thought. Think back to the last trade show or vendor-sponsored event you attended; there will have been USB memory sticks handed out like sweets, with various vendors' logos and contact details on them. I've even seen tubs of small-capacity USB memory sticks being given out for free to guests as they checked into a hotel.

Using USB devices with malware on them is another form of social engineering attack: using company logos and designs to make the USB stick appear genuine and placing them in areas where you would normally expect to grab some free swag are much easier routes to plant malware than trying to break into a computer system or email malware to a victim.

Why do we trust these freebies? Think about where and how you would plant some malicious USB sticks and what you would do to make them enticing to your victims:

- Where?
- How?
- What?

As part of some work I did for a client supporting their employee security training, I left a large wicker bowl full of USB memory sticks in the reception area of their building. I had the company's logo printed on them and a small script installed on them. When a victim inserted the USB stick into their computer, the script would run, popping up an alert box thanking them for taking part in the test and asking them to return the USB stick to the chief information security officer (CISO).

I left 30 USB sticks in the bowl, and 30 people came to the CISO to hand their sticks back in after they got a message telling them to. Playing to people's inner voice of "Ooh, cool, free stuff!" is a great way for an attacker to get a foothold inside an organization.

Everyone should have some sort of antimalware software running on their computers, but this can sometimes fail to spot sophisticated malware. Modern operating systems shouldn't automatically run software from an inserted storage device, although many will still ask if they can. Many companies go further and ensure that all their computers are configured to disable their USB ports for storage devices and to always refuse to run software on any attached storage devices.

5.2.2 BadUSB: USB devices that attack your laptop and phone

With so many devices being charged by USB—laptops, mobile phones, tablets—many people forget that USB isn't just a standard for a connector; it's a standard for data transfer. A USB socket or plug has four connectors on it: two for power and two for data transmission. Micro USB connectors also have a fifth pin, which is used by mobile phones for USB on the go (OTG); this allows the phone and USB device to work out which is the host device—although for the purposes of BadUSB attacks, we can ignore this (see figure 5.5 and table 5.1).

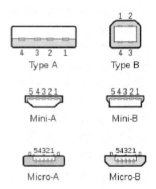

Figure 5.5   The different types of USB connectors, numbered pins showing

Table 5.1   Four pins in USB connectors uses

Pin	Signal	Color	Description
1	VCC	Red	+5 volts (power)
2	D-	White	Data -
3	D+	Green	Data +
4	Ground	Black	Ground (power)

When we plug our laptop in at our desk to charge or plug in our phone at home, we don't think that there's any danger. We're using our own chargers and cables in our own environment. Unfortunately, this lulls us into a false sense of security. When people are getting low on battery power and see a USB charging station at an airport, a coffee shop, or on the train, they won't think twice about plugging their device in. How do we know that the data lines aren't connected?

This type of attack is called *BadUSB*: a USB device (a charging port, a power adapter, or even a cable) has been repurposed, with the data lines connected, to appear as a keyboard. When connected to your laptop or phone, the BadUSB device rapidly sends malicious commands or installs malware on the victim's laptop or phone. The devices to do this are tiny, and can even be embedded within an actual USB cable. I've seen USB cables that have embedded Wi-Fi circuitry to compromise a laptop and then wirelessly give the attacker access.

The biggest danger comes from public USB charging points, where we have no idea what is actually behind the USB charging point, who controls it, or what it will do. There are two ways we can address these sorts of attacks:

- *Always carry and use your own chargers.* Never directly connect to a public USB charging station; always use your own charger and plug it directly into a main socket.
- *Use a USB condom, also called SyncStop.* These are small USB adapters that plug between a cable and your laptop, and they have the data lines disconnected. By ensuring that only power is sent through, they stop any BadUSB device from attacking your laptop or phone.

5.2.3 Evil maid attacks

A variation on these USB attacks is called an evil maid attack, a phrase coined by security researcher Joanna Rutkowska when she first wrote about this attack in 2009. Allowing an attacker physical access to our computer makes it easy for the data to be copied off. This has resulted in full-disk encryption (FDE), where the entire computer's hard drive is encrypted and can only be unlocked at boot time with a special, unique passphrase.

The idea is that if we leave our laptop unattended (e.g., in our hotel room), an evil maid could use an external USB device to compromise the laptop's firmware, ensuring that malware is loaded every time the machine reboots. In particular, malware could be installed in the firmware that would bypass the disk encryption. The evil maid then returns later on to copy the now unencrypted data off the laptop.

In 2007, former US Commerce Secretary Carlos Gutierrez left his laptop unattended during a trade talk in Beijing; he claimed that he was the victim of an evil maid attack, with the attacker trying to access sensitive data linked to the trade talks that was stored on his laptop's encrypted hard drive.

A variation on this attack is where an evil maid connects a special device to a desktop computer, between the keyboard and the machine, that records every key stroke the user enters. This is called a keylogger, and the evil maid just has to return the next day and download the data from the device—which will include every username and password the user typed in during the day.

In 2005, a criminal gang tried to steal £220 million from Sumitomo Mitsui bank in London. Members of the gang joined the contract cleaning team, and during the night, installed keyloggers in the USB ports of dozens of desktop and laptop computers across the office. They also got access to the CCTV system and replaced surveillance tapes with blanks. In the resulting panic, a number of banks in London started to superglue keyboards and mice to their desktop PCs in departments that handled sensitive data.

The golden rule here is never, ever leave your laptop unattended—at a hotel, at a conference, in the airport, even in the office. Physical access to a computer always means an attacker can completely compromise it; evil maid attacks allow them to do this without any evidence, even when your data is encrypted.

5.3   *Targeted attacks: Phishing*

In chapter 4, we looked in detail at XSS attacks. One of the most common ways these are delivered is via a targeted attack called *phishing*. Before we get into the details, let's revisit how one type of XSS, reflected XSS, works (figure 5.6):

1   The attacker sends a malicious web link to the victim.
2   The victim clicks on the malicious link, loading a valid website but executing the attacker's malicious script.
3   The malicious script sends the victim's session cookie (the data that tells the website that the victim is logged in) to the attacker.
4   The attacker can then use the session cookie to access the website as the logged-in victim.

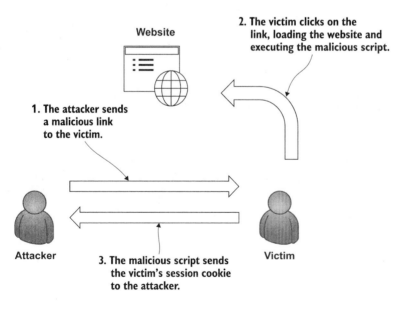

Figure 5.6   How a reflected XSS attack works. When a user is successfully logged in to a website, their browser stores a "session cookie," a string of data sent to the web server with every request, confirming the user is already logged in.

NOTE   The term *phishing* comes from a hacking term dating back to the 70s. Hackers who exploited vulnerabilities in public phone systems were called phone freakers; this term got shortened to just phreaks, and their activities were called phreaking. This form of munging language is called elite speak and is why an attack that is essentially fishing for credentials is actually called phishing.

The obvious problem for the attacker is how to get the malicious link to the victim. This is where phishing comes in. A form of social engineering, phishing is the art of sending a user a valid-looking email that takes them to a valid website vulnerable to an XSS attack. When the user logs in to the website, the malicious XSS is used to steal their session cookie. Phishing, and its more targeted version, *spear phishing* (phishing attacks aimed at specific, key individuals in a company, like the CEO), are very common because they're highly successful and easy to execute.

Phishing attacks don't always use XSS; sometimes they leverage complete clones of valid websites, with a slightly different address (URL), designed to trick the victim into entering sensitive data, like their bank account details or a social security number.

Phishing attacks are now ubiquitous, and we've all come across them at some point. How many of the following examples do you think are phishing attacks?

- An email from the tax authorities claiming you are due for a refund and that you need to click on the link to log in with your social security number.
- An email from your company's HR team saying that your bank account details need to be updated immediately or you won't be paid this month. Click the link to log in to the HR system with your employee ID.
- An email from a courier company saying they have a package to deliver, but there are some excess customs charges to be paid first. You're invited to click on a link and enter your credit card details.
- An email from your local council saying that you owe unpaid utility charges. A handy link is included that takes you to their payment portal, where you can enter your credit card details.
- An email from your security team asking you to take part in training to spot and defend against phishing attacks. Your company is working with an external training provider; click a link to log in with your company ID and password.

The sad truth is that all of these examples are real-world phishing attacks (even that last one!), but every single one is also a valid email that has been legitimately sent. When valid emails and phishing attacks look the same, how can we defend against them?

Many email clients will now automatically flag suspicious emails based on the links that are included. Usually, we can also hover our mouse over a link and double-check the website address that we would actually be sent to. Most modern web browsers will also warn us if we try to access a suspicious web page or a website that is a fake. None of these methods are foolproof, but we still have three key ways to address phishing:

- *Never click on a link in an email.* Ever, no matter how valid or plausible the email seems, no matter who it claims to have come from. Manually type the address of the website into your browser and then log in. Don't be tempted to take the lazy route and click a link directly.
- *Don't reply to the email, but forward it directly to the person or company who is claimed to have sent it.* Ask them to verify that this is a valid request. Even better, call them directly and ask. There is nothing wrong with being cautious and checking that a request is valid. But never use the contact details that may be included in the suspicious email.
- *Companies: Never send out emails with links in them.* Make it clear to your customers that no communication from your company will ever include clickable links and that you will never ask customers for personal data. You're not making life hard for your customers; you are actively protecting them from phishing attacks. Make this clear.

In addition to stealing credentials to enable further attacks on an organization, phishing is also the middle part of a string of attacks that attackers use to turn user data into hard cash. In chapter 7, we'll look at the Dark Web and see how attackers can get paid for stealing this data.

5.4   *Credential theft and passwords*

As we saw at the start of this chapter, the most effective way to break into an organization is by using a valid user account. It's much easier to use already existing credentials than to try and find software bugs or vulnerabilities in a system.

The big problem is that passwords suck. They are rubbish, they have always been rubbish, and they will continue to be rubbish. A password that can be easily memorized is one that can be easily guessed. A password that can't easily be guessed is too complex to be memorized. We need different passwords for the hundreds of different systems we now access online, and how infuriating is it to be forced to change a password every 30 days? There are also the constant irritating failure messages about passwords having to contain silly characters and mixes of numbers, letters, and capitals. The whole thing is a user-unfriendly mess.

There are three main things we can do to make the situation with passwords a bit better:

- Store passwords more securely.
- Make it easier to use unique, complex passwords.
- Stop relying on just a password to protect our accounts.

5.4.1 *Store passwords more securely*

Initially, computer systems and applications used to store passwords in plain text, in either text files or databases. These were very easy to steal, so developers and administrators came up with a way to hide passwords using a technique called *hashing*.

Hashing is a one-way transformation; we use a hashing algorithm to convert plain text into a nonsense string of letters and numbers (hashed string). However, we can't convert this hashed string back to plain text, which is good.

Encryption is a two-way transformation: encryption software uses algorithms (a cipher) to convert plain text into encrypted nonsense (ciphertext). However, the point of encryption is that data can be decrypted to be read, so the same encryption algorithm is used by the software to convert the ciphertext back to plain text. For a great introduction to encryption and cryptography, I highly recommend David Wong's book *Real-World Cryptography*, which is also published by Manning. Encrypting passwords is bad, because an attacker has a way to convert the encrypted text (ciphertext) back into plain text. Figures 5.7 and 5.8 show the differences between encryption and hashing.

Figure 5.7 How encryption works. Note that it's reversible: encrypted data can be unencrypted.

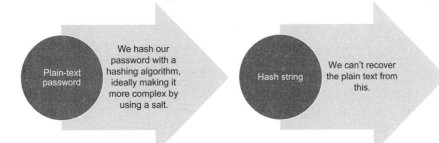

Figure 5.8 How hashing works. Note that hashing is one-way: we can't "unhash" a hash string. We can make the hashing stronger by adding another random string—called a salt—to the hashing algorithm. This adds an extra level of randomness to the result, which means unless the attacker also has the salt, it will be almost impossible for them to calculate the correct hash.

So, if hashing is a one-way function, how do we know that the password a user types in is the same as the hashed nonsense that our application or system has stored?

When we enter a password into a webpage (or an online app, or a system login), this is hashed by software on the web server with its hashing algorithm. The hashed string that's then generated is compared to the one stored by the system; if they match, we have entered the correct password. Hashing is an efficient and secure way to protect passwords, but it does depend on the hashing algorithm used. A weak hashing algorithm is fast, but that means an attacker can generate random hashes very quickly and try to guess their way into discovering a password. A stronger hashing algorithm is slower but makes it more difficult for an attacker to guess the hash. The great thing is that as end users, we don't need to concern ourselves with hashing our passwords or choosing the algorithm that matches the one the server uses; the hashing and comparison of hashes all take place within the application on the remote server.

Let's look at how an attacker can guess hashed passwords:

1   The attacker steals (or buys) a list of hashed passwords.
2   The attacker starts with a text file full of random words. This is called a *dictionary file.*
3   The attacker feeds the dictionary file into a password-cracking program, which can also combine the words with random numbers and symbols.
4   The hashing program generates a hash from the source word and compares it to the hashed passwords that the attacker has stolen.
5   When it finds a match, it remembers the source text; that's the password.

This process is called *brute forcing* (see figure 5.9).

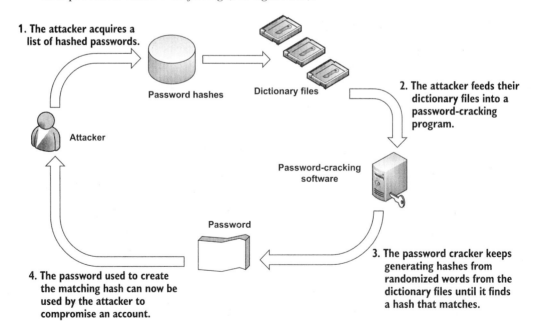

1. The attacker acquires a list of hashed passwords.

Password hashes   Dictionary files

2. The attacker feeds their dictionary files into a password-cracking program.

Attacker

Password-cracking software

Password

3. The password cracker keeps generating hashes from randomized words from the dictionary files until it finds a hash that matches.

4. The password used to create the matching hash can now be used by the attacker to compromise an account.

Figure 5.9   Brute forcing password hashes to guess a password

Graphics cards (also called graphics processing units or GPUs) carry out some hashing functions in their hardware as part of the work they do to generate images. Utilizing these hashes is very, very fast because it's carried out in the specialized hardware of the GPU. About 10 years ago, I built a password-cracking machine that had three GPUs, which I fed with four different 4 GB dictionary files. It could generate and compare 900,000 password hashes per second. The entire setup cost around £600—very cheap given the power of the end result.

Hackers also trade precomputed hash tables, with a list of plain-text strings and the resulting hashes already worked out. This makes it even easier to try and match a password and guess a string.

Using a more complicated hashing function means an attacker can't utilize cheap GPUs to brute force a hashed password match. More complex hashing algorithms also use a special string—called a *salt*—to further complicate the hashing process, making it too difficult to try brute force. A salt adds an extra level of randomness to the resulting hash: unless the attacker also has the salt, it becomes computationally impossible to calculate the right hash, even with the most complex and powerful GPUs.

In 2015, a hacking group called the Impact Team broke into the website of Ashley-Madison, a site used to arrange and conduct extramarital affairs. In addition to stealing around 60 GB of data, the attackers also stole roughly 36 million passwords hashes. Although the majority of those passwords were hashed by the relatively strong bcrypt algorithm, around 11 million had been hashed by the very old and weak MD5 algorithm; these passwords were recovered within a few weeks.

5.4.2 Make it easier to use unique, complex passwords

The more complex a password is, the harder it is to memorize. The harder it is to memorize, the more likely we are to use the same password across multiple accounts and to write it down on a Post-it note stuck to our monitor. Yet, security professionals and websites keep demanding that we use unique, complex, hard-to-guess passwords.

The solution is to use a password manager. A password manager is software that stores and manages the usernames, passwords, and other information you need to log in to websites and online accounts. Password managers require a single, strong password to manage access, and for extra security, all the passwords, usernames, and websites they store are all encrypted. Password managers like LastPass and Bitwarden are available as standalone programs for your laptop or phone, as well as browser plugins, and can synchronize data across multiple accounts.

Enterprise versions are available for companies to run themselves, allowing them to centrally control and manage the passwords their employees use to access internal systems.

This is an example of how using encryption to store passwords is a good idea: because the password manager isn't processing thousands of login requests a minute, the software can use a very strong—but very slow—encryption algorithm. Thinking back to our three concepts of a cybersecurity strategy, using encryption in this way is relevant, proportional, and sustainable. Even if an attacker managed to steal the password manager's data store, the strength of the encryption makes it almost impossible to decrypt with the password. In the next section, we'll see how to make even that more secure while still remaining usable.

5.4.3 Stop relying on just a password to protect your accounts

In chapter 4, where we looked at SMS interception and spoofing, we touched on multi-factor authentication (MFA). MFA adds an additional authentication mechanism on top of your password. There are several different ways to add MFA to make your accounts more secure.

SMS authentication involves sending an SMS with a time-limited access code to your mobile phone. You type in your password, then the SMS code, and get access to your account. As we saw in chapter 4, SMS is easily intercepted and spoofed, so you should never rely on SMS MFA to secure your accounts.

Hardware authentication involves a token, usually a USB device, that generates a complex, time-sensitive code when activated. The most common are made by YubiKey and RSA. YubiKeys are small devices, like a slimmed-down memory stick (see figure 5.10); they are plugged into the USB port or use near-field communication (NFC) to talk to your phone. Pressing your finger on the device activates it, and it generates a code that is automatically entered into your web browser. RSA tokens (figure 5.11) are hardware devices that constantly generate a new, random code. They are usually used by large enterprises, are centrally managed, and are quite expensive. YubiKeys have an advantage because we can also use them to apply MFA to our password manager, thus adding an extra layer of security. Obviously, we need to ensure we have more than one so we have a backup in case one gets lost.

Figure 5.10   YubiKeys come in a number of different sizes and formats, enabling one to be used with any laptop or mobile device you have.

Figure 5.11   The classic RSA token, although due to their cost, you're likely to only see them being used in sensitive corporate environments.

One-time passwords (OTP) are a bit like RSA tokens, although they are usually software that runs on your phone. A simple app, they constantly generate new, unique numeric codes (usually every 30 seconds), which you have to enter along with your password to access an account. OTP apps can also be used with a password manager. Some OTP apps use the time of day when generating codes, so it becomes important to ensure the time is correctly synchronized on the mobile device running the OTP app and the remote server or application.

Hardware tokens and OTP software all have to be supported and enabled by the company managing the services you're trying to access, but Google, Microsoft, Facebook, Twitter, banks, and other online services all now support them. They are simple and easy to set up and are powerful, secure, and easy to use with password managers.

I've used YubiKeys, OTP apps, and password managers. They are the simplest and easiest way to securely manage unique, complex passwords.

5.5 Building access cards

We don't normally think of building access cards as a security risk. After all, their job is to restrict access to sensitive areas. Surely that's supposed to improve security? But what makes them dangerous is the context in which they are used.

As we've already discussed, building access cards are commonly also combined with an ID card, which has our photo, name, company, and sometimes security clearance levels printed on them. There's a lot of information there. Employees are used to carrying them at all times, clipped onto their belts or on lanyards around their necks. You've probably come across many employers whose security policies demand that their ID be clearly displayed at all times while inside a building. The problem is that people forget to remove their ID once they leave the building.

Unless we work in sensitive government sites, our building access cards will be one of two types:

- *Mag stripe*—These are like a credit card; they have a magnetic stripe on them that contains some simple encoded data—normally just a number or a string of text. When we swipe the card, this number is read by a card reader. The number is then transmitted to the building access control software. This software does a quick look-up to see if we're on the list of numbers authorized to open that door. The software then either unlocks the door or trips an alarm.
- *RFID tag*—Radio frequency identification (RFID) uses cards that have a miniature circuit embedded in them, called a *tag*. An RFID tag consists of a tiny radio transponder (a combined radio receiver and transmitter). RFID works by being placed close to a reader that sends out a weak electromagnetic signal. This signal is picked up by the RFID circuit in our card, which then powers on and weakly broadcasts its ID. The ID is picked up by the reader, and then the same process we use for mag stripe cards is used to verify the ID and unlock the door.

RFID access cards are now the most common, and they're easily identifiable by people impatiently slapping them against a reader and then getting cross when the card isn't recognized the first time.

We've already looked at how surreptitiously taking photographs of someone's ID helps with our social engineering attacks. Another route can be taken that relies on exploiting an advantage (and a flaw) with the entire concept of RFID. RFID tags work by picking up a weak electrical signal and then broadcasting back an equally weak reply. All we need to do is either get close enough for our own reader to activate the RFID tag or find a way to activate the tag.

Getting close is easy; RFID readers are very small and portable. I've had great success in hiding them in my suit pocket and accidentally bumping into people (sorry, blame rush hour!). Criminals in Germany carried out a similar attack a few years ago by going around with a contactless payment card reader in their coat and pushing up against commuters to silently charge their contactless payment cards a few euros. They managed to steal tens of thousands of euros this way before being caught as (ironically enough) suspected pickpockets by the German transport police.

Cheap antennas are available, which can be plugged into a mobile phone's USB socket, enabling an attacker to activate and read an RFID tag from up to two meters away. Again, the antennas are small enough to hide in your coat or suit pocket, and the range is more than enough to enable you to mingle in a reception area, collecting RFID tags.

The cards themselves are cheap, as are color label printers. For some client work eight years ago, I created a number of cloned employee RFID cards at a cost of £6 each.

When I headed up an R&D lab, the team and I tested building access security by surreptitiously cloning someone's RFID card remotely. The ID was then reprogrammed into another RFID tag, which we put inside a squeaky rubber chicken toy. The rubber chicken was then pushed against a door card reader, which smoothly unlocked, accompanied by the despairing wail of our rubber chicken toy.

Newer versions of RFID cards are designed to block cloning and use technology similar to a chip-and-pin bank card. However, as these cards are more expensive—and building access cards are often lost or damaged—few companies use them.

EXERCISE

To round off our social engineering work, we'll work through a real-life physical penetration test I carried out a few years ago for a global asset management company. At key points, I'll ask you to write down what you would do next and why, giving you a chance to practice your OpSec and social engineering skills.

Let's call our asset management company Worldwide Asset Managers (WAM). I had explained to WAM's CISO, Alice (not her real name), that I thought there were issues with physical security—specifically their RFID staff ID tags. Knowing my fondness for good rum, the CISO bet me a bottle that I couldn't exploit this to copy some confidential data and bring it to her.

As you should always do in these situations, we both signed a certificate of permission, making it clear I would be doing this with the full knowledge and support of the CISO, and that also outlined some basic rules:

- Don't break anything.
- Don't do anything destructive.

- Commit no physical theft.
- Don't set off any alarms.

Let's work through this together. WAM is based on a small, private campus site, composed of three large buildings. There are car parks near each of the main entrances of each building. Our goal is to get access to a building, find some confidential data, and either copy it or take the original to the CISO. Each building is nicely labeled for us, with signs everywhere. The easiest one for us to target is the main building, which has the CISO's office, the Retail Investment Department, the Pension Fund Management Department, and the HR team—lots of targets inside, with a lot of confidential information for us to acquire.

Breaking this down into steps, we need to do the following:

1 Gain access to the building.
2 Gain access to a restricted area.
3 Find, copy, or take some confidential information.
4 Make our way to the CISO's office.
5 Hand over the confidential information. (And claim our rum!)

And we need to do it all without being challenged, stopped, or kicked out:

- Where would you start with this challenge?
- What information would you collect and why?

I started off by arriving very early in the morning and parking my car as close as possible to one of the main building entrances on their campus. Keeping my mobile up against my ear to make it look like I was on an important call, I used my SLR camera to take sneaky snapshots of people's ID cards. I stayed there until around 10:00 a.m., making a note of the times there were the most employees trying to enter the building: 8:15 to 8:30 a.m. seemed to be the sweet spot.

Once I knew what the right format was, I went home and printed some labels onto my own stash of RFID cards. I got a retractable cable so that I could attach one to my belt, and I also printed off some A4 sheets with WAM's logo and information. I also printed a WAM logo and stuck it onto my trusty clipboard:

- Armed with this collection of equipment, how would you try to get access to the building?
- What are the risks that you would face? How would you deal with them?

The next day, I went back to the campus and headed to the main entrance at peak rush hour: 8:20 a.m. I made sure I was cradling my phone between my shoulder and my ear, while one hand clutched a brief case and the other a stack of papers and my clipboard.

Joining the queue at the door, seeing that I was otherwise fully occupied, a helpful lady held it open for me. No kind deed should go unpunished, so I followed her through three more secure doors, until I ended up in an open plan office that, according to the signs, housed the Retail Investment Team. I mouthed a quick "Thank you so much!" to the very nice lady and then headed toward an empty desk:

- You're in. Bearing in mind what we've learned already about social engineering, what information would you gather next?
- How would you use this information to get closer to your goal of stealing some confidential data?

After ending my "phone call," I quickly looked around. There were secure disposal bins and shredders dotted around and large signs on the walls reminding people to shred printouts with confidential data and to place all other paper into the secure disposal bins. Like most open-plan offices, there were name plates at each workplace. I looked for somewhere quiet, without too many sitting nearby, and settled on the desk of Badluck Bob, fund manager (obviously not the poor chap's real name).

WAM used an older version of Windows, where the login screen helpfully displays the username of the last person to log in. Stuck to the monitor was a nice label that gave the phone number for people to call to reset their password—clearly an event that happened often enough for there to be a dedicated support team:

- You could try your social engineering skills and work at getting Bob's password reset. Or maybe you want to get some more information first. What will you do next?

Rather than going straight to trying to take control of Bob's account, I thought I'd rifle through his desk first. Like most people, Bob had some drawers under his desk and some filing trays filled with paperwork. Moving the "Clear desk policy: all paperwork to be stored in a locked drawer" sign out of the way, I tried his desk drawers. All were locked. Although they would be easy to force, that would break the agreed rules of not causing any damage.

Bob's filing trays were a gold mine, however. Stacked with client investment forms, they had people's names, addresses, the amount invested, and which funds they were invested in. There was even a printout of an email with a client's bank details on it, along with a Post-it note reminding Bob to talk to the finance people to chase a payment that hadn't cleared to the client's account:

- Clearly, we've got some confidential information, but is it enough? We could still try to take over Bob's account and get even more goodies. Maybe other people were equally careless about storing their paperwork. What would you do next?

Like all good heists, the key to success is knowing when to cut and run—when enough is enough. I gathered up some prime material from Bob's filing trays, collected my stuff (making sure my hands were full), and headed for the door.

Exiting was easy enough, but I had to pass through another two security doors to get to the CISO's office. My ID card looked valid, but I hadn't cloned someone's RFID tag, so I couldn't open the doors myself. Instead, I repeated the trick with the urgent phone call and loitered until someone unlocked the door and held it open for me.

Both times they looked at my fake ID card attached to my belt, but it looked genuine, and I was helpfully waved through. A few minutes later I was in Alice's office asking for my favorite rum.

This was a fairly straightforward test: there was no barbed wire, no slavering security dogs, no beefy security guards armed with tasers. Regardless, it was still possible to breach the company and steal some confidential data.

Go back through the process, review your thoughts at each stage, and write down what you thought the OpSec failings of WAM were—and how you think they can improve things.

Think back to the start of the chapter, where I spoke about how social engineering affects us personally and how we can apply that information to our colleagues and employees to make them more secure. Having carried out a social engineering exercise ourselves, we can now apply what we've learned to make an organization more secure and more resistant to social engineering attacks.

There are a number of areas where WAM could improve:

- Reinforce, with all employees, the need for diligence when entering and exiting secure areas. Make it clear that it's okay to err on the side of caution and shut the door on people.
- Have a security hotline number and email address, and encourage employers to report any suspicious behavior they see. WAM already puts the helpdesk number everywhere; share the security hotline number in the same places to ensure everyone knows it and uses it.
- Installing CCTV at each secured door could help identify and track security breaches.
- A security guard at each entrance could ensure that each employee uses their card to enter.
- Additionally, the security guard could remind people that they must remove and hide their ID before leaving the building—and enforce this.
- Although there were lots of reminders of good security hygiene, they weren't being followed. For secure areas where confidential data is regularly handled, a clear desk policy could be enforced by trusted cleaning contractors removing and securely shredding any paperwork left on the desk at the end of the working day.
- They need to update and modify their Windows desktop configuration so that user IDs aren't automatically displayed on the login screen.
- Adding CCTV and number plate recognition—or even a security gate that can only be opened with an employee ID card when entering or exiting the car park—could provide added security for the car park areas.

Arguably, using social engineering to carry out these sorts of attacks is easier and less dangerous than trying to break software or hack into a company's network. All you really need is some confidence and to have carried out some background information gathering. This is precisely why Kevin Mitnick was so successful, and why he generated so much fear and mystique among law enforcement.

As we've seen in this chapter, combining technical attacks with social engineering to target people is a devastatingly successful way to breach an organization. These are sophisticated attacks—sophisticated cons—and in the next chapter, we'll look at what attackers do once they have inside access to their target.

Summary

- Social engineering techniques can be used to bypass security controls to gain access to personal information such as IDs, usernames, and even projects that person is working on. This information can be used to get an IT helpdesk to reset the user's password, allowing the attacker access to critical data.
- OpSec is a process that identifies critical information, determines if this information could be useful to our adversaries, and then applies specific measures to reduce (or eliminate) the ability of our adversaries to exploit that information.
- Malicious USB chargers can be used to attack our laptops or mobile phones:
  - SyncStop and similar devices are small USB connectors that we place between a charger and our device; they disconnect the data lines on the USB connection so that only power gets through.
  - A variation on this is the evil maid attack, which involves a malicious USB device being inserted into our laptop or desktop computer by an "evil maid" while we're away from our machine.
- Phishing attacks find ways to get victims to click on a web link that appears to be a valid website but will actually trigger a malicious script, or trick the user into revealing personal information such as social security numbers, credit card details, or login credentials.
- A hashing algorithm provides a one-way transformation to convert plain text into nonsense strings of letters and numbers to protect passwords from potential attacks.
- Encryption provides a two-way method of protecting passwords. First, it uses a cipher to convert plain text into encrypted nonsense, and then the data can be decrypted to be read. The weakness is that an attacker may find a way to decrypt the encrypted text back into plain text.
- A password manager is software that stores and manages usernames, passwords, and other information we use to log in to websites and online accounts. The data they store is encrypted and can synchronize data across multiple devices.
- We can use physical security tokens (like YubiKeys) as well as password managers to help stop credential theft.
- By understanding how attackers can chain multiple small security flaws and OpSec failings to achieve a data breach, we can then more effectively analyze our own situation.

Internal attacks

6

Expanding on the technical hacks and social engineering we discussed in chapters 4 and 5, this chapter looks at the next stage: what hackers do once they have broken their way inside your organization. We'll also look at another common attack route: insider threats.

6.1   *What happens after they get in?*

Back in chapter 2, we looked at the fundamental building blocks of any security strategy (figure 6.1):

- What assets do we have?
- Who would want to attack them?
- What defenses do we already have?

Figure 6.1   Three factors of cybersecurity. These three questions—and their answers—are the cornerstone of any successful cybersecurity strategy.

Understanding what assets we have and want to protect is key to understanding how attackers will behave once they've got a foothold in our organization. Knowing who wants to attack us—where the risk comes from—also gives us further insight into how an attack develops. For attackers who want to deface a website (by uploading their own images or slogans to replace valid content), the initial hack is normally all that's required for them to upload their defacement and move on.

For an attacker who is after our sensitive data, the initial hack is normally enough for them to establish a foothold; they will then look at how to exploit this further to get to the sensitive data they want. We call this *lateral movement*, and the best way to visualize this is to refer back to the sample corporate network diagram we used in chapter 4. Infrastructure diagrams normally present a north-south view, with the external (internet) connection at the top (north) of the diagram and the most sensitive data on the internal networks at the bottom (south) of the diagram. Let's revisit our sample corporate network (figure 6.2).

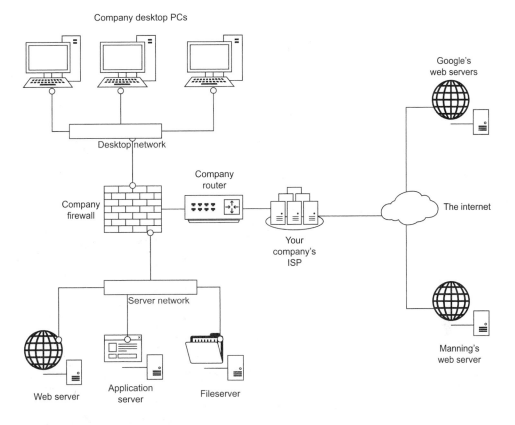

Figure 6.2   Our sample corporate network diagram from chapter 4

We want our internet connection to be at the top, the north, so with a quick 90-degree change, we get our revised north-south view of the company infrastructure (figure 6.3).

With this changed view of the infrastructure, it becomes clear what lateral movement (or east-west movement, as it is sometimes called) means to an attacker: they want to break out from their original breach point and move through the infrastructure to get to the sensitive data we're trying to protect. Let's look at a typical scenario, something featured in the news recently with the high-profile Twitter hack: an attacker using a phishing email to breach internal data stores. Using our sample company infrastructure, where every user has access to a central fileserver where documents are stored, we can see that an attacker who has breached a user's workstation with a phishing email can move laterally to the fileserver (figure 6.4).

We can further understand how this sort of attack works by using our three factors of cybersecurity. Even if we have some security protections in place, reviewing

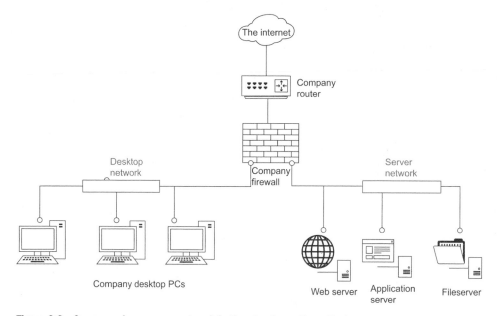

Figure 6.3   Our example company network in the classic north-south view

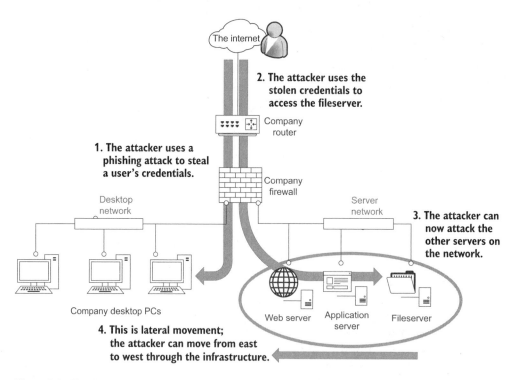

Figure 6.4   How lateral movement works: an attacker first moves from north (the internet) to south (the company infrastructure). Having compromised a system, they can move east to west (laterally) within the company.

them via the three factors will help us understand if these provide the level of protection we need:

- What assets do we have?
  - We have some sensitive documents on our fileserver that contain confidential company information.
- Who would want to attack us?
  - Criminal gangs would want to steal this confidential company information so they can sell it to competitors or use it to take advantage by, for example, shorting or buying stock.
- What defenses do we have?
  - Only users logged in with valid company credentials can access the fileserver.
  - The company firewall filters traffic between the desktop and server networks and blocks viruses and malicious attacks.

Bringing together both our understanding of how attackers work as well as our view of the three factors of cybersecurity, we can understand how breaches like the Twitter hack happen, even when we appear to have some security defenses:

- What defenses do we have?
  - Only users logged in with valid company credentials can access the fileserver.
  Problem: By using a phishing email attack, the attacker has stolen a user's valid credentials. This allows them valid access to the fileserver.
  - The company firewall filters traffic between the desktop and server networks, and blocks viruses and malicious attacks.
  Problem: The attacker isn't launching an attack between the desktop and server networks: using the user's stolen credentials, they can directly access the fileserver with normal network requests for files.

If we revisit our model of the three concepts of a cybersecurity strategy, what changes would you make to block how this attack works? What relevant, proportional, and sustainable changes could you make to protect the sensitive documents on the fileserver (figure 6.5)?

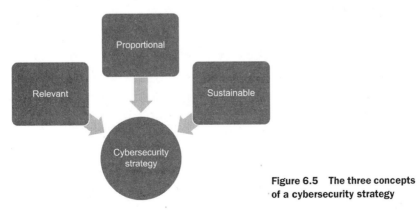

Figure 6.5   The three concepts of a cybersecurity strategy

Rather than budgeting for and buying even more security technologies, by under-standing how an attack works and what our attackers are after, we can make the most of our existing defenses to protect our assets. If the attacker is accessing the fileserver from the internet, we can configure our firewall to block any fileserver requests that are coming from the internet (figure 6.6). We can also enable MFA (as you learned about in chapter 5) so that even if an attacker steals a user's credentials via phishing, the second step of authenticating that MFA gives us prevents them from accessing the fileserver.

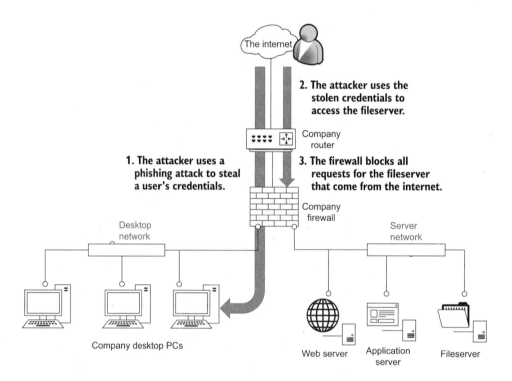

Figure 6.6   We can increase our defenses by configuring the firewall to block any requests to the fileserver that come from the internet.

Now that we've looked at how we can start pulling together what we've learned so far, let's dig a bit deeper into the other most common ways attackers steal data once they've breached an organization.

6.2   *Gaining more control: Privilege escalation*

As we learned in chapters 4 and 5, XSS and phishing are powerful attacks that, when combined, make it easy for an attacker to steal a user's credentials. We also looked at how MFA is a way to protect against using a user's stolen credentials to access sensi-tive information. However, attackers have another way to use stolen credentials:

gaining access to administrative accounts that have greater access privileges. This is called *privilege escalation.*

To understand how this works, first let's have a quick refresher on how XSS attacks work (figure 6.7). Specifically, for this example, we're most interested in a reflected XSS attack and how it's leveraged by phishing. As we discussed in chapter 4, a successful reflected XSS attack involves the following steps:

1   An attacker sends a valid-looking email to a victim.
2   The email contains a link to a website that's vulnerable to XSS.
3   The victim clicks the link, loading the vulnerable website and executing the malicious XSS script.
4   The XSS script captures the user's credentials and sends them to the attacker.

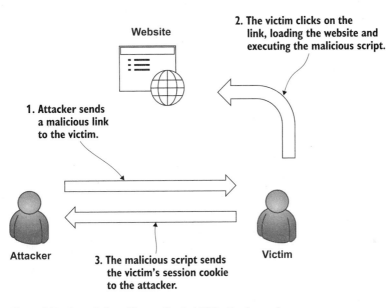

Figure 6.7   A reminder of how reflected XSS attacks work

As we've already seen, we can use MFA to protect against stolen credentials when accessing a sensitive service like a fileserver. Privilege escalation is when an attacker doesn't use the stolen credentials directly, but instead uses them to launch an attack against another user or account that has, for example, administrator privileges. Phishing remains very powerful here, as the attacker can use a user's stolen credentials to send emails as that user. Another popular attack is for the attacker to send malware, usually embedded in a business document stolen from the user, via a spoofed email from the user to an administrator.

Within a modern company infrastructure, there's usually a central data store containing user credentials, which are then used by multiple systems. Using your Google account to sign in to your phone and Google apps or using your Microsoft account to access Outlook webmail and Office Online are examples of centrally held user credentials that can be used to authenticate against other applications.

Many organizations, though, have many different user accounts that are used to access different company services, with the credentials stored in different data stores. This is not only a pain to administer from an IT management perspective, but also from a security point of view, as this increases the complexity of tracking, auditing, and protecting user access. Multiple systems with multiple levels of security containing similar user data that is then used to authenticate against different systems? Nightmare. The worst example of this I had to work with was an organization that had no fewer than 27 different sources of user authentication data, spread across eight different providers and data centers.

Given the following list of user credentials that an organization may have, reorder them in terms of least to most important (or valuable) to an attacker:

- Email login
- Laptop login
- VPN credentials
- Server administrator login details
- Mobile phone passcode
- Timesheet system login

The reality is that although some credentials might look more attractive to an attacker than others, the one with most value is the one that is easiest for attackers to steal. Once they have some valid credentials, a path is opened to leverage those into privilege escalation, resulting in lateral movement within the enterprise.

A classic example of how powerful this can be is the story of how Kevin Mitnick broke into DEC (Digital Equipment Corporation) in the early 1980s. Some of Mitnick's friends had managed to find a phone number that allowed DEC employees to remotely dial into DEC systems. They passed the number to Mitnick, thinking it worthless without a DEC employee's username and password, as well as a special dialup password used for remote access. Mitnick found out the support phone number for DEC and called the system manager. Pretending to be Anton Chernoff, one of DEC's lead engineers, Mitnick successfully tricked the system manager into resetting Chernoff's password and reading it out to him over the phone. Doubling down on his social engineering skills, Mitnick then persuaded the system manager to "remind" him of the additional special dialup password needed for remote access.

This not only got Mitnick access to DEC's key development system; he also had the credentials to dial in and access it remotely from his home computer. On top of that, by having Chernoff's username and password, Mitnick was able to access the system as an administrator—with full access to everything that the system held.

Unfortunately for Mitnick, he showed off his newfound access to his friends who had given him the initial dialup phone number. They promptly downloaded confidential source code to DEC's RSTS/E operating system, before phoning DEC's corporate security department and pinning the data theft on Mitnick.

6.3 *Data theft*

Data theft is, quite literally, where the money is. We've already seen how attackers can use one user's identity to try and steal another's, in very targeted ways, to gain access to more confidential data. Obviously, if attackers can steal credit card or bank details, they can withdraw cash from an ATM or make purchases against the card. But it's not just financial details that are valuable: social security numbers, passport and driving license details, even utility bill details—an attacker can make money from all of these by selling them off to criminals.

We've already seen some common attacks—XSS, SQLi, and phishing—that can be used to steal login details for online banking applications. These are very much smash-and-grab attacks, where it can be obvious that a breach has occurred, and the attacker has to move quickly to cash in on the theft. A more insidious, long-term attack is called an *advanced persistent threat* (APT).

6.3.1 *Advanced persistent threat*

An APT occurs when an attacker breaches an organization and remains undetected for a long period of time, stealthily and slowly siphoning away data. APTs are usually motivated by economic as well as political gain; many APTs are conducted by state actors, who have the resources to spend years planning, building, and deploying such attacks.

An important measurement used when looking at APTs is the *dwell time*: the amount of time the attack goes undetected. A report from cybersecurity company FireEye in 2019 showed that the median dwell time varies across regions: 71 days in the Americas, 177 days in EMEA (Europe, the Middle East, and Africa), and 204 days in APAC (Asia Pacific).

Arguably the most famous APT was the Stuxnet worm, a cyberweapon jointly built by the US and Israel. Stuxnet was developed in 2005 but wasn't uncovered until 2010. It was designed to attack the control components in centrifuges used by Iran to separate nuclear material used in the uranium enrichment process as part of Iran's nuclear program. The centrifuges were made by German manufacturer Siemens, and Iran bought them on the black market. They were controlled with Windows workstations, with a special bit of hardware used to program the centrifuge's controller; it was this that Stuxnet targeted.

Due to a programming error, Stuxnet infected an engineer's computer and then spread across more machines and networks when the engineer took their infected laptop home. This led to antimalware companies spotting a new strain of malware, leading to them reverse-engineering the code and discovering the true purpose behind Stuxnet.

HOW WE CAN MONITOR FOR AND DETECT APTs

Although APTs are designed to avoid detection for as long as possible, they still have a couple of roles to carry out: cause damage or steal data. With Stuxnet, the damage caused was subtle: the centrifuges were reprogrammed to spin at a different speed, causing the separation of nuclear material (or the centrifuge itself) to fail. To Iran's nuclear engineers, this looked like either bad materials or poor components, and as Iran didn't buy the centrifuges legally thanks to international sanctions, it's not like they could call Siemens and ask for support.

Even if an APT isn't directly causing damage, it will siphon data out of our organization and to the attackers. This becomes a real "needle in a haystack" problem—any organization's IT infrastructure is there for one purpose: to shift data around.

One approach we can take is to refer back to the three factors of cybersecurity (figure 6.8), which you learned about in chapter 2. As part of the discovery process, we need to understand the answer to the first and most important factor ("What assets do we have?"). We can also address the related questions:

- Who would want to attack you? (the next factor)
- Who *should* be accessing these assets?

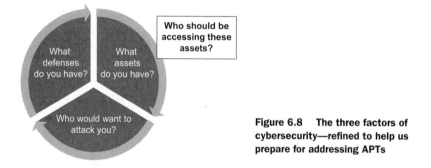

Figure 6.8   The three factors of cybersecurity—refined to help us prepare for addressing APTs

As we've seen from our example company infrastructure, if we know which users need to access which services (and which assets those services hold), we can control and manage that access. By going a step further and configuring our firewall to block not just incoming traffic to the fileserver, but also outgoing traffic from the fileserver to the internet, we can stop an APT from sending our confidential data outside the company (figure 6.9).

Of course, an APT is rarely this easily stopped, and the attackers who write and deploy them are much more sophisticated. We'll look into some more complex defenses we can build later on in this chapter when we look at defense in depth. In part 2 of the book, we'll dig into more detail on the processes and technologies we can use to manage, monitor, and secure access to our assets. In the meantime, now that we've looked at how attackers try to steal data, we can dig into how and why data theft is so lucrative and is such a lure for attackers.

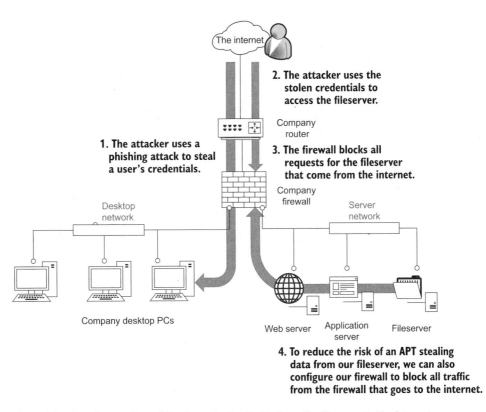

Figure 6.9   By using our firewall to stop outgoing traffic from the fileserver to the internet, we can stop an APT from sending our confidential data outside the company.

6.3.2   *Making money from stolen financial details*

Jeremy Clarkson, British motoring journalist and host of *Top Gear* and *The Grand Tour*, had decided the loss of 25 million UK citizens' bank details by the UK tax authorities, HMRC, was no big deal. In his column in UK newspaper *The Sunday Times*, in 2008, he wrote, "I have never known such a palaver about nothing. The fact is we happily hand over cheques to all sorts of unsavory people all day long without a moment's thought. We have nothing to fear."

To underscore what a palaver this all was, he published his bank account details, as well as some other information, including how to find his address and what car he was currently driving. After all, how could an attacker exploit that to steal money from his bank account? The outrage over the massive loss of data by HMRC was clearly a fuss over nothing.

Several weeks later, however, Clarkson published a retraction and did a complete about-face after it was revealed that an enterprising hacker had set up a £500 direct debit (automatic payment) from Clarkson's bank account to the British Diabetic Association charity. At the time, some direct debit authorizations only needed correct bank account and address details, making the prank trivial to set up.

To his credit, Clarkson had his eyes very publicly opened to how much of an impact theft of financial details could have. He wrote, "The bank cannot find out who did this because of the Data Protection Act and they cannot stop it from happening again. I was wrong and I have been punished for my mistake."

Setting up illicit payments against a bank account was easy enough, but stolen credit and debit card details are a bit more difficult to use. Normally, an attacker is directed by a controlling gang master to steal the list of card details and then farm them out to a network of accomplices. The accomplices—called *mules*—then coordinate withdrawing small amounts of cash from different ATMs (usually around £500 or so). The mules get to keep a small fee (20% is common), and the rest of the cash is funneled back to our mastermind. These transfers rely on classic money laundering mechanisms; for example, the mule will buy a low-value item like a collection of socks, or old mobile phones, at a very high price, which the gang master is selling on a marketplace like Amazon or eBay. The usual money-laundering mainstays of nail and tanning salons, car washes, and restaurants are all used, as well as digital currency and purchasing and transferring Bitcoin (see figure 6.10).

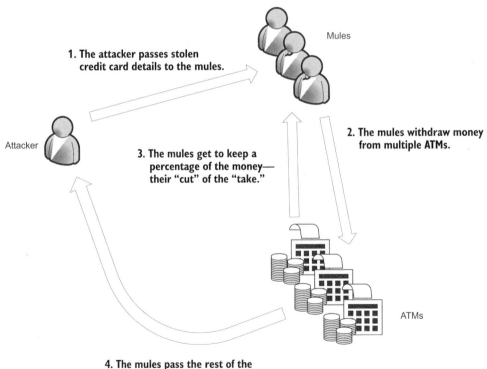

Figure 6.10   A simplified view of how money laundering works. While this process was successful in the 80s and 90s, with antifraud technology from the banks becoming more sophisticated, the modern money-laundering process can be much more complicated.

6.3.3   *Making money from ID theft*

Like stealing financial data, stealing someone's ID can be just as lucrative. Social security numbers (SSNs), tax registration codes, passport details, driver's licenses—these are all examples of personally identifiable information (PII), and all of these are used around the world to prove we are who we say we are. Consequently, all of these have value for criminals.

One of the most spectacular examples of ID theft in recent years is the Marriott International breach, which is a bit unfair, because it arguably wasn't really Marriott's fault. Marriott International is a global chain of high-end hotels and resorts. In 2015, Marriott bought the Starwood Hotels and Resorts chain in a monster $13 billion deal. Unfortunately for Marriott, it turns out that attackers had compromised Starwood's systems—in 2014—although it wasn't until 2018 that Marriott found out and the breach became public. The size of the data theft was shocking: details on around 500 million guest stays had been stolen.

At the time, most of the press focused on the huge size of the data breach and speculation on who the attackers were. What wasn't noticed, at first, was that the Marriott chain is used by departments of the US military when attending conferences and government events. Everyone has to present ID when checking in, which meant that among the stolen data were passport details, addresses, and government IDs of US military personnel and contractors.

Investigators finally traced the attack back to a larger intelligence-gathering spree by hacking teams suspected of working for the Chinese civilian spy agency, the Ministry of State Security. This puts a very different slant on the breach: instead of being about stealing credit card details for short-term theft, this was actually one of several APTs that collected IDs belonging to US military personnel—some of whom were very senior. Obviously, this data had immense value to Chinese spies (if it really was them behind the attack).

Stolen ID can be used to open bank accounts, apply for overdrafts or loans, apply for credit cards—even (most brazenly) to buy luxury sports cars. As someone's ID can be used in so many different ways, criminals can also make money more easily by simply selling the stolen IDs to other criminals or nation-states.

Given the following list of PII, how would you order them from least to most valuable to criminals?

- Passport
- Driving license
- Debit card
- Home address
- Utility bill
- Social security number (US) or national insurance number (UK)
- Credit card
- Bank account number and sort code

Looking at this list, the interesting thing is that the value of each item can vary over time and depends on how it can be used (as Clarkson found out). No item is intrinsically more valuable that the others; as with trading any other commodity, supply and demand also affects price. We'll cover how and where criminals trade this information in chapter 7 when we look at the Dark Web.

6.4   *Insider threats*

Verizon's yearly Data Breach Investigation Report found that in 2019, 34% of all data breaches involved insider threats—a percentage that has been increasing steadily over the last five years. Twenty-nine percent of breaches involved stolen credentials, and 15% came from legitimately authorized users. It's no longer enough to protect the edges of a vulnerable organization; attackers are combining different methods—technical and psychological—resulting in even more devastating breaches.

Insider threat is the term we give to attackers who are actually our colleagues, people who work alongside and with us. Christopher Grupe, IT administrator for the Canadian Pacific Railway, is one of the best examples of how damaging an insider threat can be.

Grupe had a troubled relationship with his employers, struggling with insubordination issues as well as consistent poor performance. In December 2015, he was suspended for 12 days, and when he returned to the office, he was told he was being fired. Grupe managed to convince his employers to let him resign instead and agreed to return his laptop, remote access authentication token, and access badges.

What Grupe actually did was log in remotely, change administrator passwords, delete key configuration files, and change the account passwords on the company's networking hardware. He then destroyed all access logs and deleted all data on his laptop before returning it to the company. As an IT administrator, Grupe was in a trusted role and had administrative access to a multitude of internal systems.

A few weeks later, the company had a network issue and found that they were locked out of their systems. IT teams were forced to shut down all their internal networks, factory-reset all network hardware, and manually rebuild configuration files. The company estimated that this episode cost them over $30,000. After an investigation by a digital forensics team, they traced the password changes back to Grupe. He was arrested, convicted of one count of intentional damage to a protected computer, and jailed for a year.

Out of the following list, which do you think are reasons for an employee to hack their employer?

- Being passed over for promotion
- Being told they will be fired for poor performance
- Being bribed by a competitor
- Being told they will be made redundant
- Being bribed by criminals
- Being blackmailed by criminals

- Being jealous of a coworker
- Being a secret spy

If you guessed "all of the above," congratulations. All of these were reasons for insider attacks—employees attacking their companies—in the last 3 years. And if "being a secret spy" seems far-fetched, think again. With constant advances in technology enabling companies to corner new markets, corporate espionage has never been so tempting.

The US company AMSC (formerly American Superconductor Inc.) found this out, to their detriment. In 2011, a Chinese company, Sinovel, provided three quarters of AMSC's revenue. Sinovel decided that they wanted to cut out the middle man and make the money themselves, so they bribed AMSC employee Dejan Karabasevic.

Karabasevic headed up the automotive engineering department at AMSC and regularly made business trips to China. During one of these trips, representatives from Sinovel made him a compelling offer: steal AMSC trade secrets for $20,000 and then land a six-year, $1.7 million contract with Sinovel.

Karabasevic agreed, handing in his resignation to AMSC. As is usual when resigning, he was required to work out his notice, which he did by copying cutting-edge turbine software and documentation and emailing it to his Sinovel contacts. The Sinovel team used the software and installed it on a number of wind turbines they had ordered from another company in the US. Luckily for AMSC, engineers at that company noticed the similarities with the AMSC code and informed AMSC.

Having been found out, Sinovel rejected orders they had placed with AMSC and refused to pay outstanding invoices. Having lost their largest customer, AMSC stock dropped by 40% in a single day, falling a further 84% over the next few months. AMSC ultimately lost over $1 billion in shareholder equity from the stock collapse, and 700 staff who had been hired to work on the Sinovel project lost their jobs.

It took AMSC almost seven years to get some justice, with a court finally imposing a $1.5 million fine on Sinovel in 2018, as well as ordering a $57.5 million payment to AMSC and $850,000 in damages to other victims.

EXERCISES

Spotting insider threats is incredibly difficult. Even experts like government spy agencies don't always get it right (as we'll see later on). However, looking for patterns of suspicious behavior and having a healthy dose of caution can help reduce the risk. Let's look at three different employees and think about how much of an insider threat they pose:

1 Barbara heads up the software engineering team. She regularly travels to China and India to meet with the developers who are based there. Although her employer relies heavily on the licensing revenue from their software, the company pays below average wages to their software engineers; management and the sales team, however, get regular bonuses and pay raises. As head of software engineering, Barbara has access to all of the company's source code.

Do you think Barbara could be an insider threat?

What makes Barbara suspicious?

What could Barbara do that could damage the company?

What could you do to prevent this from happening?

2 Michael is an IT manager with a high-paying salary. However, he's been promoted far beyond his skill level: he doesn't really know what he's doing. On top of that, he's a poor manager, with weak interpersonal skills and a fragile ego, and is jealous of his talented team. HR has received a number of complaints about Michael taking credit for other people's work and the poor quality and lateness of his work. As an IT manager, Michael has privileged access to all of the company's internal systems. Rumor has it within the company that Michael has been put on a performance improvement plan but that he's failed to improve and is about to be let go.

Do you think Michael could be an insider threat?

What makes Michael suspicious?

What could Michael do that could damage the company?

What could you do to prevent this from happening?

3 Robert is a failing salesperson. He's yet to make any sales this year and has consistently failed to make his quarterly targets since he started. His assigned customers don't like him, and he's unlikely to make any sales in the future. Eighty percent of his package is based on sales commission; his base salary is very low. However, Robert just bought a new car and has been showing up in the office in designer suits and sporting a nice new Rolex. He also bought himself a new top-of-the-line phone and is heading on an all-expenses-paid holiday to the Caribbean next month. Working in the sales team, Robert has full access to the company's entire customer list, along with internal confidential product pricing, product roadmaps, and copies of all production software.

Do you think Robert could be an insider threat?

What makes Robert suspicious?

What could Robert do that could damage the company?

What could you do to prevent this from happening?

All of our example employees could be insider threats. Each of them has some suspicious behaviors, and they all stand to gain by stealing confidential company data. As you can see, spotting and managing insider threats is complex. So, what are some precautions we can take to try to minimize the damage?

- *Move swiftly to remove access*. Once the decision has been made to remove someone from the company, immediately disable all their accounts and disable access. Don't delete their accounts; you may need information from them for projects or business continuity, and you may need to check them for suspicious activity.

- *Take back company property as quickly as possible.* Similarly, take back employees' laptops, mobile phones, remote-access tokens, and other company-issued equipment. Again, don't wipe them; take backups of all data and keep the equipment in storage for at least three months after the employee has left in case you need to recover data or carry out an investigation.
- *Put people on gardening leave.* Fired employees get shown the door immediately, but it can be tempting to let people work their notice once they resign. Instead, put them on paid gardening leave for the duration of their notice period. They won't be able to come in to the office, nor can they work for another company, but they will be paid to sit out their notice period at home. This limits any possibility of mischief by a disgruntled employee.
- *Regularly check and review system access.* I left an automotive client after building a major new production system for them. I returned a year later to carry out an audit, only to find that my account was still active, with the same password as when I left. Make it a habit to review accounts and system access at least every six months, and build and enforce a robust joiners-movers-leavers (JML) process that ensures accounts are properly shut down and removed.
- *Be on the lookout for suspicious behaviors.* In the film *Superman III*, Richard Pryor's character Gus Gorman embezzles money from his employer, Webscoe. He would have gotten away with it, too, except he used the stolen money to buy himself a new Ferrari 308 (to be fair, a great choice). Gorman is busted when Webscoe's CEO, Ross Webster, spots him pulling up outside the company in his sweet new ride.

There might be many reasons why an employee or colleague comes into some money or good fortune. However, there may be a pattern of purchases that matches up with suspicious behavior, which warrants further investigation.

6.5 *"Blast radius": Limiting the damage*

There's an unfortunate trend among security companies and pundits within the security industry to try to apply terms from physical warfare to cybersecurity. Not only are these terms inaccurate, they're also aimed at tapping into heightened fears of an attack as a way to sell more stuff. One of the most egregious terms is *blast radius*, which refers to the sphere of damage/impact an attacker has. But—despite the silly name— the underlying concept is an important one and forms a big chunk of how we can build protection that is relevant, proportional, and sustainable.

If we look again at our original example company infrastructure, we can see the blast radius caused by an attacker breaching the fileserver (figure 6.11). As the fileserver, application server, and web server are all on the same network, the attacker is freely able to attack them all. Additionally, because users will be accessing those systems, the attacker has the opportunity to install malware on the servers, which would further infect individual users' machines.

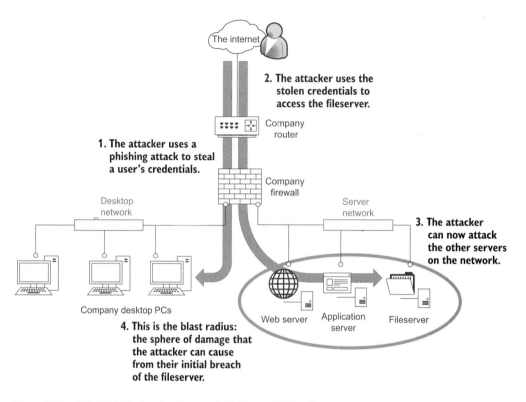

Figure 6.11   What the blast radius from an initial breach looks like

When people talk about blast radius, what they're really saying is "How can we limit, or reduce, the amount of damage an attacker can do after an initial breach?" Very often, our own architecture and infrastructure design decisions make it easier for attackers to cause more damage than they should.

Let's look at an unfortunately all too common scenario. The application server in our example company infrastructure has three classes of users who access it:

- *Administrators*—Users with full access who look after the running, patching, and updates of the system
- *Developers*—Users with full access who can deploy updated versions of software and configure the application server itself
- *End users*—Users with limited access who interact with the web applications running on the application server

A common, recurring problem I've seen over the years, across many clients, is that while end users all have individual accounts, the administrators and developers each share a single account respectively among their teams. Let's think about how this impacts the blast radius of an attacker.

EXERCISE

If we have 2 administrators sharing a single account, 20 developers sharing another single account, and 200 end users with individual accounts, what problems does this give us when trying to trace an attacker's unauthorized access?

If an attacker's goal was to compromise the application server via privilege escalation, what class of user would they initially target for attack? What class of user do you think the attacker would target next? What could we can do to spot this and to minimize the impact? If the attacker successfully compromises the administrator or developer accounts, what else could they do inside the company?

Normally, an attacker would target an end user, usually via a phishing attack, and steal their credentials. With so many other valid user accounts, and considering how subtle phishing attacks are, this is relatively easy to do and difficult to spot.

Next, the attacker would want to escalate their privileges by attacking either a developer or administrator account. By sending phishing emails that appear to come from the compromised end user account, it is relatively simple to craft a convincing attack. Because the administrative and developer accounts are shared between multiple users, it becomes incredibly difficult to spot malicious or unauthorized use, or even to track which user did what on the system.

We have a further problem: administrative and developer accounts are often shared across multiple systems. It's highly likely that the same administrative and developer credentials can be used to take control of the company's web server and fileserver as well.

Our first steps to limit the damage should be as follows:

1. Remove the single administrator and developer accounts, and instead give each admin and developer user their own dedicated account. This allows you to track who logged in, when, and what they did on the server.
2. Enable MFA on all user accounts, protecting them from credential theft in the first place.
3. Have separate administrative and developer accounts for each system (web, application, and fileserver), stopping credential usage across systems.

Once we've tackled the basics like this, we can then look at infrastructure improvements that will further improve the security of our systems. First, though, let's look at some of the ways we shouldn't try to limit the damage from attackers.

6.5.1 *AI, machine learning, behavioral analysis, and snake oil*

In the 18th century, shady European entrepreneurs sold snake oil as a magic cure, an amazing elixir that could cure everything from tuberculosis and rheumatism to cancer. Snake oil was essentially mineral oil, with entertaining additives such as cocaine, amphetamine, alcohol, opiates, chilies, and camphor.

Just like the snake oil salesmen of old, security companies today promote all sorts of fabulous products—magical security elixirs—to deal with insider threats.

AI

There's actually no real artificial intelligence in anybody's products. To qualify as AI, a program must pass the Turing test, where the program has to answer a long series of questions from a human interrogator until the human is convinced the program is actually human itself.

When vendors talk about AI, what they actually mean is "some code (an algorithm) that pattern-matches against known actions." Vendors will also use the phrase *machine learning*; all that means is that their pattern-matching algorithms can improve their accuracy by learning from their results. AI in cybersecurity tools is neither automated nor intelligent; all of these tools still require ongoing manual management to be effective.

The most common example of this is WAFs. Like a normal firewall, a WAF sits between our application and the internet. However, a WAF examines the actual requests and responses being sent between a user's browser and the web server and pattern matches those requests against known attacks, generating an alert (or blocking the request) when it finds a match.

WAFs are notoriously unreliable, mostly because a lot of web applications aren't well written; something that looks like an XSS attack actually turns out to be a poorly implemented way of updating a user's shopping cart. WAFs also don't work well with encrypted traffic, adding latency and slowing down the speed of a website while they decrypt, analyze, and re-encrypt the requests and responses.

Managing, tuning, and updating a WAF is a full-time job, and many web applications will deal with millions of requests a day. Agile delivery methods might, in the same day, deliver three or four application updates—all of which could change the nature and content of those requests. Clearly, keeping on top of this is neither proportional nor sustainable, which is why companies rarely enable anything other than the basic checks in their WAFs.

BEHAVIORAL ANALYSIS

Some vendors will go a step further and talk about user behavioral analysis. This is when a tool looks at a regular event—for example, people logging in to the email system—and then flags behavior that falls outside of what it normally sees as needing investigation. The most common example is tracking logins: most employees will get into the office between 8:30 and 9:30 in the morning and then log into the email system. Similarly, the majority of employees log out between 4:30 and 6:00 in the afternoon. There may be the odd login and logout activity outside of these busy periods, but a large number of logins at, say, 11:00 a.m., triggers an alert and alarms from the monitoring system.

There are two big problems with this that make these systems (at best) highly unreliable:

- *They work in isolation.* If there was a major accident on a motorway or severe train delays due to a breakdown, as humans, we'd expect to see a large number of people logging on much later on in the day. Automated tools, however, will still create alerts and alarms.
- *These systems have to be trained.* Every company and organization is different and has different working patterns and practices, so naturally there's a long period of time where these automated systems have to be trained, where human intervention is required to investigate the alerts and then flag them as false. This all works on the assumption that an attacker isn't already inside the organization. If there is already hostile activity on your network (e.g., logins at odd times), the behavioral analysis will note this as normal "background noise." Rather than making us more secure, such systems are easily tricked into hiding actual security breaches.

Despite their downsides, these tools do have their place in organizations that have highly automated, mature security functions, where the business decision to invest lots of time and money for a small increase in security capabilities is a good trade-off. For the majority of us, though, these tools are just modern snake oil, and we *can* do better. In chapter 2, we focused on the real basics of building a long-term cybersecurity strategy. Now we'll look at how we can design and improve infrastructure to better deal with internal threats.

6.6 Building your castle: Defense in depth

In chapter 1, we looked at Warwick Castle and how its evolution over the years in the face of increasing and changing threats kept its inhabitants safe. We're going to look at this in more detail, comparing the three main security strategies people have used to protect from internal and external threats.

6.6.1 Perimeter security: Build a wall

When we first started connecting systems and networks to the internet, the situation was much simpler. Attacks were relatively unsophisticated, and we could get away with putting a barrier between the network and our private systems and networks. Firewalls were created, allowing simple traffic analysis, and blocking or allowing certain types of requests and protocols to specific systems.

This was called perimeter security and was exactly like a basic castle design: stick a moat and a big wall between the outside attackers and our valuables—with a single gate that allows approved traffic to go in and out (figure 6.12).

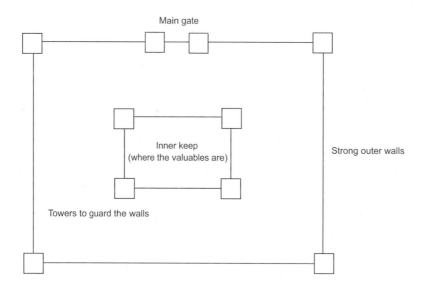

Figure 6.12   A simplified view of a basic fortified structure

As attacks increased in sophistication, we needed to add more layers of defense. Just like Warwick Castle, defensive security infrastructure has developed and improved over time. Castles evolved to have more defensive layers (figure 6.13):

- A barbican (a heavily fortified two-level gate)
- Moats around the castle (usually filled with water or nasty wooden spikes)
- Multiple fortified internal structures (e.g., stables, grain storage, barracks)
- Inner walls around some of the more important fortified structures
- A further inner wall around the keep
- Raising the keep and protecting its foundations
- A second, smaller fortified gate, called a sally port, so that defenders could exit the castle safely and launch a counterattack

One of the secrets of the success of fortified centers like Warwick Castle is that they have evolved over time to take into account the evolving threats they face, created a constant feedback loop that analyzes the threats they face, and adapted their security measures to match them. Adding layers of security and new security technologies means we don't rely on one type of defense; we're not relying on something like one gate, which is a single point of failure. *Defense in depth* is a concept fully embraced by

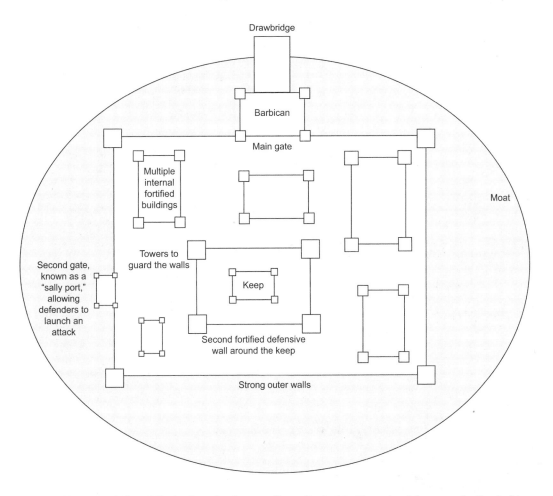

Figure 6.13 An evolution of the basic perimeter security castle design. The extra defenses make the design more complex but add much more security.

Warwick Castle: when an attacker breaches one layer of defense, they have to start their attack all over again to breach the next level. We can apply the same idea to our example corporate infrastructure. As it stands, there is a single point of failure: a single, central firewall (figure 6.14).

Our firewall is a single point of failure—our one gate protecting the castle—and if attackers breach it, they have free reign to pillage our company. How would you change our sample company infrastructure to build in some defense in depth?

Think about how users and customers access company information:

- Where do the access/data requests come from?
- What sort of services are being accessed? By whom?
- How could we control or manage that access?

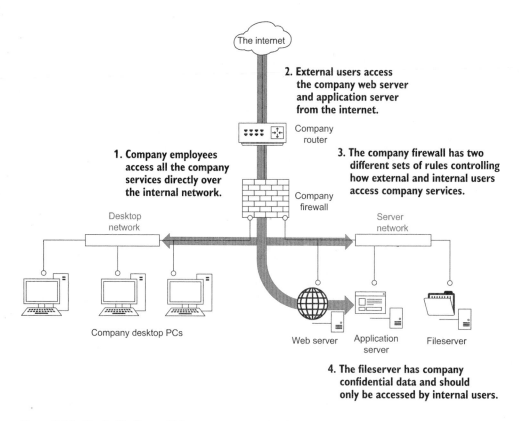

Figure 6.14   The traffic flows within our company network

Grab a pencil and some paper and update the sample company infrastructure to build in some extra security. Think back to what we covered in chapters 4 and 5: the different types of attacks and how we can mitigate those attacks. We'll strip our example company infrastructure to just the basics (figure 6.15). Take those and redraw the infrastructure with some defense in depth.

There are several different ways to do this, and as always, no one single right way, so try to be creative, taking into account what we've already looked at in this chapter.

One way that this could be done is by splitting the networks up further based on the type of data they will hold and who will access that data (figure 6.16). We can add some more firewalls, ideally from different manufacturers so that a bug or security flaw in one doesn't affect everything. By putting the servers that are accessed by external users into their own network, we make it harder for an attacker to move laterally in the organization and attack the fileserver. External server networks such as this are often called a DMZ, after the military term demilitarized zone. A DMZ is a network where we have a lot of defenses to protect it from known attacks, while at the same time having a lower level of trust in the services that are placed there.

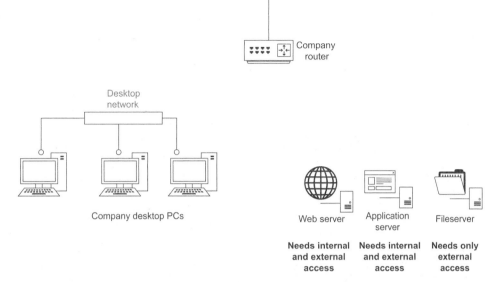

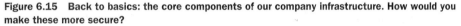

Figure 6.15   Back to basics: the core components of our company infrastructure. How would you make these more secure?

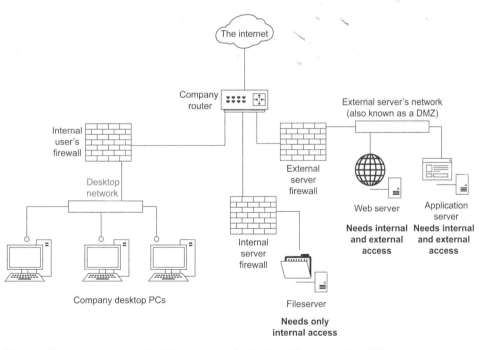

Figure 6.16   One way to start building a defense-in-depth architecture is by splitting up our services and isolating them based on who would be accessing them.

This helps limit lateral movement within the organization from an attacker's initial breach. Even if we don't stop the attacker fully, the extra defenses will slow them down long enough for us to spot the attack and do something about it. This is a simplification of what could be done; defense-in-depth solutions could also include secure remote access, MFA services, cloud-hosted email services, cloud-based security monitoring, and more. We will look in much more detail at defense-in-depth architecture and solutions in part 2 of this book when we look in more detail at how to protect our company, people, and data.

6.6.2   *Zero trust: The attackers are everywhere*

It is all great when the attackers are only coming from outside, from the internet. But, as we saw at the start of this chapter, a large and growing percentage of attacks are coming from inside our organizations. Insider threats stem from bribed or dissatisfied employees who already have access to systems and data sources internally.

In 2013, a security analyst based in Hawaii and working for security contractor Booz Allen Hamilton had access via his work to various internal systems of the NSA, the US spy agency. Using his access, and allegedly getting colleagues to share login details with him, he copied an estimated 1.7 million highly classified documents and files. These covered everything from secret internal NSA catalogues detailing custom spy equipment used by the agency to data access/analysis operations, and even included secret documents from UK and Australian spy agencies who were working alongside the NSA on sensitive projects.

Selected documents were shared with and published by journalists from around the world. Although some of the documents that were shared provided proof of cyber capabilities within the NSA that had already been guessed, other documents highlighted new and sophisticated programs, along with detailing embarrassing revelations about the NSA spying on US allies. The breach was described as "the most damaging ever" for the NSA, with a former director of GCHQ (Government Communications Headquarters, the UK spy agency) claiming that the breach was a strategic setback that had damaged the UK, US, and NATO. The security analyst's name was Edward Snowden.

As an employee of a security contractor, Snowden had limited access to some NSA systems. Anonymous sources and NSA memos have claimed that Snowden used social engineering to get colleagues to share their login details with him, as he needed access "to do his job."

Despite part of the NSA's remit to protect sensitive US government networks and systems, it's clear that they failed to adequately protect their own systems from an internal attack.

Thinking back to one way we learned to stop attackers from using someone else's login credentials and passwords, what's one technology that the NSA should have ensured was implemented across all their systems that could have limited Snowden's access?

Zero-trust architecture is the name given to an infrastructure design approach that assumes every device on a network, every system in an organization, is potentially under the control of attackers and is therefore hostile. As the *X-Files* showed us, trust no one.

In the UK, the National Cyber Security Centre (NCSC) is a government agency within the UK's spy agency, GCHQ, that provides advice and support to the private and public sector on security issues. NCSC has come up with six key principles that underline a zero-trust architecture:

- *Single, strong source of user identity*—User information is held and updated in a secure, central repository.
- *User authentication*—Along with strong passwords, MFA is used to authenticate user access.
- *Machine authentication*—Not just users are authenticated; machines (laptops, servers, even printers) should have secure identities, like digital certificates, which are checked and validated before allowing access to a service.
- *Additional context, such as policy compliance and device health*—If our laptop or a server we're accessing is running out-of-date or unpatched software, then it should be automatically denied access to more secure systems.
- *Authorization policies to access an application*—Don't just rely on usernames and passwords, but also use group membership to allow access to applications. For example, someone in the finance department doesn't need access to the system that programs building access cards.
- *Access control policies within an application*—Even if you can authenticate to and access an application, that doesn't mean you should be able to access all the data within the application—or even make updates to the data. For example, access-control policies can ensure that certain people only have read-only access to a very limited subset of the full data in an application.

None of these are new or ground-breaking ideas, but by combining them and trusting none of the components within our company infrastructure, we can ensure we are prepared for both internal attacks as well as the results of an external breach.

From this list, which of the six zero-trust principles, if implemented fully by the NSA, could have limited the information Snowden had access to? Thinking back to how Snowden was able to access and copy so much data, it's clear that although the NSA had implemented the first principle (single, strong source of user identity), they hadn't implemented all the others fully across their systems. Using all of them together could have severely limited Snowden's access—and made it easier to spot his efforts at trying to get access to data.

Let's take our example defense-in-depth company infrastructure and see how we can improve things. We've already segmented networks and installed separate security devices to block and spot attackers' actions. Our revised company infrastructure is much more secure than it was initially. For comparison, figure 6.17 is our defense-in-depth architecture.

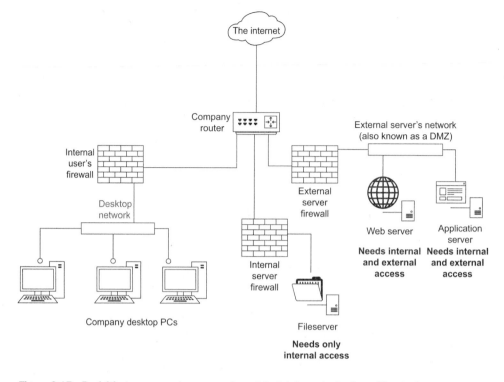

Figure 6.17   Revisiting our example company's updated defense-in-depth architecture

Zero-trust architecture means that we trust none of our infrastructure; we need to treat everything as if it were potentially compromised. For example, when a user's desktop computer requests a file from the fileserver, we should use the zero-trust principles to

- Force the user to authenticate (with MFA)
- Force the user's machine to authenticate
- Check that the user's machine is allowed to access the fileserver
- Check that the user is allowed to access the fileserver
- Check that the user is allowed to access the specific directory and file on the fileserver

Zero-trust architecture can be a massive and complex investment. We can see the impact it has on our example corporate infrastructure. We need to have a highly secure source of authentication, and we need to have a highly secure source of identity for devices that manages the creation, distribution, and revocation of digital certificates for each device on the network.

An example of what a zero-trust architecture could look like is shown in figure 6.18. As you can see, the infrastructure is a lot more complex:

- We have two of each, key router and firewall, to spread the load of managing the traffic and to ensure that things keep running if something happens to one of them.
- We have vulnerability and malware scanners on each network that handles normal user traffic.
- We have a separate, secure network, where we centrally store and analyze the logs from every device in the company.
- This network also hosts the service that deploys, revokes, and manages the individual identity certificates given to every device.
- We have another separate, secure network, that holds our MFA service.

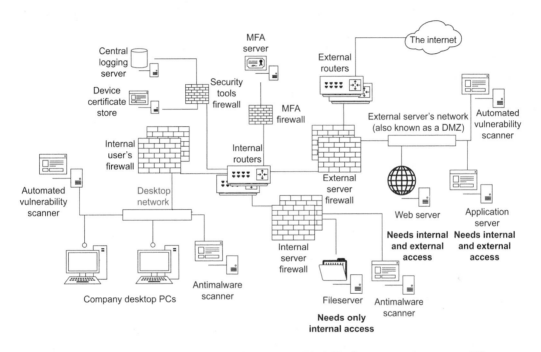

Figure 6.18 An example of what zero-trust architecture could look like for our example company. Things are much more secure, but they also more complex, which means more expensive. Is this overkill given the assets we have and who we think would want to attack us?

This extra leap in complexity is why we looked at the three concepts of a cybersecurity strategy in chapter 2—that it be relevant, proportional, and sustainable. Obviously, if you're a spy agency like the NSA, zero-trust architecture ticks all those boxes: the nature of the data being stored and processed justifies the cost and complexity. For many other organizations, however, zero-trust architecture might not be worth it, or it may make sense to partially apply it.

A common area where zero-trust architecture principles are often used is when companies deploy a BYOD network to allow employees to use their personal mobile phones and tablets to access company resources. Zero-trust principles can be applied to just the BYOD network and the devices connected to it, while the company continues to implement defense in depth across the rest of their infrastructure.

Another area where zero trust is being used more often is in the cloud. Infrastructure within the cloud is often available as prepackaged services that can be deployed and configured automatically. By removing some of the administrative overhead of deploying and managing these extra services, it's easier to design the cloud infrastructure with a zero-trust approach. Cloud services can also be removed and rebuilt automatically, which makes removing and rebuilding a potentially compromised service much easier.

If the NSA had properly implemented zero-trust architecture, the damage from Snowden would have been severely limited. And it's much more likely he would have been caught long before he fled with the NSA's crown jewels. This serves as a timely reminder that very often the organizations tasked with giving security guidance (the NSA in the US, and the NCSC in the UK) are unable to implement even the basics themselves. Their guidance is very often "Do as we say, not as we do."

As we've seen, fully implementing a zero-trust architecture, over and above defense in depth, can be complex and expensive, which is why the core concepts of a cybersecurity strategy—that it is relevant, proportional, and sustainable—are so important to bear in mind when looking at our personal and company security. Zero trust may sound good, but for many organizations, it might be a step too far for them, where merely beefing up their infrastructure to properly provide defense in depth might be a more suitable option.

Summary

- Infrastructure must be built and modified to address not only external attackers who have breached our defenses, but also to deal with insider threats from colleagues and other employees.
- Privilege escalation is when an attacker uses stolen credentials to gain control of an account with higher access, for example, an account with administrator privileges.
- Phishing can be used in privilege escalation attacks. An attacker can send an email using stolen credentials or send malware to an administrator, often embedded in a business document stolen from the user and sent via a spoofed email.
- An advanced persistent threat occurs when an attacker breaches an organization but remains undetected for a period of time. These types of attacks are used to secretly obtain data over time and can be motivated by either economic or political gain.
- Criminals can profit from stealing data by using the victim's credit cards, accessing their bank accounts, or stealing the victim's IDs, thereby allowing them to open bank accounts, apply for loans, or apply for credit cards—all at the victim's expense.

- Insider threats refers to attackers who are colleagues.
- There are several methods to prevent insider attacks when employees are let go:
  - Once the decision has been made to remove someone from the company, all their accounts should be disabled to prevent malicious attacks.
  - When an employee is released, recover laptops, company-issued mobile phones, remote access tokens, and other company-issued equipment.
  - Regularly check and review system access to make sure old accounts and system access are properly shut down.
- Ways to limit the "blast radius" of attacks include the following:
  - Give each administrator and developer their own dedicated account, thus removing shared accounts. This will allow you to track who logged in when and what they did on the server.
  - Enable MFA on all user accounts to prevent credential theft.
  - Have separate administrative and developer accounts for each system.
- Defense in depth leverages our understanding of what assets we have, and who needs to access them, to ensure we build a secure infrastructure that is relevant, proportional, and sustainable.
- Zero-trust architecture is where we assume every component could be compromised and force authentication and authorization checks at every level. While the most complicated approach, it's also the most secure way to design infrastructure.

The Dark Web: Where is stolen data traded?

This chapter covers

- Learning the difference between the three main Dark Web protocols
- Demonstrating how to download TOR and access the TOR Dark Web and hidden onion sites
- Understanding how, where, and why encryption and anonymity do and don't protect you on the Dark Web
- Learning how the desire for anonymity and security drove both the development of the Dark Web and bitcoin
- Understand how bitcoin is—and isn't—related to the rise of dark markets

There's no point in understanding what motivates attackers and how they work if you don't understand what the payoff can be. What is the point of stealing millions of credit cards or millions of social security numbers? How can an attacker successfully cash in on all that stolen data? Understanding the payoff and why it motivates attackers is the key piece of the puzzle in understanding how attackers think. It's what shifts the focus of the breach at Marriott from the theft of information on over 500 million guest stays to a potential state-sponsored attack aimed at stealing information on US military personnel and contractors.

In this chapter, we'll look at the main destination for attackers to trade, sell, and store their stolen data: the Dark Web.

7.1 *What is the Dark Web?*

The Dark Web is also the subject of a huge amount of hype and misinformation, much of it driven by security consultants and security software vendors who want us to buy expensive security solutions based on fear of the unknown. The Dark Web is presented as something subversive and dangerous, a shadowy threat to our data. There are also a lot of terms being shared around by marketing teams and ill-informed journalists about the Dark Web, the Deep Web, and even the underbelly of the internet.

This is all nonsense. The internet (or the World Wide Web, as it is often called) isn't just one, single thing. It's a number of different protocols and data streams, layered on top of each other. When we access a website, our request is actually sent across many different networks, all interconnected. If we want to load the website of my publisher, Manning Publications, for example, our request is sent between a number of different networks (figure 7.1). In my case, the request has to travel from Italy, across the Atlantic, and from there to Manning's hosting provider in the US—seven or eight different networks, run by different companies, yet still all the internet.

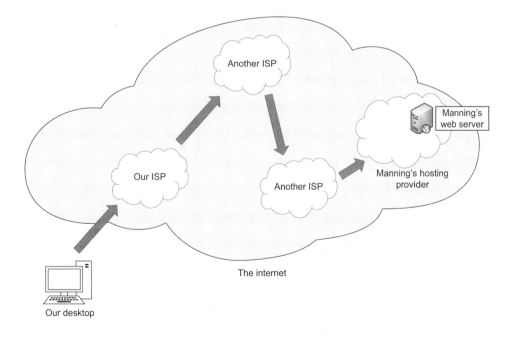

Figure 7.1 How a request from our desktop actually ends up at Manning's webserver. The internet isn't one single network; it's a series of connected networks from many different companies and organizations that have agreements to route traffic between them.

While many people think of the internet as just being used to access websites, there are actually a number of very different communication protocols that we use to access a wide range of other services:

- *TLS (Transport Layer Security)*—Any time you see HTTPS being used, you're actually seeing TLS—a method of encrypting an HTTP conversation to secure the contents. TLS can also be used to encrypt other protocols.
- *NTP (Network Time Protocol)*—This is used to synchronize our computer and phone clocks and make sure we have the right time set.
- *SMTP (Simple Mail Transfer Protocol)*—SMTP is used by all email clients and email servers to send and receive email.
- *IMAP and POP (Internet Mail Access Protocol and Post Office Protocol)*—These two protocols are used by our email clients—for example, Outlook—to collect email from our email servers.
- *FTP (File Transfer Protocol)*—This is not so common any more, but it is used to download and upload files to an FTP server, basically a fileserver on the internet.
- *SSH (Secure Shell)*—SSH is a secure, encrypted way to remotely access servers. Because it's encrypted, it has almost completely replaced Telnet, which was similar but had no encryption and was highly insecure.

The internet itself uses a networking protocol called TCP/IP (Transmission Control Protocol/Internet Protocol), sometimes called the Internet Protocol, which was always designed to be flexible enough for other protocols that handled specific applications to work on top of it. As we can see in figure 7.2, TCP/IP allows all the protocols we listed to "piggyback" on it.

Networking in general, and TCP/IP specifically, is a fascinating and complex subject that any budding security engineer will need to really come to grips with. More detail is firmly outside the scope of this book, but I highly recommend *TCP/IP Illustrated*, Vol. 1, by W. Richard Stevens (Addison-Wesley, 1994), the first in a definitive three-volume series covering how TCP/IP and associated protocols work.

The flexibility of the TCP/IP protocol is what has allowed people to build hidden internets—the so-called Dark Web. There isn't one single Dark Web, and each Dark Web doesn't communicate with each other. They each use different tools and protocols, are accessed in different ways, and have been built with very different goals in mind. Each Dark Web hosts its own internet-like services: search engines, discussion boards, email servers, website hosting, and so on. All the Dark Web protocols have one thing in common: they have been designed to be as secure as possible and to provide as much anonymity to users as possible.

Often, Dark Webs are referred to as *darknets*, and the normal internet is referred to as the *clearnet*, due to its lack of privacy and anonymity. Let's look at the three main Dark Web protocols currently being used and developed.

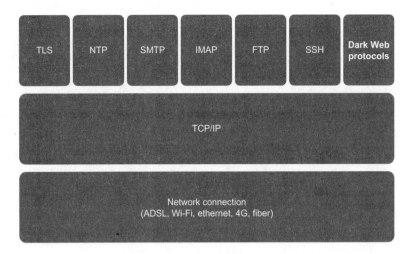

Figure 7.2   A (very) simplified diagram showing the relationship between the IP, TCP/IP, and other commonly used protocols–including Dark Web ones—that piggyback on TCP/IP

7.1.1   TOR

TOR is an acronym for "the onion router," and it had a very strange beginning. In the 1990s, the US Naval Research Laboratory began to research how a network of computers around the world could be used to route secure, encrypted communications from spies back to their handlers. In 1997, the US Defense Advanced Research Projects Agency (DARPA)—the team that brought us the internet (which was originally called ARPANET and was for use by defense and research bodies)—also got involved.

The two US government agencies appeared to face problems with developing and deploying TOR, and so, in a surprise move, they released the source code. A core team of three were sponsored by digital civil rights pioneers, the Electronic Frontier Foundation (EFF), to continue developing TOR, leading to setting up the Tor Project, which continued to develop TOR and related applications.

TOR uses a concept called onion routing to encrypt and transmit its traffic through thousands of volunteer-run machines connected to the internet. Onion routing is a way of wrapping the data in multiple layers of encryption; each layer can only be decrypted and read by the next machine to transmit the data (see figure 7.3).

In this way, when using TOR, it's possible to access normal internet websites and services, with a degree of anonymity. However, the connection from the final machine on the TOR network (called an *exit node*) and the rest of the internet might not be

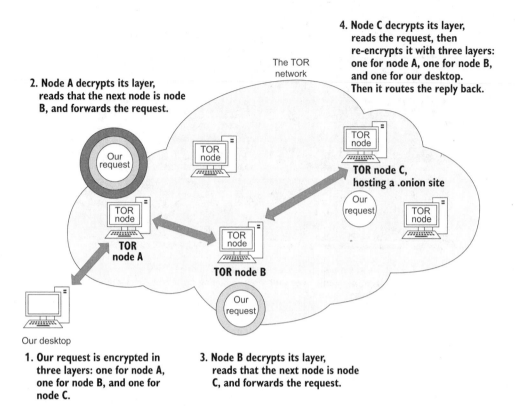

Figure 7.3 How TOR's layers of encryption protect our request and its reply. At each step, each TOR node only knows which previous node sent it the data and which node it has to send the data to next. Being unable to trace the entire flow of data makes the request anonymous.

encrypted and is likely to be heavily monitored (see figure 7.4). The most security comes from accessing websites and services that are completely hosted within the TOR network.

Controversy has long surrounded TOR: the TOR Project receives significant funding from US government agencies. In 2012, 80% of the Tor Project's $2 million annual budget came from DARPA, the US Naval Research Laboratory, the US State Department, and the National Science Foundation. The US and UK spy agencies (the NSA and GCHQ, respectively) have both contributed code and bug fixes to the project, with the NSA claiming TOR is "the king of high-secure, low-latency Internet anonymity." Such hefty government involvement has made many suspicious that spy agencies have defeated the security and anonymity that TOR provides.

Documents leaked from the Snowden breach (covered in chapter 6) make it clear, however, that although NSA and GCHQ researchers have found ways to reduce the anonymity TOR provides, they are unable to completely break it.

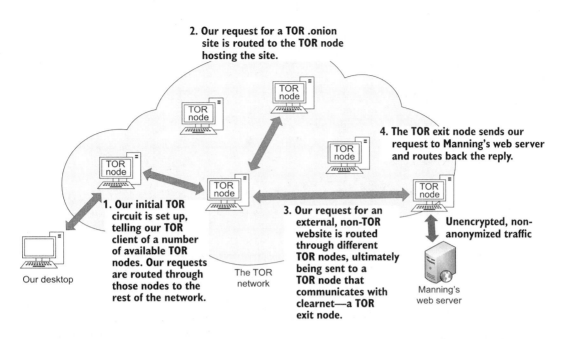

2. Our request for a TOR .onion site is routed to the TOR node hosting the site.

4. The TOR exit node sends our request to Manning's web server and routes back the reply.

1. Our initial TOR circuit is set up, telling our TOR client of a number of available TOR nodes. Our requests are routed through those nodes to the rest of the network.

Our desktop

The TOR network

3. Our request for an external, non-TOR website is routed through different TOR nodes, ultimately being sent to a TOR node that communicates with clearnet—a TOR exit node.

Unencrypted, non-anonymized traffic

Manning's web server

Figure 7.4 How traffic is routed internally with the TOR network and how exit nodes route traffic through to the clearnet. Traffic sent from the TOR exit node to the clearnet is not anonymous or encrypted and can be intercepted.

The design goal of TOR to allow individuals to anonymously and securely communicate has also brought controversy: infamous dark markets like the Silk Road and Dream Market could only be accessed by TOR and sold illegal drugs, malware, weapons, and stolen financial details. Currently, TOR is the most popular example of the Dark Web and is the easiest to access.

7.1.2   I2P

The Invisible Internet Project (I2P) was started in 2003 as a way to enable secure, encrypted, peer-to-peer communications. I2P works by setting up a number of encrypted connections (called *tunnels*) to other I2P users (called *peers*). Each I2P user can configure how many tunnels to set up and how many I2P peers each will route through. These decisions affect the security, latency, and transfer speed of your communications.

In figure 7.5, we can see the I2P communications between two users, Alice and Bob. Both have set up two I2P tunnels—one for outbound communication and one for inbound communication. Alice's outbound tunnel is configured to route via three I2P nodes. Bob's outbound tunnel is configured to route via four I2P nodes. Note that the nodes don't have to be unique.

I2P is mostly used for communications, allowing secure, anonymous connections to Internet Relay Chat (IRC) servers. IRC has been around since the late 1980s and is a flexible, scalable, text-based chat system, comparable to modern alternatives

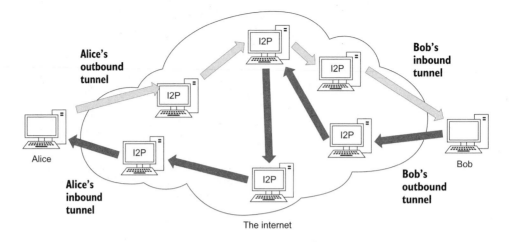

Figure 7.5   A simplified view showing how two users, Alice and Bob, communicate using I2P

like Slack. IRC has long been the preferred communications platform for hackers, developers, and engineers and was a natural focus for I2P to add security and anonymity too.

I2P has also developed to allow anonymous website hosting and browsing (like TOR), and work is ongoing to add support for other services, like a distributed data store, file-transfer applications, and a blogging platform.

I2P has been anonymously developed by volunteers. Although it's been around since 2003, the code is still viewed as beta, with usability and stability issues.

7.1.3   *Freenet*

Freenet is a peer-to-peer platform, initially developed by Ian Clarke to be censor-resistant and provide anonymous freedom of speech. Clarke initially developed the idea behind Freenet as a student project while at the University of Edinburgh in 1999; it's been in constant development since 2000.

Freenet works by every computer (node) in the network storing lots of small snippets of encrypted data, working like an enormous, secure, distributed cache system. Unlike like peer-to-peer and Dark Web protocols, Freenet doesn't provide much in the way of functionality. It does, however, provide an application programming interface (API) called Freenet Client Protocol (FCP). Other programs can use this API to provide services like online chat, file sharing, and message boards.

When we want to store some data, a request is sent to the nearest node. This, in turn, sends a request to the other nodes in the network. For storage, the data is divided up into small chunks, encrypted, and then stored on a number of nodes. The data can be duplicated across many nodes as well (see figure 7.6).

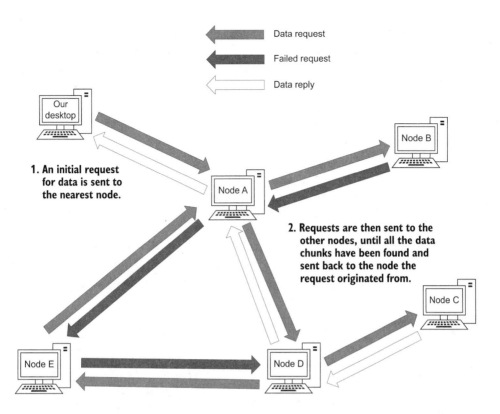

Figure 7.6 How data is requested across the Freenet network. An initial request is sent to the nearest node, which then passes the request to the other nodes until all the chunks of data have been found, which are then sent back to the node that originally requested the data.

To retrieve the data, a request is sent to the nearest node. This, in turn, sends the request to the other nodes until all the data chunks are found. These are then sent back to the node that originally requested the data (in this instance, our desktop), where the data chunks are decrypted and reassembled.

Due to its nature, Freenet is mostly used for file storage and is popular for sharing censored or repressed information like books, guides, and manifestos, as well as for normal document storage by people who want to contribute to a censorship-resistant information network. Thanks to its distributed data, Freenet is very resistant to censorship or having parts of the network shut down. The downside is that the network can be quite slow.

As we can see, the different design goals behind I2P and Freenet mean they both work in very different ways from TOR, and the funding and scale of TOR means that it has overshadowed other Dark Web protocols. Let's look at how we can use TOR to access some Dark Web sites.

7.2   How to access the Dark Web

Reading about how the Dark Web works only goes so far, so now we'll work through the steps to install the required software and start using the Dark Web ourselves. When learning how to access the Dark Web in this section, we'll focus specifically on TOR. This is partly because of its popularity and partly because the TOR Project has put significant effort toward addressing the ease of use problems.

7.2.1   Precautions

There is nothing inherently bad or dangerous about using TOR. As an interested end user, the use case—and the risks faced—are very different from those faced by an under-cover spy, journalist, or democracy campaigner in an oppressive regime. The Dark Web gives these users anonymity, and even simple things like registering for a down-load, accepting website cookies, or registering a user on a Dark Web forum can all leak information that would compromise their anonymity. There are a few common-sense steps you should follow, though, as you should when dealing with any new or potentially untrustworthy website:

- Never enter personal details (e.g., your name, address, or email address) on a Dark Web site.
- Don't download anything.
- Make sure your antimalware software is up to date and running correctly.

These are all the same straightforward precautions we should normally take when accessing a new website or online service. However, the Dark Web is more similar to the Wild West internet of the early 90s than the modern-day, policed, and controlled internet we all use. Identity theft and malware are the reasons some dark markets exist. Scammers are taking advantage of the flood of interested users who have heard about the Dark Web and want to experience it for themselves. Browser plugins that block suspicious websites won't work on the Dark Web, and antimalware software that works with our web browser will also struggle to work. So, some extra precautions— and some healthy distrust—are required to ensure we stay safe.

Before we dive in, let's remind ourselves how TOR works (figure 7.7). As Shrek points out, like onions and ogres, TOR is composed of layers. The onion router wraps layers of encryption around data that is sent and received. Each node or peer on the TOR network decrypts the layer meant for them to work out which node to send the request to next. This is done for each request sent and each reply received, and each node can only decrypt the top layer to see which node to send the data on to next.

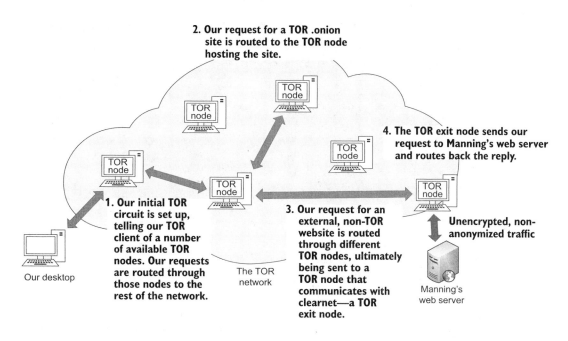

Figure 7.7 A reminder of how the TOR network routes traffic internally and externally. Internally routed traffic is secure and anonymous.

EXERCISE

The best way to learn about the TOR Dark Web is to try it for yourself. Let's work through the process of getting TOR running, accessing a search engine, and then accessing a list of Dark Web sites.

1   Install the TOR Browser Bundle.

To make it easy to use TOR, the TOR Project has developed the TOR Browser Bundle. This is a self-contained version of the Firefox web browser, bundled with the configuration and tools needed to run TOR. This can be installed alongside your existing web browsers and won't impact any of your existing configuration.

2   Go to the TOR Browser Bundle download homepage at https://www.torproject .org/download/.

Click one of the download links that matches your computer's operating system; the page will look like figure 7.8.

3   Once the file has downloaded, run the installer.

You'll be asked to confirm your language and the location to install the Browser Bundle. Because the TOR Browser Bundle is self-contained, you can install it anywhere—on a USB stick, on your desktop, or in your Documents directory.

Once the install is complete, make sure the "Run the TOR Browser" box is ticked and click Finish.

Figure 7.8   The TOR Browser Bundle download page should look like this.

4   The TOR Browser will now start.

You'll see a small pop-up screen that talks about *establishing a circuit*; this is the TOR client software connecting to other TOR nodes and peers. After this has closed, you'll be presented with a standard web browser. By default, the browser will load a special home page for the TOR-hosted site of the Duck-DuckGo privacy search engine.

5   Access a TOR search engine.

Instead of .com or .co.uk, websites hosted on TOR end in .onion. The first site we want to look at is the TOR search engine, TORCH. TORCH is available on the standard internet (the clearnet) at torsearch.net, but we want to access the TOR version.

6   Type the following address into the address bar and press Enter to load the site: http://cnkj6nippubgycuj.onion/.

After a small pause, you should see figure 7.9.

Figure 7.9   The TORCH (TOR SearCH) web page should load, bringing back instant nostalgia if you remember AltaVista.

If you're as old as me, you'll notice that TORCH looks a lot like the pre-Google Altavista search engine: a search box with a load of advertising banners. Already, you can get a feel for how most people use TOR, based on TORCH's suggestion of the most common search terms.

However, we want to look at a directory of Dark Web sites and forums, and for that, we want to load the site Dark Fail.

7 In the address bar of the TOR browser, type the following address and press Enter to load the site: https://dark.fail.

After a small pause, you should see figure 7.10.

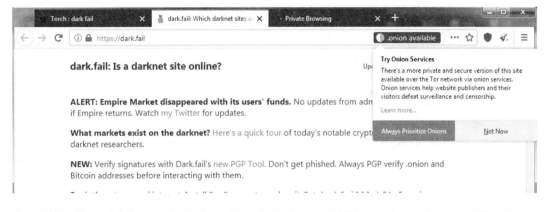

Figure 7.10 The dark.fail clearnet website and the offering from our TOR browser to use the secure TOR .onion version

Notice the pop-up to the right of the screen. The TOR browser has worked out that we're accessing a common site on the clearnet and that there is a secure version available as a .onion service. Ideally, we'd like the browser to automatically load .onion sites over clearnet ones.

8 Click "Always Prioritise Onions."

On the current version of the TOR Browser, this saves a preference to always load .onion sites rather than clearnet sites.

Also notice that the page reloads and the address in the address bar has changed (figure 7.11).

dark.fail is designed to be simple, quick to load, and easy to use. You'll notice that there are no graphics, no complex forms or icons, just a plain-text description of the site, some news and warnings, and then a list of common .onion sites.

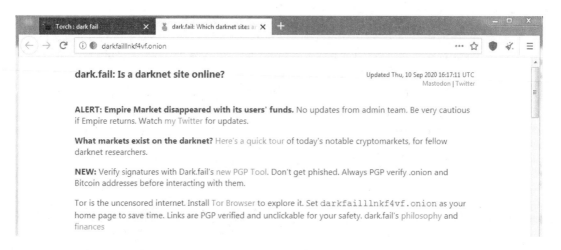

Figure 7.11   Loading dark.fail, a popular website on the TOR Dark Web

9 Scroll down the page.

You'll notice that although there are lots of listings for dark market sites, there's also links to

- VPN providers
- Mainstream news sites like the BBC and the *New York Times*.
- Links to secure service providers, like email provider ProtonMail
- And even links to Dark Web sites run by the FBI, CIA, and the National Police of the Netherlands

10 Feel free to explore.

Visit some of the sites on the list and see how they compare to clearnet versions. You'll quickly notice that sites like the BBC function very differently; this is because technologies that could be used to compromise our security or track us (like JavaScript scripts and cookies) are all disabled by default.

It should be clear that there's far more to the Dark Web than illegal drug distribution and hackers selling stolen information. There's a whole ecosystem of services, much like a shadow internet. Let's look at other ways the Dark Web is used.

7.3   *How is the Dark Web used?*

Having browsed the Dark Web a bit, you have hopefully started to get a feel for how it works and what is hosted on there. Let's dive into the various famous and infamous services typically offered by TOR Dark Web sites.

7.3.1   *Illegal weapons*

During a live demo, as part of a talk I was giving on the Dark Web, I was browsing through one of my favorite dark markets (which has sadly since been shut down by the

FBI). Much to the delight of my audience, we came across an auction listing by some enterprising Ukrainians who were selling off fully functional captured Russian tanks and armored troop transports. For between $8,000 and $40,000, you, too, could buy your own personal, fully functional, and armed BMP-8 armored transport or a T-80 tank.

A dedicated dark market called The Armoury, focused purely on weapons sales, was active between 2011 and 2013 in various forms, before finally being shut down.

7.3.2 Illegal drugs

Possibly the most famous Dark Web site is the original Silk Road, run by Ross Ulbricht, who went by the pseudonym of The Dread Pirate Roberts. Launched in 2011, Silk Road quickly rose to prominence. Functioning a lot like eBay, the site used user feedback and seller reputation scores and secure payment via escrow services and implemented payment via the secure digital currency bitcoin.

Best described in the words of the FBI, Silk Road "emerged as the most sophisticated and extensive criminal marketplace on the Internet at the time, serving as a sprawling black market bazaar where unlawful goods and services, including illegal drugs of virtually all varieties, were bought and sold regularly by the site's users. While in operation, Silk Road was used by thousands of drug dealers and other unlawful vendors to distribute hundreds of kilograms of illegal drugs and other unlawful goods and services to well over 100,000 buyers, and to launder hundreds of millions of dollars deriving from these unlawful transactions."

Silk Road was shut down in 2013, and Ulbricht was arrested after making the somewhat careless mistake of publicly using the same email address to administer Silk Road and take part in chat forums on the regular internet. At the time of its closure by the FBI, Silk Road had around 10,000 products for sale by vendors, 70% of which were drugs, and was processing an estimate $15 million in transactions yearly.

7.3.3 Hackers for hire

There are five recurring urban legends associated with the Dark Web:

- You can hire hitmen and arrange assassinations.
- You can view "red rooms" and witness murder to order.
- You can hire elite hacker teams.
- You can hire terrorist cells to carry out attacks.
- People-smuggling is rife, and you can buy trafficked slaves online.

None of these are true. Terrorists, hitmen, and people smugglers are not the most tech savvy of people, and on top of that, their entire way of working is built on trust and verifiability. Anonymous online communications, where it's impossible to prove an introduction via a trusted third party or to verify where orders are coming from, fundamentally undermine how these people operate. Buying drugs on an eBay-like site, with user feedback, product quality, and vendor reliability ratings is one thing, but that model translates poorly to arranging an assassination or smuggling slaves across a border.

However, you can often find hacking tools and services being offered on dark markets. Software tools like ransomware, bank account–stealing Trojans, botnets for launching DoS attacks, and undiscovered software security flaws (called *zero days*) are all offered for sale.

Some of these are offered as services, which you can rent by the hour, day, or week. Some are even offered as professional services, with 24/7 support phone lines, money-back guarantees, software updates, manuals, and support forums.

7.3.4   *Hacktivism*

We came across hacktivism in chapter 3 when we looked at the different types of hackers. Hacktivists use their knowledge of technology and security in support of activist activities—everything from civil disobedience to jury-rigging portable Wi-Fi broadcasters for use in Tibet to evade Chinese censorship. Many groups like Anonymous, rocked by arrests and betrayals of key members, have migrated to using the Dark Web to secure their communications. Some public clearnet communications services, like IRC, are still used, but via TOR or I2P in order to safeguard the user's anonymity.

With the rise of censorious and proto-fascist regimes around the globe, the ability to secure and anonymously communicate and share information has never been more important. Groups like Distributed Denial of Secrets use the Dark Web to expose political corruption and law enforcement abuse, taking data from breaches and making it freely available.

7.3.5   *Evading censorship*

The original purpose of TOR was to enable spies to send information securely back to their handlers, without the threat of interception or discovery. This is still a reason for privacy activists, reporters, and oppressed minorities to use the Dark Web today.

TOR has proven particularly effective at bypassing the Great Firewall of China—the state-implemented censorship that stops Chinese citizens from accessing information the ruling communist party doesn't want them to see. It's for this reason that the UK's BBC launched a TOR .onion website, making their uncensored journalism available to the Chinese.

Investigative journalists in China have used TOR to share details about the ethnic cleansing, suppression, and genocide of the Uyghur minority in China, as well as details about human rights abuses in Tibet, and journalists from Zimbabwe and Belarus have shared details of government oppression and censorship from their countries.

7.3.6   *Making money from stolen data*

In earlier chapters, we looked at how hackers breach organizations and steal confidential data, with some examples of some of the larger cases. Apart from obvious traditional money laundering, the remaining question is "How do attackers make money from their stolen data?"

This is where the dark markets once again come in. Rather than risk arrest trying to use stolen credit card details or create fake identities, it's much easier for an attacker to sell the stolen data to specialists.

Privacy Affairs carries out yearly research on the average price of stolen information on Dark Web markets. Their 2020 survey revealed the prices in table 7.1 for financial information.

Table 7.1   Privacy Affairs 2020 average Dark Web price for stolen financial information

Stolen information	Average Dark Web price (USD)
Credit card details, account balance up to $1,000	$12
Cloned Mastercard with PIN	$15
Credit card details, account balance up to $5,000	$20
Cloned VISA with PIN	$25
Cloned American Express with PIN	$35
Stolen online banking logins, minimum $100 on account	$35
Stolen online banking logins, minimum $2,000 on account	$65

Compare that to the prices being charged for using stolen IDs to generate forged identity documents (table 7.2).

Table 7.2   Privacy Affairs 2020 average Dark Web price for forged identity documents using stolen IDs

Forged identity document	Average Dark Web price (USD)
Wells Fargo bank statement	$25
US driver's license, average quality	$70
Wells Fargo bank statement with transactions	$80
US driver's license, high quality	$550
European national ID card	$550
US, Canadian, or European passport	$1,500

Think back to the Marriott International data breach we looked at in chapter 6—especially the stolen passport details belonging to those in the US military. Comparing the cost to stolen credit card data, it's clear that the criminals could make much more money from selling the passport information. For the account holder, getting a new passport is infinitely more difficult than cancelling and re-issuing a credit card; for the thief, the passport holds more value to the various spy agencies who were behind the Marriott breach.

7.3.7   *Bitcoin*

Bitcoin is the first and most famous digital currency. Combining cryptographic security with almost complete anonymity, plus its purely digital nature, so-called "cryptocurrencies" like bitcoin could have been tailor-made for the Dark Web. Bitcoin—and its associated transactions—are recorded on a giant, distributed ledger, known as a *blockchain*. Computers run software as part of the bitcoin network, constantly generating hashes (a string created by a cryptographic algorithm), which proves mathematically that a bitcoin exists or that a transaction has occurred.

Although not connected to the Dark Web in any way, bitcoin is a common sight on dark market websites. Combined with the anonymous and secure nature of the Dark Web, bitcoin has become an almost de facto payment method. Normally, the trail of sending bitcoin from one person to another can be tracked. If that payment is for illegal drugs or a stolen Russian tank, everyone involved is in trouble.

Because bitcoin is digital, it can be used with anonymizing services, called *mixers*, or tumblers. Much like a digital money-laundering operation, a mixer functions to hide the ultimate destination of your bitcoin payment. Payment is sent to an account held with the mixer. The bitcoin is then exchanged for many other different ones, hiding their source and origin. Payment can then be sent out to the vendor, with its true origin hidden and impossible to guess.

Bitcoin mixer services are common on the Dark Web, and some are even specifically recommended by dark markets. Anonymizing the source and destination of a digital payment in this way, with the whole transaction carried out over a secure and anonymous network, makes it impossible to track down buyers and sellers, making bitcoin (and other less popular digital cryptocurrencies) ideally suited for use on the Dark Web.

Thanks to its digital and pseudo-anonymous nature, bitcoin is also used by scammers to receive payment for their ransomware, which is where most of us will normally come across bitcoin (apart from the various breathless news stories about the current bitcoin USD exchange rate, or when another bitcoin exchange has been hacked). Although most popular and most closely tied to the Dark Web, bitcoin isn't the only cryptocurrency that has been developed: all of them are useful for pseudo-anonymous digital transfer of money from victims to scammers.

Summary

- There is not just one Dark Web, and the individual Dark Webs do not communicate with each other.
- Each Dark Web has been designed to be as secure as possible, while providing anonymity to their users.
- All Dark Web protocols use encryption and a network of machines—called nodes—to anonymize data traffic and hide both users and Dark Web sites.
- Technologies like JavaScript in web pages can be used to undermine the anonymity of a Dark Web protocol, and exit nodes—where Dark Web traffic becomes

normal internet traffic—can be monitored and compromised by third parties to spy on our communications.

- The desire for anonymity, security, and censorship-resistant communications and data sharing drove both the development of the Dark Web as well as bitcoin and other cryptocurrencies.
- The digital and pseudo-anonymous nature of bitcoin has fueled the rise of dark markets.

Part 2

Part 2 of this book deals with the flip side of part 1: how we can build out relevant, proportional, and sustainable defenses against the attacks and attackers we met in part 1.

Each chapter looks at important elements that contribute to a successful cybersecurity operations capability. Chapter 8 dives into a commonly misunderstood but important area of cybersecurity: risk management. Chapter 9 then shows how to test your own systems and discover vulnerabilities and covers penetration testing, bug bounty programs, and dedicated hacking teams. Chapter 10 builds on chapters 8 and 9 by describing how security operations work and covers the key areas of monitoring, alerting, and incident response.

Finally, chapter 11 describes how to protect our most valuable asset—and our biggest danger—our people. Chapter 12 wraps up the book by looking at what to do after the inevitable hack—how to recover, whom to get help from, and how to improve our defenses and responses for the next attack.

Understanding risk

As we kick off part 2 of the book, we start looking at things from a purely defensive point of view and dive in at a deeper level to see how to protect ourselves and our organizations from attackers. Although it would be useful for you to have read the first half of the book, this chapter can be treated as a standalone reference that can be read in isolation. You might find it helpful to read chapter 2, where we talk about building a cybersecurity strategy.

8.1   *Issues vs. vulnerabilities vs. threats vs. risks*

One of the biggest areas of confusion in cybersecurity, and one of the biggest barriers to effectively communicating cybersecurity concerns, is the confusion around definitions and key terms. Vendors will often (sometimes deliberately) conflate these terms, using them interchangeably, so let's lay down some definitions:

- *Issue*—An issue is an underlying problem or potential problem—for example, it could be a software bug, a hardware fault, or a server misconfiguration. We don't know yet if it can used by an attacker.
- *Vulnerability*—A vulnerability is a known weakness that can be exploited by an attacker. An issue that we know can be used by an attacker is a vulnerability.
- *Exploit*—An exploit refers to some code, an application, or a sequence of steps that an attacker uses to execute a successful attack.
- *Threat*—A threat is a circumstance or action with the potential to cause harm or damage. Malware and disgruntled employees are both examples of threats.
- *Risk*—A risk is the potential for loss or damage when a threat exploits a vulnerability. This could be loss of data, reputational damage, or even loss of life.

How are these four tied together? And how do they help us understand risk? Let's look at a couple of examples:

- **Example 1**

  We'll use our XSS knowledge from chapter 4:
  - *Issue*—We are not checking the data entered into the username field in a web form.
  - *Vulnerability*—The issue has been tested, and we know that XSS is possible by entering JavaScript code into the username field.
  - *Exploit*—Someone has written instructions on how to successfully execute an XSS on our web form.
  - *Threat*—Attackers are trying to steal user credentials to take over user accounts.
  - *Risk*—A malicious attacker could use the XSS vulnerability on our web form as part of an attack to successfully steal a user's credentials, resulting in data loss and reputational damage.

- **Example 2**

  Let's look at another example, this time using the climatic attack on the Death Star, from *Star Wars: A New Hope*:
  - *Issue*—The reactor core in the Death Star could explode if it is hit with an explosive device.
  - *Vulnerability*—There is an exposed exhaust port that leads directly to the reactor core.
  - *Exploit*—The Rebel Alliance stole the plans to the Death Star and have a plan to fire a proton torpedo into the thermal exhaust port.

- *Threat*—The Rebel Alliance launched a fleet of attack fighters at the Death Star.
- *Risk*—The Rebel Alliance star fighters might evade the defensive turbo lasers and TIE fighters and fire a proton torpedo down the exhaust port, causing the Death Star to explode.

This shows how the risk is a combination of the vulnerability and threat. Star Wars is a rich source of cautionary tales for cybersecurity (if we ignore the space wizards):

- The Death Star staff were unaware of the exploit and vulnerability until they were under attack (much like other companies who get hacked).
- Their CEO, the Grand Moff Tarkin, made an executive decision that the risk wasn't worth doing anything about and placed too much confidence in his perimeter security: turbo lasers and TIE fighters.
- Although they had some extra defense (ray shielding to protect the exhaust port from laser fire) they hadn't addressed the vulnerability.

To paraphrase Han Solo, hokey religions and ancient weapons are no match for a good defense-in-depth strategy at your side.

EXERCISE

For each of the following, work out if they are a vulnerability, a threat, or a risk:

- A form on a website that is susceptible to SQL injection
- North Korean state-sponsored hackers
- A web server running out of data software
- A hurricane causing a power outage in our office, disrupting business

ANSWERS

- *Vulnerability*—A form on a website that is susceptible to SQL injection
- *Threat*—North Korean state-sponsored hackers
- *Issue*—A web server running out of data software
- *Risk*—A hurricane causing a power outage in our office, disrupting business

Now that we've got a good grasp on what these terms mean, let's look at a real-life example.

A bank has an online customer account management website. The customer's account number forms part of the URL used to access their own secure account management page. Attackers are constantly probing the account management website to find security flaws. Bank customers regularly receive phishing emails, but the bank has no extra login security beyond an account number and password.

Given this situation, write down what you think the vulnerability, threat, and risk are:

- Vulnerability
- Threat
- Risk

You should have worked out that the vulnerability, threat, and risk are similar to the following:

- *Vulnerability*—The customer's account number forms part of the URL (address) used to access their own secure account management page.

    The bank has no extra login security beyond an account number and password.
- *Threat*—Attackers are constantly probing the account management website to find security flaws.

    Bank customers regularly receive phishing emails.
- *Risk*—Attackers could substitute other customers' account numbers in the URL of their web browser, thus gaining access to customer accounts and causing the bank monetary and reputational damage.

This was actually the scenario with Citi in 2011. Attackers managed to get access to a single customer's online account and saw that the customer's account number formed part of the URL (address) to load the account management page. The attackers decided to try random numbers instead and were granted access to other users' accounts. Citi ended up having to send out tens of thousands of replacement credit cards to affected customers—accounting for 1% of its entire North American customer base.

8.2   *How likely is a hack?*

To help us work out how likely a successful attack will be, we can revisit our three factors of cybersecurity model (figure 8.1):

- What assets do we have?
- Who would want to attack us?
- What defenses do we have?

This is the first stage in helping us understand how likely we are to be attacked.

Let's revisit our example from chapter 2, in which we applied the three factors to a fictitious company. Our company example has two main systems: an e-commerce website and an HR payroll system.

Figure 8.1   A reminder of our three factors of cybersecurity model

The HR payroll system has the financial details of all our company's employees. It's an old system that has a number of known vulnerabilities, but it needs internet access, so we've put it behind a firewall to protect it from incoming malicious data. Only the HR team can access this system.

We also have our new e-commerce website that allows customers to buy models of Warwick Castle from us. This is completely separate from the HR system and has been developed from the ground up by a team using secure coding principles. The system is very secure. For extra protection, it's also behind a firewall to stop malicious incoming data. The development team has admin access to the system.

Applying the three factors model to the company, we can see the following:

- What assets do we have?
  - *HR payroll system*—Old, lots of vulnerabilities
  - *E-commerce website*—New, securely developed
- Who would want to attack us?
  - *Disgruntled ex-employees*—Low threat
  - *Financial fraudsters*—Medium threat
  - *Identity thieves*—Medium threat
  - *Financial fraudsters*—Medium threat
  - *Criminal organizations*—High threat
- What defenses do we have?
  - *A firewall*—Limited admin access (the HR team)
  - *A firewall*—Limited admin access (the development team)

Now that we know where we stand, we can build a simple matrix to show how likely an attack would be. At this stage, we're not looking at defenses; we just want to combine what we know about our vulnerabilities and threats (table 8.1). We will use a simple color-grading scheme to populate each field:

- *Dark gray*—High threat
- *Medium gray*—Medium threat
- *Light gray*—Low threat

Table 8.1 A simple table mapping out the risk posed to each system from our identified threats

	Disgruntled ex-employees	Financial fraudsters	Identity thieves	Criminal organizations
HR payroll system	Low	Medium	Medium	
E-commerce website		Medium		High

So far, so good. We have a good idea of where we are most vulnerable and what threats we are facing. Now let's add in some extra rows to show what defenses we have, adding in the final bit of information we've gathered by using our three factors model (table 8.2). Again, we'll use a simple color grading scheme to populate each field:

- *Dark gray*—No defenses
- *Medium gray*—Some defenses
- *Light gray*—Layered defenses (defense in depth)

Table 8.2   Now we can add in our defenses. We can instantly see that we have no defense in depth (no light gray boxes) and that the defenses we have may not be enough to protect us from medium and high risks.

	Disgruntled ex-employees	Financial fraudsters	Identity thieves	Criminal organizations
HR payroll system	Low	Medium	Medium	
Defenses	Some defenses	Some defenses	Some defenses	
E-commerce website		Medium		High
Defenses		Some defenses		Some defenses

This simple matrix gives us an easy visual guide to the current state of things in our example company. This is an effective "We are here" signpost to share with non-security people and gives a snapshot of our current security situation. More importantly, it forms a basis for us to prioritize further investigations, fixes, and proactive measures like staff training.

As we discussed in chapter 2, using the three factors model in this way, we can construct a roadmap that shows priorities and timelines for our security improvements. In the following timeline, we've prioritized work that will address the biggest security issues on the most vulnerable system first: our HR system. This allows us to reduce the likelihood of a successful attack. We're layering in defenses, building a defense-in-depth approach to address our threats.

Our priority is the HR system; we know it's old and has a number of vulnerabilities. We don't have much in the way of defense: a firewall and limited admin access. So our priorities, in order of urgency, should be as follows:

- Addressing the vulnerabilities we know about in the HR system
- Adding in monitoring for the HR system so that we know about successful and unsuccessful logins from users, as well as application errors that could be caused by attempted attacks
- Adding in monitoring for the HR system firewall so we can see how often attacks are attempted
- Either replacing or upgrading the HR system

Alongside the improvements to the HR system, we also want to invest in some security awareness training for our HR and development teams. As they have admin access to their respective systems, they will be targeted for phishing attacks. Let's prepare them for that.

Having dealt with the immediate problems with the most vulnerable system, we can then move on to the e-commerce website:

- Add in monitoring for the e-commerce website so we know about successful and unsuccessful logins from users, as well as application errors that could be caused by attempted attacks.

- Add in monitoring for the e-commerce firewall so that we can see how often attacks are attempted.

Having dealt with the pressing issues, we can then

- Hire some dedicated security staff.
- Look at investing in a threat intelligence feed that will notify us when new attacks and vulnerabilities are discovered.
- Conduct a security review: Are the changes we made effective? How has our work improved our security?

Now that we know what's required, we can plot out a simple timeline that shows not only how we're going to address the issues, but also the dependencies between the different items of work. Figure 8.2 gives an example of what this could look like.

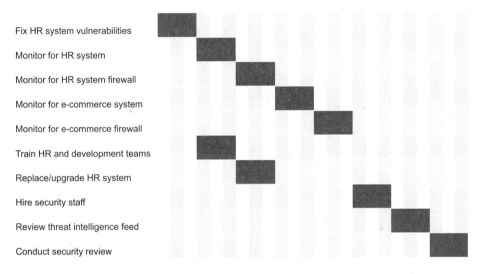

Fix HR system vulnerabilities

Monitor for HR system

Monitor for HR system firewall

Monitor for e-commerce system

Monitor for e-commerce firewall

Train HR and development teams

Replace/upgrade HR system

Hire security staff

Review threat intelligence feed

Conduct security review

Figure 8.2 Our security roadmap, showing the order in which we will implement security improvements to address the vulnerabilities we found

Bringing all of this together helps us achieve three important outcomes:

- We have identified the areas that have the most risk and are therefore most likely to suffer a successful attack.

  The HR system is out of date, and we know it has vulnerabilities, which makes a successful attack more likely.
- We've started building a roadmap for improvement.

  By patching the vulnerabilities in the HR system and then monitoring user access via the application and its protective firewall, we are more likely to notice and stop attacks.

- We have a series of easy-to-understand visual tools, which we can use to show other people in our organization the current state of our security and how (and when) we will improve it.

  Our risk matrix and security roadmap make it easy to understand the vulnerabilities and risks we face, as well as what we're doing to address them.

Any strategy or program to improve security is pointless if people—managers, teams, developers, leadership—don't understand what vulnerabilities we have, how likely they are to be exploited, and how damaging that exploitation could be. Sometimes we will find that our leadership team is happy to accept the risk because the cost of resolving the vulnerability outweighs any costs arising from a breach. Equally, our leadership team may decide that what looks like a less severe vulnerability on paper needs to be addressed sooner because a breach would affect customer confidence and lead to a loss of business. The most important thing to remember is that no one in a business can make sensible decisions unless they have actionable data that can be easily understood—and that's what every security program should be providing.

The HR system in this example is described as "having lots of vulnerabilities"; before we can effectively understand and communicate our risk, we need to know what "lots of vulnerabilities" looks like. Let's take a look at what tools and frameworks we have available to us to turn that vague phrase into some actionable data we can use to improve our security.

8.3   *How bad will it be?*

Back in chapter 2, when looking at building a cybersecurity strategy, we looked at the Common Vulnerabilities and Exposures (CVE) system and the Common Vulnerability Scoring System (CVSS) score as a way of rating and tracking the severity of a vulnerability. Let's revisit those two metrics again in more detail.

As a reminder, CVEs are used to coordinate all information around a specific vulnerability, and a CVSS score is used to rate how serious it is. This is their goal; it's not, however, the way they always work. Sometimes a CVE won't have all the details around a vulnerability. It may be that all the details aren't yet known or that when the CVE was registered, the vendor was in a rush to publish and skipped some details. Additionally, a vulnerability may have several CVEs associated with it, or a single CVE may map to multiple vulnerabilities; quite often, a CVE may not even be created for a vulnerability.

Does this mean CVEs are useless? No, but we do need to remember that while tracking just CVEs doesn't give us a full picture, using CVEs and understanding how they work is the first step toward understanding and communicating our risk levels. In the next chapter, we'll look at what else we can do to discover and manage vulnerabilities to supplement this, but for now, we'll get started by digging deeper into how a CVE works.

First, the most important point to bear in mind is that a CVE is an identifier, not a vulnerability. Let's revisit our breakdown of a CVE from chapter 2 to remind ourselves what a CVE contains. We looked at CVE-2018-0101, which describes a critical security vulnerability in Cisco ASA firewalls, and which comes with a CVSS score of 10 (figure 8.3). We can view the full details in the National Vulnerability Database (NVD) at https://nvd.nist.gov/vuln/detail/CVE-2018-0101. To start, we'll look at how that shocking score—10.0, the highest a vulnerability can get—was calculated.

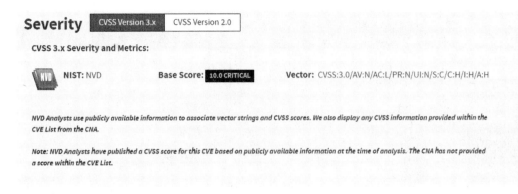

Figure 8.3   The CVSS score for CVE-2018-0101 is a shocker.

8.3.1   *Common Vulnerability Scoring System*

CVSS has been used for many years to help researchers, vendors, affected end users, and organizations to understand the details of a vulnerability. CVSS scores give us three main information points associated with a vulnerability:

- The characteristics of a vulnerability (e.g., is it a remote or local attack? Is it theoretical, or are attackers actively exploiting it?)
- The severity score (how bad it is, on a scale from 0 to 10)
- A simple description to communicate all of this

In our example, CVE-2018-0101, we can click on the value of the Base Score (10.0 Critical) to be taken to a new page, where we can see how the CVSS is calculated. The CVSS Base Score is mandatory and is calculated from two values: Exploitability Metrics and Impact Metrics. We can see here that the CVSS Base Score is calculated by combining the exploitability and impact metrics, and the value is rounded up, which gives a CVSS Base Score of 10 (figure 8.4).

Let's break down those two sets of metrics and look at the information that is used to calculate their values. For each of the metrics, a table describes the possible values and explains what they mean. In each table, the first entry generates the highest CVSS, moving down in impact to the last entry that generates the lowest CVSS (or has no impact at all, if the metric is skipped).

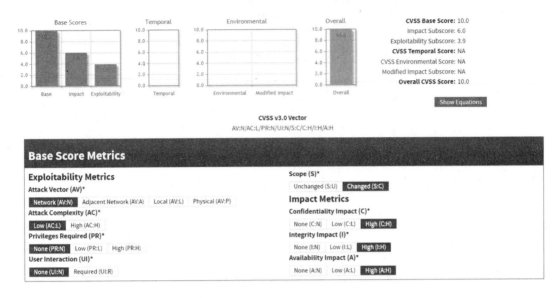

Figure 8.4   A breakdown of how the CVSS Base Score has been calculated for CVE-2018-0101

EXPLOITABILITY METRICS

The *Attack Vector* (AV) describes how the attacker accesses the vulnerable device/software (table 8.3).

Table 8.3   Definitions for the AV metric

Network (N)	The attacker can exploit the vulnerability remotely over the network (e.g., from the internet).
Adjacent (A)	The attacker can exploit the vulnerability by being on the same local network as the vulnerable system.
Local (L)	The attacker must have local access (e.g., they must be logged in to the vulnerable system or may need user interaction to execute malware).
Physical (P)	The attacker must have physical access to the vulnerable system.

Attack Complexity (AC) shows how complicated the attack is (table 8.4). A low-complexity attack could be carried out by anyone. A high-complexity attack would require specialist knowledge, skills, or experience.

Table 8.4   Definitions for the AC metric

Low (L)	There are no special conditions or circumstances to exploit the vulnerability. An attacker can have repeatable success exploiting the vulnerability.
High (H)	A successful exploit depends on something beyond the attacker's control (e.g., they must exploit another component to get access to the network, or they must guess sequence numbers or configuration settings).

For the attack to succeed, does the attacker need any special privileges (*Privileges Required* [PR]; table 8.5)? The impact is highest when an attacker needs no privileges to exploit a vulnerability.

Table 8.5   Definitions for the PR metric

None (N)	The attacker requires no privileges to exploit the vulnerability.
Low (L)	The attacker requires basic privileges (e.g., normal user access) to exploit the vulnerability.
High (H)	The attacker needs significant privileges (e.g., administrative access) to exploit the vulnerability.

Does the user need to be involved in the exploit of the vulnerability (*User Interaction* [UI]; table 8.6)? The impact is obviously higher if the attacker can exploit the vulnerability without needing to involve some form of user interaction.

Table 8.6   Definitions for the UI metric

Required (R)	A user must take some action before the vulnerability can be exploited by an attacker.
None (N)	No user interaction is needed.

The *Scope* (S) metric refers to the scope of the vulnerability—if it can be exploited and then used to attack other parts of a system or network (table 8.7). For example, if there is a vulnerability in a web server that allows the attacker to then compromise database servers, and then the scope is changed. If the vulnerability only allows an attacker to compromise the web server, and they can't attack the database servers, then the scope is unchanged.

Table 8.7   Definition of the S metric

Changed (C)	Exploiting the vulnerability affects resources and systems beyond the vulnerable system.
Unchanged (U)	Exploiting the vulnerability only allows the attacker to affect the resources and components of the vulnerable system.

IMPACT METRICS

- Confidentiality Impact (C)
- Integrity Impact (I)
- Availability Impact (A)

The Impact metrics (table 8.8) talk about the impact the vulnerability has on three main areas: confidentiality, integrity, and availability. We briefly touched on this model back in chapter 2; this is also known as the CIA triad (which is hilarious for anyone who's been following the US Intelligence Agency's adventures in drug trafficking over the years). For each of these three metrics, the measurements are the same.

Table 8.8   Definitions for the C, I, and A Impacts, within the Impact Metrics of the Base Score

High (H)	There is a complete loss of confidentiality/integrity/availability. The attacker has full control over resources, configuration, service availability, and any data.
Low (L)	There is reduced confidentiality/integrity/availability. Impact is limited.
None (N)	There is no impact.

On top of the Base Score, there are two additional optional metrics: Temporal Score and Environmental Score. Both can be used to give more detailed information about the vulnerability, and both can further affect the CVSS score.

TEMPORAL SCORE

Unfortunately, the Temporal Score isn't a mandatory part of the CVE, which is a shame, as it could be used by vendors and vulnerability researchers to give us some more detail on the vulnerability. Although rarely used at the moment, there is pressure on vendors and researchers to make more use of the Temporal Score when creating CVEs.

The *Exploitability Code Maturity* (E) metric measures the likelihood of the vulnerability being exploited, based on the availability and maturity of exploit code (table 8.9).

Table 8.9   Definitions for the E metric

High (H)	Reliable, widely available, easy to use, and automated exploits have been developed and are actively being used.
Functional (F)	Functional exploit code is available that can be used in most situations.
Proof of Concept (P)	Basic code to prove the exploit is available, but an attack demonstration is not possible on most systems. Exploit code requires substantial changes before being usable by a skilled attacker.
Unproven (U)	There is no exploit code, or the exploit is still theoretical.
Not Defined (X)	Skip this metric.

The *Remediation Level* (RL) metric defines the level of fix that is available for the vulnerability (table 8.10). Initially, when a vulnerability is reported, there is no patch, followed by workarounds, temporary fixes, and an official patch.

Table 8.10   Definitions of the RL metric

Unavailable (U)	There is either no solution available, or it is impossible to apply.
Workaround (W)	There is a temporary, unofficial, nonvendor solution available.
Temporary Fix (T)	There is an official temporary fix available from the vendor.
Official Fix (O)	A complete patch or upgrade solution is available from the vendor.
Not Defined (X)	Skip this metric.

The *Report Confidence* (RC) metric gives us the degree of confidence that researchers have in the CVE (table 8.11). Sometimes a vulnerability may be reported, but no technical details have been shared by the vendor, or the root cause is still unknown. The more confidence we have in the report—the more the vulnerability is validated by the vendor or researchers—the higher the score.

Table 8.11 Definitions of the RC metric

Confirmed (C)	Detailed reports of the vulnerability exist from multiple sources, confirmed by the vendor, and proof of the vulnerable code or exploit is available.
Reasonable (R)	Significant research is available, but the root cause of the vulnerability hasn't been confirmed, or researchers don't have access to the source code to confirm the vulnerability. There is confidence that the vulnerability can be reproduced with effort and proof of concept exploits produced.
Unknown (U)	There are reports of a vulnerability but differences on the impact or root cause. There is uncertainty of the true nature of the vulnerability, or it may be intermittent.
Not Defined (X)	Skip this metric.

ENVIRONMENTAL SCORE

You'll notice that the Environmental Score metrics are a duplicate of the Base Score metrics. That's because the Environmental Score is where we can modify the CVSS by adding in information that's specific to our own environment and infrastructure. We'll look at how that works and how we can customize the CVSS for our own environment after we delve a bit further into understanding the CVE vector.

8.3.2 *CVE Vector*

As we can see, the CVSS score can give us a lot of information on a given vulnerability. This is communicated by the CVE vector, which is a text string that combines all the important information from the CVSS score. Looking at our sample CVE, CVE-2018-0101, we can see that the vector is CVSS:3.0/AV:N/AC:L/PR:N/UI:N/S:C/C:H/I:H/A:H. This breaks down as

- *CVSS:3.0*—The CVE is using version 3.0 of CVSS to score the vulnerability.
- *AV:N*—The attack vector is via a network; this vulnerability can be exploited remotely (very bad).
- *AC:L*—The Attack Complexity is low; this is an easy attack to carry out and is easily repeatable (very bad).
- *PR:N*—Privileges Required: None. An attacker doesn't need any special privileges or to be authenticated to carry out the attack (very bad).
- *UI:N*—User Interaction: None. An attacker doesn't need to trick a user into doing something (as they would with an XSS attack) to make the attack succeed (very bad).

- *S:C*—The Scope is changed; a successful attack can be used to exploit other, unrelated devices and services (very bad).
- *C:H*—Impact on Confidentiality is high; there is a complete loss of protection, meaning the attacker has full access to all resources (passwords, configuration files) on the affected Cisco ASA firewall (very bad).
- *I:H*—Impact on Integrity is high; there is a complete loss of confidentiality, meaning the attacker can modify files and the configuration on the affected Cisco ASA firewall (very bad).
- *A:H*—Impact on Availability is high; the attacker can misconfigure or shut down the affected Cisco ASA firewall (very bad).

The CVE vector gives us an easy way to share the most important information about a CVE. When dealing with vulnerabilities, both the CVSS and CVE vector should be used to describe the criticality and attack vector of the vulnerability.

Now that we've come to grips with how to calculate the CVSS and understand the CVE vector, let's work through an example. The NVD provides a handy tool we will use to work out our CVSS and build a CVE Vector description.

Head on over to https://nvd.nist.gov/vuln-metrics/cvss/v3-calculator. You'll notice on the page that we're given an initial CVSS of 0.0, and there are some fields to start building our CVE vector. The tool will then automatically calculate our CVE vector (figure 8.5).

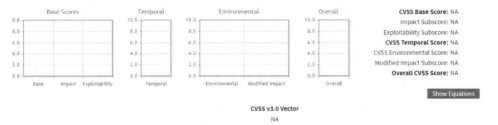

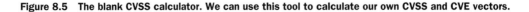

Figure 8.5   The blank CVSS calculator. We can use this tool to calculate our own CVSS and CVE vectors.

EXERCISE

Now's the chance to build out your own CVSS and CVE vector using NVD's interactive calculator:

1 We'll begin by loading up the calculator at https://nvd.nist.gov/vuln-metrics/cvss/v3-calculator.

2 Click on that link to load the page in your web browser. You'll see all values are N/A and blank.

3 We'll just use the Base Score metrics for this exercise.

4 These are the details of our example vulnerability:

   a A vendor produces firewall and network load-balancing appliances. These are configured via a web interface.

   b A vulnerability has been found in the web interface that allows a remote attacker to modify the configuration, operation, and data on these network appliances.

   c The attacker does not need to authenticate, and they do not need any user interaction.

   d The attack is easy to reproduce and execute.

   e The attack only results in compromise of the network appliance.

5 Using the information given, click on each field in the Base Score metrics part of the calculator and see what the CVSS and CVE vector are worked out to be.

With this information, you should have ended up with a CVSS of 9.8 (seriously bad!) and a CVE vector of AV:N/AC:L/PR:N/UI:N/S:U/C:H/I:H/A:H.

This attack is described in CVE-2020-5902 (figure 8.6), which is a vulnerability in network appliances from F5 and at the time of this writing is still being actively exploited, causing significant disruption. We can see the details of the CVSS and CVE Vector on the NVD website at http://mng.bz/yayp.

8.3.3 *Making things personal*

We've looked at how the CVSS and CVE vectors are calculated and how important they are to communicating the severity and impact of a vulnerability. The final thing to look at is how we can personalize this to suit our own environments. Let's look at CVE-2020-5902, the F5 vulnerability we looked at in our last exercise.

The Environmental Score metrics allow us to further customize the CVSS based on our environment. They are at the bottom of the CVSS calculator page, and you'll notice that they repeat the metrics we already have. The Environmental Score metrics allow us to further customize the CVSS and CVE vector by adding in extra information that is unique to our own environment; in other words, to customize the generic CVSS so that it's more relevant to our own organization's infrastructure (figure 8.7).

Looking at CVE-2020-5902 again, if our F5 appliances weren't directly accessible from the internet (i.e., a firewall stopped remote access to the web configuration

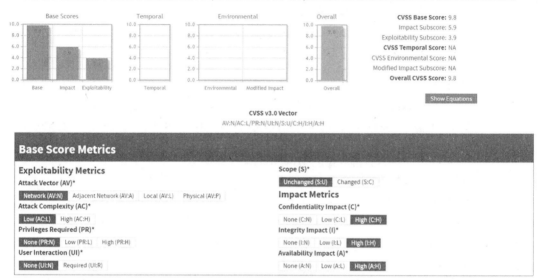

Figure 8.6   The breakdown of the CVSS value for CVE-2020-5902

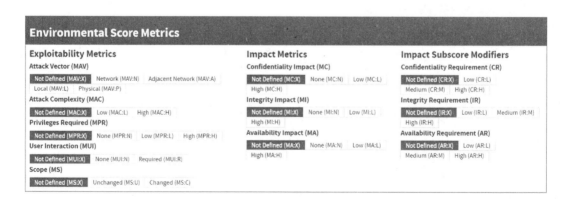

Figure 8.7   We can use the Environmental Score metrics to customize the CVSS for our own specific environment, giving us a better understanding of how the vulnerability affects us.

interface), then the nature of the attack changes. If we stopped direct access to the web interface, then two values would need to change:

- *Attack Vector (MAV)*—This would change to Adjacent Network (MAV:A), because the attacker would need to bypass our internet firewall and have access to the same protected network that the F5 appliance is on.
- *Attack Complexity (MAC)*—Needing to bypass a firewall, from another vendor, that protects the network the F5 appliance is on significantly raises the difficulty of the attack. So, Attack Complexity would be set to high (MAC:H).

If we set these values, we can see the impact this has on the CVSS and CVE vector. The CVSS has dropped from 9.8 to 7.8—still a critical vulnerability but not as serious due to our defense in depth (a firewall blocking external access to the F5 web configuration interface). The CVE vector has also changed and is now displaying and taking into account the impact of our own infrastructure environment. Figure 8.8 shows the impact our changes have on the CVSS.

▦ Common Vulnerability Scoring System Calculator CVE-2020-5902

Source: NIST

This page shows the components of the CVSS score for example and allows you to refine the CVSS base score. Please read the CVSS standards guide to fully understand how to score CVSS vulnerabilities and to interpret CVSS scores. The scores are computed in sequence such that the Base Score is used to calculate the Temporal Score and the Temporal Score is used to calculate the Environmental Score.

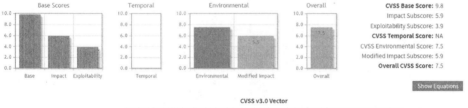

CVSS Base Score:	9.8
Impact Subscore:	5.9
Exploitability Subscore:	3.9
CVSS Temporal Score:	NA
CVSS Environmental Score:	7.5
Modified Impact Subscore:	5.9
Overall CVSS Score:	7.5

Show Equations

CVSS v3.0 Vector

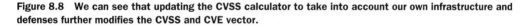
AV:N/AC:L/PR:N/UI:N/S:U/C:H/I:H/A:H/CR:X/IR:X/AR:X/MAV:A/MAC:H/MPR:X/MUI:X/MS:X/MC:X/MI:X/MA:X

Figure 8.8   We can see that updating the CVSS calculator to take into account our own infrastructure and defenses further modifies the CVSS and CVE vector.

We can see the immediate impact that our defense in depth (protecting network appliances from external access, via a firewall) has on lowering the severity of a vulnerability. We can also see how we can use the CVSS calculator to understand how CVEs will directly affect our own infrastructure. This is all valuable contextual information that we can use to assess and communicate how vulnerabilities specifically affect our own organization.

8.4   *A simple model to measure risk*

Security should always take a risk-based approach; by understanding the threats we face and the vulnerabilities we have, we can identify and address the areas with the highest risk. This is why we've focused on getting the basics of cybersecurity right—all the complex models and cybersecurity frameworks are pointless and ineffective if we don't understand the fundamentals of what we have, who would want to attack us, and what defenses we already have.

With the understanding of our basic security building blocks in place, we can start measuring and communicating risk, meaning we can tackle the highest-risk areas first, dealing with the most likely attacks before they happen. At the start of this chapter, we looked at some core definitions. We'll now build on those to understand how a simple model to measure risk works. As a reminder, the three key definitions we need here are shown in figure 8.9.

- *Vulnerability*—A vulnerability is a known weakness that can be exploited by an attacker. An issue that we know can be used by an attacker is a vulnerability.
- *Threat*—A threat is a circumstance or action with the potential to cause harm or damage. Malware and disgruntled employees are both examples of threats.
- *Risk*—The potential for loss or damage when a threat exploits a vulnerability. If the threat is low and the vulnerability is difficult to exploit, we have low risk. If the threat is high and the vulnerability is easy to exploit, we have high risk.

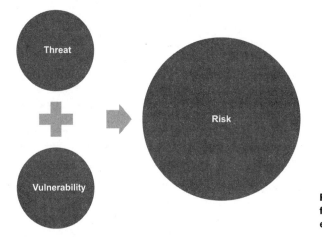

Figure 8.9   A risk is the potential for loss or damage when a threat exploits a vulnerability.

As a reminder, let's revisit our earlier example of the Death Star in *Star Wars*:

- *Vulnerability*—There is an exposed exhaust port which leads directly to the reactor core.
- *Threat*—The Rebel Alliance launched a fleet of attack fighters at the Death Star.
- *Risk*—The Rebel Alliance star fighters might evade the defensive turbo lasers and TIE fighters and fire a proton torpedo down the exhaust port, causing the Death Star to explode.

Our risk (the Death Star could explode) arises from our threat (the Rebel fleet) exploiting a vulnerability (the reactor's thermal exhaust port is vulnerable to attack). The risk level is high; the Death Star could blow up. It doesn't get more serious than that.

EXERCISE

For each of the following threats and vulnerabilities, work out

- What the risk is
- How severe you think the risk is

1 Vulnerability: An e-commerce website stores all usernames and passwords in a plain text file, which is stored on the web server along with the rest of the website's HTML files.

   Threat: Hackers use search engines to quickly and simply find common configuration files they can exploit.

   Risk:

2 Vulnerability: An organization's Wi-Fi network has had the same password for several years. The password is printed on signs inside the reception area of the building, as well as in documents on the organization's website.

   Threat: Wi-Fi signals can be picked up outside the building.

   Risk:

3 Vulnerability: A banking website's login form is vulnerable to an XSS attack. Users logging in have MFA, using a special code sent to them via SMS.

   Threat: SMS message interception and spoofing is well understood by attackers, as are XSS and phishing attacks, and all are commonly used to seize control of user accounts.

   Risk:

ANSWERS

1 Risk: It would be easy for hackers to find the text file with the usernames and passwords and then log in using customer credentials, defrauding both customers and the company. This would be easy to exploit and would have severe consequences, so the risk level is high.

2 Risk: An attacker can easily find the Wi-Fi password and access the internal network from outside the building, appearing as a valid user. This would be easy to exploit and would have severe consequences, so the risk level is high.

3 Risk: Attackers could target specific users with XSS attacks and use SMS interception to log in as the user. This would be a complex attack and would require effort to focus on a few, targeted individuals. Although the attack would have severe consequences, it is complex and requires a high level of expertise and coordination from the attacker, so the risk level is medium.

Back in chapter 2, we looked at how presenting equations and formulae without context was unhelpful and confusing. Rather than sticking "Risk = Threat × Vulnerability" in front of people and expecting them to shower us with a large budget and support our security improvements, we have a much better way to measure and communicate risks, threats, and vulnerabilities. Let's look at how that can work.

8.5   *How do I measure and communicate this?*

Now it's time to bring together everything we've learned so far in this chapter. Understanding our threats, vulnerabilities, and risks is useless unless we can clearly communicate them to the rest of the business. When we think about our cybersecurity strategy as being a direction of travel, showing the journey we are taking to make our organization more secure, we also need to enhance that with regular signposts saying "We are here."

For people to buy in and support our cybersecurity strategy—or even to support individual initiatives within the strategy that address risks—they need to be able to understand not just what we're trying to do, but also the context around it. We also need to be able to show that we're making progress—moving along our roadmap to increased security—and that means we need to be able to demonstrate some simple metrics that show how we're doing in terms of progress (figure 8.10).

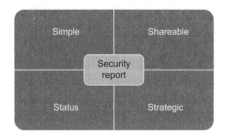

Figure 8.10   The four requirements of a good security report: it must be simple, sharable, strategic, and show status.

Our goal here is to create something that fulfills four important requirements:

- *Simple*—Easy to understand for non-cyber and nontechnical audiences
- *Sharable*—Shareable with anyone inside our organization who needs to know about updates to our security
- *Status*—Serves as our "We are here" update to support our cybersecurity strategy
- *Strategic*—Used to track how well we are making progress in improving our security

The most effective way I've seen this work over the years at all levels of security maturity is a simple four-page report. The structure is straightforward, and, in fact, we've already gathered most of the information we need in this chapter. Let's pull together the information we've gathered from working with our company example in this chapter.

8.5.1   Page 1: Our security matrix

For any information to be useful to others within our organization, we need to make sure they understand where we are at the moment. The security matrix we built earlier in this chapter provides a simple, at-a-glance view of how things currently stand (table 8.12).

Table 8.12   The first page should lay out our current security situation. The security matrix table we built earlier is a great way to show how things currently stand.

	Disgruntled ex-employees	Financial fraudsters	Identity thieves	Criminal organizations
HR Payroll System	Low	Medium	Medium	
DEFENSES	Some defenses	Some defenses	Some defenses	
E-commerce website		Medium		High
DEFENSES		Some defenses		Some defenses

8.5.2   Page 2: Our vulnerabilities

Utilizing CVSS and the associated scale to gauge the severity of a vulnerability gives us a great way to simply show the scale of the security problems we currently face. A simple graph that breaks down the numbers of low, medium, high, and critical security vulnerabilities conveys all the required information. Alongside that, we should have the graph from the previous report, so we can provide a side-by-side comparison showing how our exposure to vulnerabilities has changed over time. Obviously, it should be a change for the better, but the final page of the report is where we can provide context if things have gotten worse.

In chapter 9, we'll go into more detail about how we can discover and rate these vulnerabilities ourselves—important data that we can then feed into this part of our report. For the moment, though, an example of what this would look like is shown in figure 8.11: a simple graph that shows the number of low, medium, high, and critical vulnerabilities that our organization has. If we have the data—and if it's appropriate for our audience—we might also want a second graph that shows how the number of vulnerabilities has changed since the last report (hopefully they're all going down!).

8.5.3   Page 3: Our security roadmap

Our security roadmap is a reminder of our direction of travel; it shows our journey to improve security. The roadmap won't be static; we'd expect the sequence of security improvements to change, based on finding new vulnerabilities, work taking longer than expected, or changes in the business impacting priorities and budget (figure 8.12).

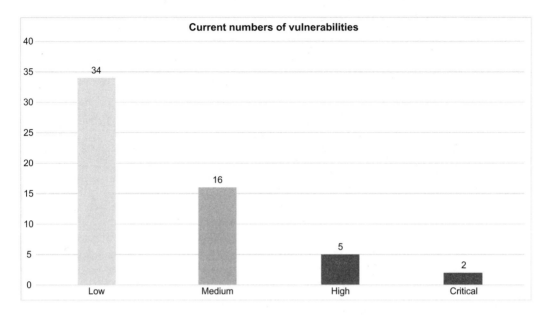

Figure 8.11   An example of how we can show the current numbers of vulnerabilities in our organization. We'll look at this in more detail in chapter 9.

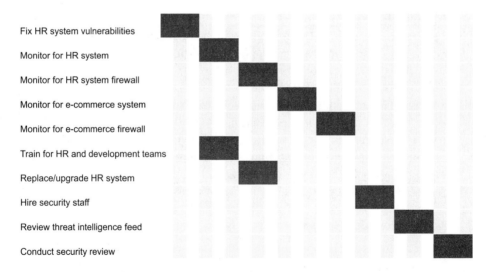

Figure 8.12   Page 3 should show our security roadmap, clearly communicating how we will improve security over time.

8.5.4   *Page 4: Information and actions*

This is where the important context for our audience goes—simple bullet points that flesh out and support the report:

- Why the number of critical and high vulnerabilities have increased (new vulnerabilities found; problem worse than we thought; vendor hasn't released patches yet)
- Changes to the security roadmap (business priorities have changed; new vulnerabilities in a critical service have been found; lack of resources to complete the work)

The important things to keep in mind are the key goals of our report: that it's simple and sharable, provides status, and is strategic (figure 8.13). We don't need an essay here, and we don't want to waffle. Four to six bullet points that contain actionable information, that either support our report or have specific requests of the audience, are all that's needed.

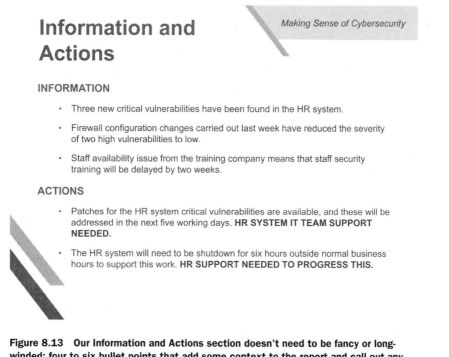

Figure 8.13   Our Information and Actions section doesn't need to be fancy or long-winded; four to six bullet points that add some context to the report and call out any actions are all that are needed.

Anything larger or more complex than this is going to lose our audience: non-security people working in other teams across the business, whose support and understanding is critical to improving security across an organization. As the maturity of a security practice within an organization grows, we'll have more complex layers of information that feed into this report:

- From internal and external vulnerability testing (covered in chapter 9)
- From a security operations team actively monitoring events in the organization (covered in chapter 10)
- From external security intelligence feeds (covered in chapter 10)

All of these extra sources of information will enrich the data we can present on page 2 (our vulnerabilities) and on page 4 (information and actions). We shouldn't expect this level of detail from day 1. Just as our security roadmap is a direction of travel to improving our security, our ability to identify and report on security vulnerabilities should also improve over time.

Reports and reporting are often viewed as boring, pointless, and a big waste of everyone's time. I absolutely agree—when they're done poorly. A vague, waffling report that needs a meeting to be explained is not only a waste of time, but will actively damage any attempt to communicate. A quick, to-the-point report that clearly shows where we are, what we're doing, and what needs to happen next—a report that fulfills our four goals (simple, sharable, status, strategic)—is not only easy to put together, but makes our jobs easier as we try to improve the security situation of our organization.

No matter how complex the data we are collecting on risks, threats, vulnerabilities, and exploits, a security status report always needs to be short, concise, and to the point. Just as with a successful security strategy, our reporting on our security status should line up with our three concepts and be relevant, proportional, and sustainable. In the next chapter, we'll look at how we can test our own systems and infrastructure and discover vulnerabilities before someone outside our organization exploits them.

Summary

- A risk is when a threat exploits a vulnerability caused by an issue.
- The CVSS helps us understand the details of a vulnerability by providing three main information points: the characteristics of the vulnerability, its associated severity score, and a simple description of the vulnerability.
- We can use environmental scores to calculate revised CVSS values that are relevant to our organization.
- Metrics and reporting are often viewed as boring and unimportant, but some of the most valuable outputs from any security work are actionable data.
- Showing what our current situation is, what we're doing about it, and how it will make our organization safer is probably one of the most important things a cybersecurity program needs to achieve.

Testing your systems

This chapter covers

- Differentiating and choosing between the different types of penetration tests
- Learning how bug bounty programs work and when to use one
- Learning why a physical penetration test is important
- Differentiating between red and blue teams to learn how they support our organization's security

We can't measure or manage risk unless we know about the vulnerabilities in our own software and systems. To do this, we need accurate, timely, and actionable data on vulnerabilities, which means a lot of testing. In the first part of the book, we learned how attackers will exploit some common physical and virtual vulnerabilities. Now let's learn about the different ways we can find these vulnerabilities ourselves, before the attackers have a chance to exploit them.

9.1   How are vulnerabilities discovered?

We can't rely on other people to tell us about our vulnerabilities; otherwise, our first knowledge of them is likely to be when they're exploited by an attacker. In that case, the first we know of a vulnerability is when we're invited to one of those panicky executive meetings where the fateful words "I think we've been hacked" are uttered.

If we're slightly luckier, IT support passes on an email from a random stranger who's found something broken on our website or infrastructure. If we're really lucky, we get timely updates of security issues and the associated patches and fixes from our various vendors, and a chance to fix the problems before someone exploits them.

I've been party to all these scenarios, and none of them are great places to be. In an ideal world, not only do we have processes in place to deal with these possibilities, but we're also actively looking for—and fixing—vulnerabilities ourselves. Before we explore the various ways we can manage finding vulnerabilities for ourselves, let's look at the three most common, unpleasant scenarios organizations usually find themselves in.

9.1.1   An attacker has exploited a vulnerability

This is a nightmare scenario for all organizations. There is a whole range of ways that an ongoing attack can be recognized. Some common ones include these:

- A system or application starts to perform poorly.
- A system or application shows signs of a high processing load.
- Network traffic, on internal networks and to the internet, increases.
- Users report that sites or applications are failing to load or are showing strange errors.
- There is an increased number of user logins, especially from privileged users.

These are all what are termed *indicators of compromise* (IoC) and are usually the first signs that an ongoing attack has breached your organization. However, these signs aren't the only notices we might get. I was hired to help deal with a security breach for a financial services client after a business partner found their confidential client list (with payment details) uploaded to a random file-hosting website. Sometimes the attackers will get in touch directly, usually to demand some sort of payment to stop the attack, via email or via on-screen messages from ransomware.

9.1.2   A stranger has found what they think is a vulnerability

Sometimes people on the internet will come across a bug on our systems or applications and get in touch to tell us about it. Although these are often the usual programming or performance issues everyone faces, they can sometimes turn out to be serious vulnerabilities. Often security researchers will be looking into a new theoretical vulnerability, trying to see if it could be exploited, and will inform organizations if they think they are vulnerable.

There are also the fraudsters: individuals or groups that scan an organization's sites and infrastructure, looking for vulnerabilities, and then get in touch to sell some security consultancy and remediation work. Their hard sell is usually a small step away from outright blackmail ("If you don't hire us to fix these issues, hackers could destroy your company!"), and I'd never recommend working with them. As we'll see later in this chapter, only a planned, authorized, and managed test of our organization's security gives us the information we need to properly address any vulnerabilities.

9.1.3 A vendor has released a security advisory

This is the most common scenario. The usual sequence of steps is as follows:

1 A security researcher finds a vulnerability in a vendor's product.
2 They contact the vendor with the details.
3 Any potential short-term remediations are worked out.
4 The vendor releases a patch.
5 A CVE is released with the details.

Sometimes a vendor ignores the security issue or drags their heels on releasing a patch, in which case the security researcher will often release the details of the vulnerability directly to warn end users that there's an exploitable problem. At other times, the vulnerability is discovered because attackers are actively exploiting it, and researchers and vendors have worked back from IoC to understand the underlying vulnerability.

Most vendors will have a regular release of security patches and updates. Microsoft, for example, has Patch Tuesday, where they release security patches for all affected products on the second Tuesday of every month. Apple doesn't appear to have a regular schedule for their patches, and Google updates some of their products so often (four or five times a month for the Chrome browser) that trying to stay on top of the updates can be overwhelming. For serious issues, almost all vendors will release emergency patches and fixes, outside of their normal release schedule.

Obviously, there are many risks in allowing other parties to randomly discover and share details of vulnerabilities in our systems. In addition to the danger of having our systems compromised via vulnerabilities we hadn't heard about, there's also the problem of managing resources to fix the vulnerabilities. When the security, application support, and IT teams are constantly having to drop their work to address new security vulnerabilities, business systems will suffer outages as they're taken offline to be fixed. Running in constant firefighting mode like this means it's more likely that critical systems will fail, and equally important work delivering updates and new capabilities to the rest of the business will be constantly delayed.

Thinking back to our three concepts of cybersecurity strategy (figure 9.1), while fixing vulnerabilities is relevant, working in a haphazard, reactive way like this is neither proportional nor sustainable.

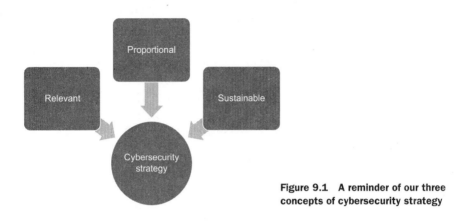

Figure 9.1   A reminder of our three concepts of cybersecurity strategy

A key part of any security strategy is the ability to check, test, and fix our own systems; managing vulnerabilities in this way is both proportional and sustainable. This process of finding and measuring vulnerabilities is called *vulnerability management*. Let's look at how we go about achieving that.

9.2   *Vulnerability management*

An entire book could be devoted to how vulnerability management is carried out—and why most organizations do such a bad job of it. Organizations with a mature security function should implement the full vulnerability life cycle management process to properly identify and remediate vulnerabilities across their organization. Less mature organizations (or those with a flawed approach to security) will just implement vulnerability scanning and patching. Let's quickly look at how they fit together.

9.2.1   *Vulnerability life cycle management*

Vulnerability life cycle management is the entire life cycle of preparing for, identifying, and remediating vulnerabilities and then working through a feedback loop to improve the entire life cycle.

The vulnerability life cycle management process is comprised of six stages that feed into each other, providing a process of continual improvement. This is the top-level process that defines and implements vulnerability management best practices across the organization:

1 *Governance*—The governance stage defines the frameworks, policies, processes, and their ownership that are used throughout the vulnerability management process. This is not an operational stage but is a definition and management stage that is required before vulnerability scanning can be carried out.

2 *Operations*—The operations stage deals with the actual process of scanning for and then alerting and reporting on vulnerabilities.

3 *Remediation*—The remediation stage deals with addressing the found vulnerabilities, defining how automated patching and configuration takes place, defining any break/fix access or processes needed, and covering all other areas of action needed to automatically remediate a vulnerability.

4 *Exceptions*—The exception stage deals with vulnerabilities that cannot be addressed automatically, requiring manual testing and approval or even creation of a dedicated project of work. For example, patching Java may have an adverse effect on Java applications running on that host. Patching a highly available application might require a longer maintenance window. The exception stage takes input from exception management processes.

5 *Measurement*—The measurement stage deals with the performance of the previous operations, remediations, and exceptions stages, reporting on and reviewing compliance with service and business *key performance indicators* (KPIs).

6 *Evaluation*—The evaluation stage reviews the entire process, verifying that KPIs, policies, and procedures are relevant and proportional, and using any lessons learned to feed back into the governance stage to improve the overall process. This is not an operational stage but a management and review stage that is carried out after vulnerability scanning and remediation.

Each of the six stages of the vulnerability life cycle management process feeds into the next so that the entire model provides a feedback loop of continuous improvement, helping organizations stay on top of vulnerability management (figure 9.2).

Managing the vulnerability life cycle properly is key to not just identifying and fixing vulnerabilities but also reducing the number of vulnerabilities we actually have in the first place. Since vulnerability life cycle management touches multiple areas of an organization outside security, it can be a complex process to embed and adopt for less mature organizations. But we need to start somewhere. What's the basic approach to finding and evaluating vulnerabilities? Let's find out.

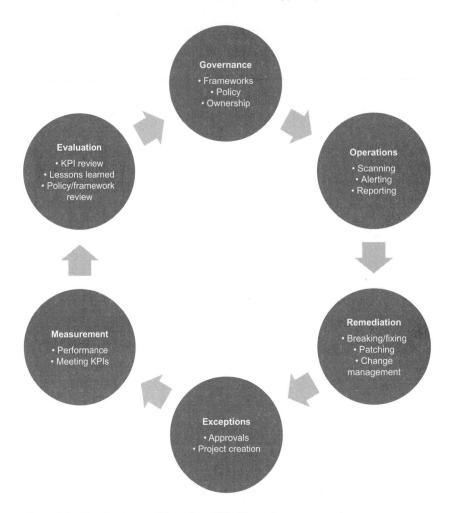

Figure 9.2   The six stages of the vulnerability life cycle management process

9.2.2   *Vulnerability scanning workflow*

Lots of organizations struggle to implement vulnerability life cycle management properly, for a number of reasons:

- Lack of organizational maturity
- Missing processes and ownership across the rest of the organization
- Lack of staff, expertise, and experience
- Poor security strategy

An alternative is to instead use the "scan, alert, patch" approach to managing vulnerabilities. This is a basic approach to dealing with vulnerabilities, but it has a number of problems:

- *This doesn't scale.* We can only run so many scanners, then deploy so many patches, before we run out of people and maintenance windows that can apply the patches.
- *This doesn't catch all vulnerabilities.* Vulnerability scanners work in different ways, and prioritize vulnerabilities and misconfiguration issues. But if a vendor hasn't acknowledged a vulnerability, the scanner won't be able to spot the problem—it won't know what to look for.
- *This is reactive.* We have to wait for a vulnerability to be discovered, understood, and communicated by the vendor and then for our scanner to be updated. During that period of time (which can be months), we are exposed to attackers exploiting the vulnerability.
- *We need to have a full understanding of our entire infrastructure to be able to effectively scan it.* For many organizations, after decades of acquisitions, mergers, and under-investment in IT, this is very difficult to achieve.

The vulnerability scanning workflow can be broken into four main stages (figure 9.3):

1 *Identify*—The identify stage defines the scope of the vulnerability scan—the assets to be scanned, their configurations, and their owners. An effective vulnerability scan depends on accurate information.

2 *Scan*—The actual scan doesn't just involve scanning for vulnerabilities; it should also categorize and prioritize the found vulnerabilities, automatically patching and remediating where possible. Where an automated response isn't possible (e.g., applications that depend on Java would need manual testing), these vulnerabilities are dealt with by the next stage: the exception stage. This maps to the operations and remediation stages of vulnerability life cycle management.

3 *Exception*—The exception stage deals with vulnerabilities that can't be automatically patched or remediated. The remediation should be escalated to asset owners, with the vulnerability scanning team working with them to communicate what is needed to remediate the vulnerability and in what timeframe, keeping in mind vulnerability management as well as business service KPIs. This maps to the exceptions stage of vulnerability life cycle management.

4 *Review*—The review stage looks at how the vulnerability scan went. Where KPIs weren't met, asset and owner information wasn't accurate, or the exception process didn't work as expected should all be noted and escalated as appropriate. This maps to the measurement stage of vulnerability life cycle management.

Figure 9.3 The four stages of the vulnerability scanning workflow

As we can see, this is a much simpler approach to identifying and addressing vulnerabilities. There are limitations compared to implementing the full vulnerability life cycle management approach, but this is a good place to start. Passive scanning is only one way to identify vulnerabilities, though. A much more enjoyable (and useful) approach is to deliberately break things via penetration testing.

9.3   *Break your own stuff: Penetration testing*

One of the earliest and most controversial types of hacking tools is the vulnerability scanner. Hackers who built these tools claimed, quite sensibly, that the only way to understand how vulnerable your systems were was to scan them yourself. Their opponents (unsurprisingly, software and hardware vendors) claimed that these tools were irresponsible and would make their way into the hands of malicious attackers, resulting in easier, mass attacks.

The hackers were right: vulnerability scanners allowed IT and security support teams to understand how and where their software and hardware was vulnerable to attack. Armed with this information, pressure was applied to vendors to clean up their act and proactively address security issues. Possibly the most famous of these tools was Back Orifice, launched with media fanfare by the hacking collective the Cult of the Dead Cow, at DefCon 6 in 1998.

Back Orifice was developed to highlight the massive security vulnerabilities in the main versions of Windows at the time: Windows 95, 98, and (later) 2000 and NT. Back Orifice consisted of a small, unobtrusive server program, which was installed on the target Windows machines. A graphical client was then used to connect remotely, giving the Back Orifice user full administrative control over the remote Windows hosts. Due to the small size and unobtrusive nature of the server component, Back Orifice was quickly used by malicious parties as well as Windows administrators, leading all antivirus vendors to identify it as malware. Back Orifice was used to publicly embarrass Microsoft to the point that Bill Gates eventually penned his "Trustworthy Computing" memo to all Microsoft staff in 2002, positioning security as Microsoft's highest priority.

When we talk about penetration testing software, applications, and infrastructure, there are three different types of penetration testing, based on the level of information the testers have:

- *White box*—White box testing is usually the most comprehensive. The penetration testers are provided with all architecture documentation, configuration details, and source code. Live systems can be thoroughly tested, from both inside and outside the organization, and the testers are also able to carry out static and dynamic code analysis on applications. Because of this, white box testing also usually takes the longest time to carry out and is the most expensive.
- *Black box*—Black box testing is the opposite of white box testing and places the penetration testers in the same situation as any attacker. They have no knowledge of any internal systems, applications, or services; no access to user accounts; and no code to analyze. While this is the most realistic penetration

test, it also means that if the testers aren't able to break into systems, they may not find the internal configuration issues and vulnerabilities that exist. Application analysis is probably not possible or will be inaccurate.

■ *Grey box*—Grey box testing is a combination of the white and black box testing approaches. The penetration testers are given limited information and access to systems—usually normal user accounts with internal accounts, so they can test from inside the organization—and some limited architecture and design documentation.

Obviously, there are some immediate limitations here. For example, a rapidly growing start-up probably doesn't have all the documentation and information to support a white box penetration test, and the company will be in such a state of flux and change due to rapid growth that any documentation they do have is probably out of date.

EXERCISE

Now that we've looked at how the different types of penetration test would work, let's think about how they would work best for different clients. Given the following different types of organization, what sort of penetration test would be most appropriate?

■ Bob's Bungees has a website that sells bungee cords that the company buys from a supplier in China.

■ MyFace is a social media network with a mobile application for Android and iOS phones, as well as a main website.

■ Widgets, Inc. produces hardware and software used in traffic management systems. The systems are connected via a private network that has no internet connection. They build their own hardware and write their own applications that run on that hardware.

Simple e-commerce websites are best suited to black box testing: an internet-facing website is constantly exposed to remote attackers, and we get the most value by understanding how and where their attacks would succeed. Companies that work with a combination of a website and mobile applications are best suited to grey box testing, where we can understand how attacks from authenticated users and from applications will work. Finally, an organization with well-understood custom hardware and software, with the most to lose from an inside attack, is best suited to a white box penetration test.

In reality, few organizations will have the information and level of detail needed to carry out white box testing. When doing a large penetration test for a financial services client, it turned out that the team supporting the website and applications had no idea how all the components worked, or even where they were hosted. The team that built the software and infrastructure had been made redundant several years ago, and it wasn't until the website crashed that the company realized they didn't have any design documentation.

For most organizations, a black box testing approach will be their reality. This has several advantages:

- The penetration testers don't start with any preconceived biases about "how things should work."
- The penetration test will probably uncover a number of systems or applications that were forgotten.
- The penetration test is as close as the organization will get to a "real-world" attack.

Let's look at the different parts of an average penetration test.

9.3.1 *Defining the scope*

One of the most important areas of penetration test is defining the scope. A well-thought-out scope defines and limits what the penetration test should cover, ensuring that we get some useful, actionable data out of the test while limiting the chance of anything going wrong.

I was contacted by a client in a panic. They had just had a penetration test carried out. The client sold items from their web store and had outsourced the entire payment management process to a specialist third party—sensible stuff, but they hadn't scoped their penetration test properly. As a result, the penetration testing provider discovered some interesting flaws in the payment process and accidently crashed the payment provider's system. The entire situation devolved into a messy three-way argument about who was liable for the loss of business.

A good scope should define the following:

- What sort of test it will be (black, white, grey box)
- Whether the test will be carried out using automated tools, manual hacking, or a combination of both
- The systems, applications, sites, and appliances that will be tested
- The times and dates or time period when these systems will be tested
- Specific systems, applications, sites, and appliances that must not be tested or affected by the test
- And lastly—and most often forgotten—when the report will be delivered

Alongside the scope, a few other useful things need to be agreed upon before carrying out the test:

- *A nondisclosure agreement (NDA)*—No one wants either party blabbing about any vulnerabilities found.
- *A limited liability agreement*—Penetration testing by its very nature is disruptive, and there's always a chance that the test will cause a service to crash or will even corrupt some data. Accidents happen, especially with badly written applications, so it's important to define the extent of any liability from either party. Absolutely get your legal team involved in this.

- *A statement of work (SoW)*—The SoW should be short, concise, and clearly say what will be done, by whom, when, how much it will cost, and what the output will be.

Any reputable penetration testing provider will provide all of these as a matter of course; if they don't, it's a warning sign to avoid working with them.

9.3.2 Carrying out the test

The golden rule of a penetration test is "Don't break anything." We've seen in previous chapters how we can simply test for the existence of XSS and SQL injection (SQLi) attacks; penetration testing tools will also query applications, services, and infrastructure to find out what software versions are running and match those against a CVE database to see if vulnerabilities exist. This is the focus of an automated penetration test, where vulnerability scanners and other tools are used to check for obvious, known vulnerabilities and misconfigurations.

If you're thinking, "But that means a lot of the vulnerabilities found are purely theoretical!" then you're right, which is where a manual penetration test comes in. Manual penetration tests consist of the penetration testing team acting more like advanced attackers, using their skills to chain multiple misconfigurations and vulnerabilities and trying to gain remote access to systems and data.

Manual penetration tests will take longer, are more likely to crash a service or application (or cause other disruption), and will be more expensive. On the flip side, they are more representative of how actual attackers will work and are therefore much more useful. Table 9.1 summarizes the differences.

Table 9.1   The differences between automated and manual penetration testing

	Automated	Manual
Price	Cheap	Expensive
Speed	Quick	Slow
Depth	Superficial	Comprehensive
Likelihood of disruption	Low	High
Usefulness	Moderate	High

Many organizations will sensibly settle for a mix of the two types of penetration tests. I regularly work with clients who have a quarterly automated penetration test (really just a more involved vulnerability scan), supplemented with a yearly manual penetration test that carries out a deep dive into their infrastructure and applications.

Of course, it's not just our external applications and infrastructure that should be regularly tested. Internal penetration tests should be carried out on a regular basis as well, although this is an area where most organizations run internal automated scanners rather than carry out manual tests.

9.3.3   *The report*

The real reason anyone carries out a penetration test is to get a report showing what's wrong and what vulnerabilities have been found. In many ways, the report we get back from a penetration test is the single biggest factor in how useful the test was.

Most reports will have pages (and pages and pages, if you're unlucky) of vulnerabilities, listed with the CVE severity level. There should be an executive summary, which has something a bit more useful than some statistics: there should be some actionable data that enables us to take the report's findings and make some improvements to our overall security.

A sign of a poor testing report is when the summary contains vague, useless statistics—like this one taken from the executive summary of a penetration test for a financial services client: "Testing showed client infrastructure is affected by 6 Critical-rated security vulnerabilities, 40 High-rated security vulnerabilities, and 82 Medium-level security vulnerabilities. Patches should be applied in-line with client's patching process."

Compare that to the actionable data contained in this summary from another financial services client I worked with: "28 systems running Windows Server 2012 are vulnerable to 4 critical security bugs, that must be patched within 7 days (affected systems and patch information detailed in Section 1). 14 Red Hat Linux systems are vulnerable to 2 critical security bugs, that must be patched within 7 days (affected systems and patch information detailed in Section 2)."

The first example is vague and unhelpful—what was the client supposed to do with this information? Any manager reading this report would be confused and worried. The results sound bad, but what should they do with them?

The next example contained actionable data: the summary made it clear how many systems were affected, what needed to be done next, and which part of the report contained more detail. If we're engaging an external penetration testing team, there's a checklist of things we can use to measure if they are any good. Can they supply

- Sample reports
- Details of their tools/testing process
- Team biographies
- Client testimonials

Let's look at each of these in more detail.

SAMPLE REPORTS

First and foremost, we need to see a sample report. There is no reason, ever, for a sample report to contain real customer data or information. With the cheap and easy availability of cloud infrastructure, populating a sample report with meaningful results that aren't client-specific is trivial. Anyone carrying out penetration testing should be able to provide a sample report as the first order of business; if they can't, walk away.

We need to check that the report contains the information we need:

- Is the executive summary useful?
- Can it be easily understood?
- Does it contain actionable data?
- Is the rest of the report ordered sensibly (e.g., grouping tested systems by application or operating system)?
- Does the detail of the report give us the information we need? There should be information about the CVE, CVSS, whether a patch is available, and how to mitigate the vulnerability for every vulnerability found.

If the sample report can't satisfy these requirements, then it's clear from this early stage that any work produced by the penetration testing team won't be of much use. We should walk away.

DETAILS OF THE TOOLS THEY ARE USING

The details of the tools being used are especially important for an automated test, but also useful to know in a manual test, where tools are always used to supplement the work of the tester. Some tools may not be able to accurately or reliably test some aspects of security that are important to us. For example, can the tool match a vulnerability with its associated CVE? Or can the tool examine server certificates to check if they are valid or about to expire? Is the tool able to combine (or chain) multiple attacks together to more accurately reflect how an attacker would work?

Any supplier claiming that they use a custom, in-house-developed scanning tool, and they can't possibly share the details, is blowing smoke. At the very least, we need to know how the tool works to understand if there is any danger of it crashing older infrastructure or poorly written applications.

BIOGRAPHIES OF THE TEAM

Why are we engaging this penetration testing team? What makes them different from anyone else offering this service? Any provider should want to showcase the skills and experience of their team. When I prepare a summary of my teams for clients, I keep it to a maximum of two paragraphs per person. When reading through the team bios, we should get a clear feel for their mix of experience, where else they have worked, and their specialties within cybersecurity.

TESTIMONIALS FROM OTHER CLIENTS

Many companies do a poor job with testimonials when looking at a penetration testing provider. The customer testimonials need to be from the same industry and show that the penetration testing provider understands our company and also understands the specific threats each distinct industry faces.

Having a glowing testimonial from a meat-packing client in South America is wonderful PR but has no relevance if our company is in the private health care sector. If a penetration testing provider can't provide a testimonial from a client organization in the same industry we are in, the first questions we should be asking them are "So, are we the first company in this sector you've worked with? If not, why does no one else want to share a testimonial or case study?"

The important word here is *trust*. If a penetration tester can't provide the checklist items, does it help us trust them, their team, and their service? We're asking an external company to try to break into our infrastructure, break our applications, and see if they can steal our data. Penetration testing is a high-stakes engagement, and we need to be able to trust our provider can not only do the work, but to not cause damage in the process.

Penetration testing feeds into vulnerability management. First, we need to find the vulnerabilities in our systems, and then we can understand how to prioritize patches, fixes, and remediations. This vulnerability management, in turn, feeds data into our risk management efforts. Penetration testing is the first step in a process (see figure 9.4) that helps us manage our risks.

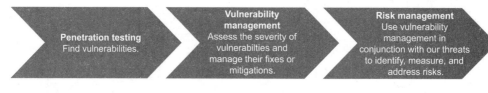

Figure 9.4   How penetration testing supports vulnerability management, which in turn supports risk management

While a penetration test is the first auditable sign of "This is how bad things are," having a penetration test is just the first step to testing our own organization. Merely having a penetration test and then assuming the organization is secure is a recipe for disaster, as Trustwave and their client Heartland Payment Systems found out.

Heartland was the victim of a data breach in 2009 that exposed 130 million US credit and debit cards—at the time, the largest recorded data breach. Trustwave was engaged by Heartland to carry out a Payment Card Industry Data Security Standards (PCI DSS) audit, measuring and documenting that the security processes and systems in place were adequate and in line with the PCI DSS requirements. However, the two insurance companies who provided cybersecurity insurance to Heartland sued Trustwave, alleging that because Trustwave had carried out PCI DSS assessments, vulnerability scans, and compliance testing services for Heartland since 2005, Trustwave's scans and audits should have spotted that a breach of Heartland's systems occurred in 2007, with malware planted in 2008 that was used to steal the credit and debit card data.

In chapter 2, where we looked at how to build a cybersecurity strategy, we discussed how our strategy was our direction of travel: how we move from our current state of security to an improved state of security. Vulnerability and risk management are both part of the measured security improvements that help deliver our cybersecurity strategy (figure 9.5), giving us actionable data that helps us to improve our level of security.

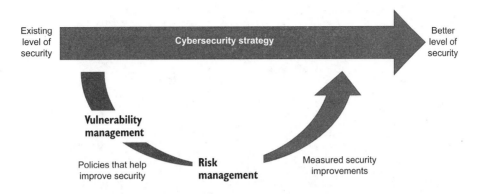

Figure 9.5   How vulnerability management and risk management provide measured improvements to security as part of our cybersecurity strategy

While penetration testing is the first (and, sadly, for many organizations, the only) step in vulnerability management, we have some other options to improve our ability to spot and fix vulnerabilities. Let's look at a way we can improve on penetration testing: running a bug bounty program.

9.4   *Getting expert help: Bug bounties*

With so many security researchers and hackers doing good work uncovering vulnerabilities and exposing security failings, it's only natural for a leadership team to ask, "Why can't we get these people to help us with our security?"

Bug bounty programs, which offer rewards to researchers and hackers who find and tell us about security vulnerabilities, are immensely popular. Rather than have expensive security researchers on staff, harnessing that expertise while only paying on results makes sound financial sense.

BEFORE WE BEGIN

There is no point in starting a bug bounty program if our teams aren't prepared and able to address the security issues that may be found. Starting a bug bounty program because "We're too busy to find all the problems ourselves" is a recipe for disaster; we'll just end up with more security problems that are known but are not being fixed.

Not only do we need the bandwidth from developers and engineers to fix any bugs that are found, but we also need buy-in from across the organization to support the bug bounty process. Our executive team needs to understand what the bounty program is, what it will (and won't) cover, and why we even need it. We also need to make sure that our legal and marketing teams are involved. We need to define NDAs, reporting and communication channels for discovered security issues, payment processes, and coordinated public disclosure processes. Figure 9.6 shows all of the components our organization needs to have in place for a successful bug bounty program.

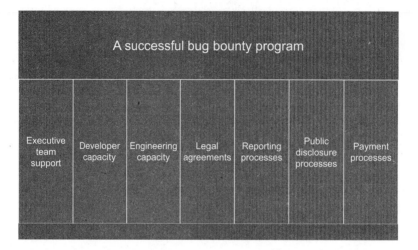

Figure 9.6   The components of a successful bug bounty program

WHAT ARE WE TRYING TO FIX?

Many organizations try to start a bug bounty program, which then fails, because they aren't clear about which areas of their business should be covered. There can also be confusion about what the output should be or how useful it is.

A bug bounty program will always be a black box testing scenario. We are relying on external third parties, and they are only going to have the same access to our services, applications, and infrastructure that any other external user will have, so we can expect them to attack websites and applications but not be able to carry out the full code audit and analysis we'd expect to see from white box testing. This is still very useful, but we need to remember the context a bug bounty program has to operate in, because this immediately puts limits on the types of bug that will be found.

MAKING IT ALL SOMEONE ELSE'S PROBLEM

There's a lot to address here, and for many organizations—especially small or fast-growing ones—this can be overwhelming. Luckily, there are a number of third-party organizations that have been set up specifically to outsource and manage a bug bounty program.

HackerOne is probably the most mature and reliable platform for this. Founded in 2012, HackerOne has a global community of hackers who can carry out code analysis, penetration tests, and security assessments. HackerOne also provides prebuilt processes and workflow to allow third parties to accurately define and report security issues to your organization. Outsourcing the provision and management of a bug bounty program to a third party like this makes a lot of sense, especially if the reason for looking at a bug bounty program in the first place is because of a lack of internal security resources.

EXERCISE

Now that we've looked at what bug bounty programs can and can't provide, let's work through a quick exercise to see where a bug bounty program could be useful. Given the three companies listed, which ones would benefit from a bug bounty program? Should they build their own or outsource it?

- *A fast-growing social media start-up*—Their focus is on growth and market share, so their DevOps team is under delivery pressure and has a large backlog of work. There is only one security person in the organization, and she has her hands full just trying to ensure that basic security processes are in place.
- *A global financial services company*—They've been in business for decades, with dedicated development and security teams across the world. Their business is a tempting target for attackers, so their websites and mobile applications are under constant attack.
- *An EU-based e-commerce company selling online insurance*—Their operations are limited to the EU, and they are compliant with local regulations like GDPR. With a single product (insurance), they have a single website and mobile application managed by a modest development and security team.

The first company, our fast-growing social media start-up, is a poor fit for a bug bounty program. Lack of maturity in the company and the focus on growth mean they will struggle to manage basic security problems, let alone a bug bounty program.

The second company, our financial services firm, is a good fit for a bug bounty program. They will be under constant, focused attack, and with global teams dedicated to security and development, along with a mature business, they are well placed to manage a bug bounty program.

The third company, our EU insurance broker, is a good fit for an outsourced bug bounty program. They will benefit from external bug hunters' expertise but probably lack the capacity to sustainably manage their own program.

Bug bounty programs can be a good way to take advantage of a global pool of talented hackers, but we need to make sure—as with all areas of security—that it's relevant, proportional, and sustainable.

In chapter 5, when we discussed social engineering, one of the main goals for attackers was to get physical access: to a laptop, a data center, or a building. We don't just need to test for virtual vulnerabilities; we need to test for physical ones as well with physical penetration testing.

9.5 *Breaking in: Physical penetration testing*

In chapter 6, we first looked at physical penetration testing. Physical access to a computer will always mean a determined and capable attacker can get at our data, which leaves us with a quandary: If physical access is so powerful, why do so few companies carry out physical penetration testing?

One of my clients was a government department that was in the process of a whole-sale migration to a new computing platform. This was a multimillion-pound project that involved half a dozen top-tier servers from Sun Microsystems costing £4 million each. The department rented space in a professional data center for their production systems, and they also had a small data center on the ground floor of their main building.

This data center had been well designed: key cards and number pads to gain access, multiple access doors to make your way through, and CCTV cameras recording anyone exiting or entering the data center room. The data center also had some secured double doors, which led to the street and garage, so that the massive Sun servers and storage arrays could be delivered.

Unfortunately for this particular project, the government department wasn't accurate when calculating how much cooling the data center's air conditioning could provide. Once it had been filled up with two large Sun servers and four big storage arrays, all running at full tilt, the air conditioning system became overwhelmed, and equipment began to overheat.

I went into the data center early one morning to check on the night's backups and found that the building contractors had wedged open the double doors to let some cold air in. Even better, I found that a homeless man and his dog had wandered in and were happily asleep, curled up against a £4-million server. The backup tapes had been making noise overnight, apparently disturbing his sleep, so he'd pulled them out, leaving them scattered around his makeshift bed.

9.5.1 *Why is physical penetration testing not carried out?*

Physical penetration testing is often missed because companies assume that because they have security guards and a reception desk, they are protected. Organizations forget about all the other ways someone can get access to their facilities.

Too much faith is placed in CCTV, sign-in registers, reception desks, and the odd security guard. There are many parallels between lax physical security and cyber-security (table 9.2).

Table 9.2 Comparing the flawed assumptions about cybersecurity and physical security

Cybersecurity assumptions	Physical security assumptions
"We have firewalls that will stop attackers from breaching our web applications."	"We have security guards that will stop attackers from getting access to our facility."
"We use usernames and passwords to limit access to sensitive applications."	"We use ID cards to limit access to sensitive locations."
"We carry out yearly security training for all staff."	"We carry out yearly training for our security guards."
"We log all user access, so obviously we can detect a malicious login."	"We get all visitors to sign in at reception, so obviously we can detect a break-in."

This is all very familiar: the same arguments and approaches to computer security map to physical security—and their shortfalls and gaps are just as devastating. The approach to solving these security issues is the same. We can reuse our three factors of cybersecurity model to address physical security issues as well (figure 9.7):

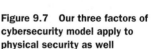

- What assets do you have?
- Who would want to attack you?
- What defenses do you have?

Figure 9.7 Our three factors of cybersecurity model apply to physical security as well

EXERCISE

Let's look at a normal office building with a fairly standard setup:

- We have a security guard in reception.
- We have a reception desk where visitors can sign in.
- We have an open plan office, with a hot desk area, where building visitors and employees can sit and work. There is a mixture of desktop and laptop computers. There's the usual clutter of paperwork, mobile phones, printers, and filing cabinets.
- There are some executive offices, with laptops and paperwork inside.
- There are some meeting rooms.
- There are whiteboards in the meeting rooms and executive offices.

How would you map the three factors model to physical security?

- What assets do you have?
- Who would want to attack you?
- What defenses do you have?

An example mapping could look something like this:

- What assets do you have?
  - Mobile phones in the open plan office—easy to steal
  - Mobile phones in the executive offices—easy to steal
  - Laptops in the open plan office—easy to steal
  - Laptops in the executive offices—easy to steal
  - Desktop computers in the open plan office—we could try and log in to them
  - Lots of paperwork everywhere—easy to steal
  - Whiteboards with confidential information (possibly) leftover from meetings
- Who would want to attack you?
  - Competitors
  - Disgruntled employees

- What defenses do you have?
  - Doors to the meeting rooms and executive offices might have locks or PIN pads to access them.
  - We have a security guard at reception we could use to enforce ID checks.
  - Visitors need to sign in at reception, which is another place we could enforce ID checks.

As we discovered in chapter 5 when looking at social engineering, the techniques and models we use for computer security apply equally effectively to physical security.

9.5.2   *Why does physical penetration testing matter?*

Having physical access to a computer or mobile device means having full control over it. No matter what passwords or encryption are used, an attacker who physically has our device will always be able to access the data that's stored on it.

Physical penetration testing is our means of seeing how easy it is for an attacker to get that physical access. This might be by gaining entry to an office or stealing a laptop from a shared workspace, or even something as simple as being able to stand outside the office and pick up the Wi-Fi signal.

A large UK government department has a massive, fortified building in London. Built to withstand terrorist attacks at the height of the "Irish Troubles," the building is reinforced against bomb blasts, has a filtration system to protect against a gas attack, and has an airlock-style entrance system, which can instantly lock someone inside if it detects explosives or weapons.

They also have a single Wi-Fi network internally for all the different groups based inside—and this Wi-Fi network can be picked up outside on the street, in the middle of one of London's bustling tourist hotspots. This internal Wi-Fi network is protected with a password, but due to the number of suppliers, contractors, and visitors, this password is widely shared. In fact, a quick search via Google will reveal several indexed documents that show the password, along with a map and full address, given out to visiting guests.

Back in chapter 4 we covered the use of malicious Wi-Fi access points. All the physical security measures put in place by this government department can be bypassed by someone standing outside the building with the other tourists.

9.5.3   *What should a physical penetration test cover?*

Our approach to defining and managing a physical penetration test should cover the exact areas of our cyber penetration test. We need to solve similar problems, with similar assumptions, so we can use the same approach:

- Scope
  - What's the scope of our test?
  - Can the testers fake an ID?
  - Or steal an ID?

- Which facilities, locations, and areas within those locations are they allowed to access?
- How do they prove access?
- Do we want to target a specific office of an executive?
- Testing type
  - Black, white, or grey box?
- Should we give the penetration testers
  - Copies of valid ID?
  - Building plans?
  - Details of where our CCTV cameras are?

Everything we've learned so far for cybersecurity testing—our models, approaches, and even the hacker mindset—maps nicely over to the physical testing side as well. The techniques around social engineering, covered in chapter 5, apply perfectly to physical access. By ensuring we are properly scoping and testing physical access, we ensure that the good work being done on the cyber side isn't undermined.

Now that we've learned how we test for both physical and virtual vulnerabilities, the next challenge is to make this sustainable. This is where red and blue teams come into play.

9.6 Red teams and blue teams

Once organizations have established a process for regular internal and external penetration testing, as well as how to address the vulnerabilities discovered, the next stage is to formalize this with dedicated teams. Alongside the dedicated teams come dedicated attack/defense simulations. Organizations that move to red and blue teams should have at least a yearly gaming exercise, simulating a full cyberattack, allowing them to test their defenses and processes while learning and improving.

9.6.1 Red team

The concept of red teaming came out of military war games: to properly test defenses, a group was needed who could effectively carry out the actions of attackers. The idea behind this has been carried over to cybersecurity. A red team goes beyond a penetration test: they think, plan, and act as if they were attackers, providing a test not just of an organization's defenses, but also their communications and processes.

Red teams will be engaged to achieve a specific goal during a test or simulation: gain access to specific confidential data or successfully disrupt a key business service, or even gain access to the information held and managed by a specific individual within the organization. Often a red team will be tasked with campaign-based testing: emulating an attacker's actions over a series of weeks or months to thoroughly test the security and security response of a critical service or piece of infrastructure.

A penetration test will look for vulnerabilities in our software, applications, and infrastructure. But how do we know that our processes for responding to and dealing with attacks, service outages, and data corruption work? Disaster recovery, business continuity, and business resilience planning rarely go beyond the paper stage. Having a red team thoroughly test our defenses means we can work through, test, and then review the processes and communications that we have put in place to support our organization when facing a service outage.

9.6.2   *Blue team*

On the opposite side is our blue team. Blue teams go beyond a team of security analysts that monitors for attacks and raises alerts. If the red team is there to simulate a proper attack, the blue team is the counter that simulates the full defense process. One of the main tasks for the blue team is following (and therefore testing) escalation and communications processes, ensuring service availability and business continuity.

Blue teams should move beyond reactive defense ("We have seen an attack and will now respond"), and instead be able to provide proactive defense ("We think like attackers; understand the vulnerabilities, threats, and risks we face, and will plan and act to reduce those risks"). This is why part 1 of this book dealt with thinking like an attacker and looking at the most common attacks: only by thinking like an attacker can we proactively defend against the risks our organization (and we as individuals) face.

We'll look in more depth in chapter 10 at how security operations work and how a blue team capability builds on that. The United States' National Institute of Standards and Technology (NIST) published a cybersecurity framework (http://mng.bz/M0dQ) that defines five core functions for defensive teams:

- *Identify*—Develop an organizational understanding to manage cybersecurity risk to systems, people, assets, data, and capabilities.

This maps to the three factors of cybersecurity: What assets do we have? Who would want to attack us? What defenses do we have?

- *Protect*—Develop and implement appropriate safeguards to ensure delivery of critical services.

This maps to the three concepts of cybersecurity strategy—build and deploy relevant, proportional, and sustainable defenses and processes for our organization:

- *Detect*—Develop and implement appropriate activities to identify the occurrence of a cybersecurity event.
- *Respond*—Develop and implement appropriate activities to take action regarding a detected cybersecurity incident.
- *Recover*—Develop and implement appropriate activities to maintain plans for resilience and to restore any capabilities or services that were impaired due to a cybersecurity incident.

These core functions aren't standalone actions a defensive team takes (figure 9.8). A good blue team should be using these as a feedback loop, taking the output from the recover function and using it to improve the rest of the functions.

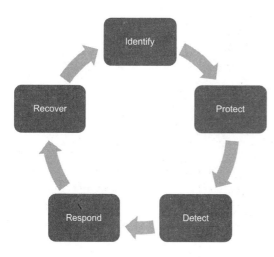

Figure 9.8 The five core functions from the NIST cybersecurity framework

RECOVER: LESSONS LEARNED

The most important part of the process is communicating what went well, what could be improved, what is missing, and what is needed—the lessons learned from the exercise. These should cover all aspects of the organization's response to the attack; not just technology issues, but processes, communications, incident management, and even the involvement and availability of the senior leadership team.

9.6.3 Other "colors of the rainbow" teams

In the never-ending quest for vendors to sell more software, technology, and services, they have come up with a host of other colored teams. Some that you may hear mentioned are these:

- *Yellow teams*—Responsible for building defenses and defensive processes
- *Green teams*—Responsible for changing yellow team behavior based on blue team (defender) knowledge
- *Orange teams*—Responsible for changing yellow team behavior based on red team (attacker) knowledge
- *Purple teams*—Responsible for changing blue team behavior based on red team knowledge

These form part of the (very accurately named) *BAD pyramid*: the build, attack, defend pyramid (figure 9.9).

None of these should be needed in any organization that has properly thought out their cybersecurity strategy and that has effective communication and support between

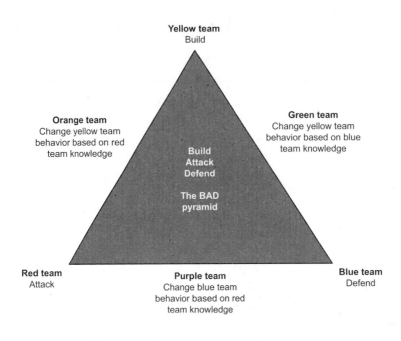

Figure 9.9   The BAD pyramid, showing the technicolor rainbow of different types of security teams the industry has created

teams. We don't need dedicated build teams if our IT teams are educated and supported by our security team. We don't need a dedicated purple team if our red and blue teams are working effectively, sharing their knowledge and delivering business and process improvements after each simulation.

Like much of the IT and security industry, these extra teams have been floating around to make organizations believe that they are missing something or doing an incomplete job; therefore, buying some extra software and training is going to improve their situation. This isn't the case if we're tackling the basics properly and we understand the purpose and context of the various parts of a cybersecurity function.

This is why the lessons learned as part of the blue team process are so important: communicating and sharing improvements across our organization, based on an attack simulation, is how every area of the organization can improve their security and business resilience. We'll look into this important activity in detail in the final chapter of this book.

9.6.4   *Keeping your staff*

One of the biggest problems that organizations face is how to keep their staff. People entering the cybersecurity profession want to be red teamers; they "want to hack." Blue team staff often feel sidelined and tasked with the grunt work, as opposed to the glamour of exposing vulnerabilities. Hiring and onboarding new staff is exponentially more expensive than keeping existing team members, so how can we achieve that?

POSITIONING

Too often, a career in cybersecurity is sold as being a white hat hacker, spending your days as a penetration tester, hacking into exotic systems of world-famous clients. The much more prosaic reality is that a lot of time is spent in meetings and writing reports. Beyond that, some of the most skilled and demanding work is within a blue team. Blue team members need to think like attackers—to understand how a red team operates—but they may also need to

- Manage communication across diverse internal teams and staff
- Communicate directly with senior stakeholders within the organization, but also with partners and clients
- Coordinate defenses and responses from across an organization
- Work with executive, legal, and HR teams
- Support management when dealing with the press (and, in some cases, work directly with the press)

The reality is that many people's cybersecurity career will follow the profile of

- Starting as an analyst, monitoring systems and alerts (more on this in the next chapter)
- Moving to a penetration testing role
- Then moving to a security engineering/architecture role, as part of a wider blue team

Make it clear to staff that understanding and carrying out attacks—being part of a red team—is only a part of a career in cybersecurity and is a stepping-stone to the more complex and challenging work. Helping people understand that there is much more than launching attacks and that there are other career options if they are not cut out for that is the first step to retaining staff within our organization.

CONFERENCES

Too often conference attendance is handed out to senior staff, viewed as a reward for years of warming a chair and treated as a "jolly." Now is the time to rethink that attitude, because good security conferences for good security people are very different affairs.

Organizations I've worked with that have had high security staff retention rates have followed these golden rules for conferences:

- Everyone gets to attend at least one conference a year, regardless of seniority.
- Everyone who attends a conference has to give a half-hour presentation to the rest of the security team to share what they've learned.
- Don't just attend, present. Encourage all seniority levels to submit conference talks to share the good work they're doing.

That last point is particularly important. The easiest way to hire new, top-tier talent is by word of mouth. If our organization is doing great things in security, why aren't we telling everyone about it? Our security teams can be one of the most effective engines to drive new talent to our organization. Every presentation carries with it the subtext "You, too, could be working with us on this cool stuff."

TRAINING AND CERTIFICATIONS

HR teams and managers are hardwired to assume that professional development means training courses, but I firmly believe that's because no one has taken the time to educate them on the alternatives. The last time I attended a training course was back in 1993, when I learned how to administer Lotus cc:Mail. Yes, I'm that old, but this goes to show that people can continue to learn and grow their skills without needing to sit in a classroom with 20 other people for 5 days.

The most effective training I've seen for security people is the hands-on workshops that are provided at the better security conferences. These are usually single-day affairs that pack a huge amount of knowledge transfer into a challenging and educational environment. Combining hands-on training workshops with conference attendance presents excellent value for money, and by getting everyone attending a conference to present their learning and thoughts to the rest of the team, we generate the sort of knowledge-sharing and cross-fertilization of ideas that traditional training courses can never provide.

Does it work? At companies where I implemented these ideas, they enjoyed 100% staff retention within the security teams. Feedback from staff performance reviews cited training and personal development through the team's conference presentations as one of the main reasons they felt engaged and valued.

In the next chapter, we'll look at the security operations center (SoC); this is where the information we find from vulnerability management and testing our systems gets turned into useful, actionable data we can use to improve our security.

Summary

- Vulnerability life cycle management comprises the life cycle of preparing for, identifying, and remediating vulnerabilities, and then applying a feedback loop to improve the life cycle.
- Bug bounty programs entail paying third parties to test our software and paying them a cash reward for vulnerabilities they discover. We need to understand when a bug bounty program can be relevant and proportional for an organization.
- Penetration testing can be used to secure our organization by testing our software, applications, systems, and infrastructure for security vulnerabilities. The different types of penetration tests include the following:
  - White box testing, where the testers have full access to source code, architecture diagrams, and system configuration
  - Black box testing, where the testers have no knowledge of any systems or code

- Gray box testing, which combines white and black box approaches by giving the testers a limited knowledge of architecture and documentation
- Attack/defense simulations provide a powerful method of testing cybersecurity. These simulations are carried out by two teams:
  - Red teams play the role of the attacker. They think, plan, and act as attackers, testing not only the organization's defenses, but also their communication and processes.
  - Blue teams play the role of the defender. They are tasked with countering and preventing attacks. They are also required to think like attackers so that they can provide a proactive defense against the risks the organization faces.
- Retaining skilled cybersecurity team members is key to a successful security operations capability. The roles need to be clearly defined up front, and continued training and certifications are valuable methods of keeping employees sharp and engaged.

Inside the security
operations center

10

This chapter covers

- Differentiating between logging and monitoring, applying our three concepts of cybersecurity

- Working through some real-life security incidents, learning how to apply the observe, orient, detect, and act (OODA) loop and the three concepts to incidents

- The different external intelligence data feeds we can use, how they work, and how they can be both beneficial and detrimental to our security capability

Visibility of security events gives defenders a head start on addressing security incidents and is the difference between reading the news or being on the news. Our security operations capability is the best view we have of how effective our IT (development, spend, and strategy) is and feeds into our business strategy to show us where we should be investing more in technology.

Managing risk is about making informed decisions, and for that, we need actionable data, which is what a good security operations capability should provide. Let's look at how we achieve this.

10.1 Know what's happening: Logging and monitoring

There is no point in investing in security if we don't have visibility into what's happening across the organization. Without that visibility, we're essentially throwing money at ghosts and scary noises in the night. To effectively know what's happening, we need to put three things in place:

- A security operations team
- Relevant, proportional, and sustainable logging
- Relevant, proportional, and sustainable monitoring

Let's start by looking at the main building block: our security operations team. Traditionally, organizations build out a security operations center (SOC). A SOC is meant to be a team of security analysts and engineers who use a collection of security tools to log, monitor, analyze, and provide alerts for suspicious events occurring within the organization. Unfortunately, the SOC seems to have morphed into a vanity project, where the C-suite can point to a secured room with a glass wall and a battery of big screens showing impressive and scary graphics and statistics.

This leads to the current sad state of affairs where there's a huge amount of support from the C-suite for building out an SOC, but the focus is on showing partners, customers, and shareholders a flashy room full of serious geeks in polo shirts. Any security effort gets diverted into these vanity projects that deliver very little apart from some PR.

Ignoring the shallowness of an executive's PR win, there are a number of reasons why an SOC is no longer relevant to an organization:

- *The majority of infrastructure is now cloud-based.* Having infrastructure and services in the cloud doesn't just make them cheaper and more scalable; it also means these services can be accessed from anywhere. The same is true for security tools. What used to require dedicated client software can now be accessed from a web browser, or even a mobile application.

  There will continue to be exceptions: some organizations (like government departments and manufacturing or research and development [R&D] facilities) will require secured, dedicated data centers, with tools and applications that can never be cloud-based.

  However, when even spy agencies like the UK's GCHQ or the US' NSA are hosting data and applications in the cloud, it's clear that "cloud first" is a technology strategy that's here to stay.

- *Remote working and distributed teams are the new normal.* One of the biggest lessons from the COVID-19 pandemic is that, for many people, working 100% remotely is perfectly possible. For people working in cybersecurity, where the systems we monitor and protect have always been remote, working away from the office (and a big operations center) makes perfect sense. And, because security teams have always had to work remotely from the systems and applications they protect, redundant and secure communications are already in place. Even small start-ups now have "follow-the-sun" models, where there are teams in each major continent, allowing the smallest of companies to operate around the clock 24 hours a day.

- *It is not cost effective.* Building out a flashy operations center was rarely cost effective, and with cloud-based solutions and remote working, a centralized security operation makes even less financial sense. Money spent on expensive office space that can only be used by a small number of people is more effective at increasing security by being allocated to VPNs, password managers, and MFA devices for staff.

Rather than having a single, centralized operations center, effective security teams are now distributed and remote and are able to more flexibly address the security needs of an organization. So, to make sure that our security investment is relevant, proportional, and sustainable, we instead need to change the conversation and start talking about *security operations capability.* From here on, when I talk about an SOC, I'm talking about our security operations capability.

One of the areas where many organizations come unstuck is confusing logging with monitoring. Let's look at the two and learn the differences between them—and why they both matter to SOC.

10.1.1 Logging

Every application, service, and appliance will store a log of events and actions. The goal of a SOC is to identify which log events could be useful from a security point of view and then ensure that the relevant application, service, or appliance is correctly configured to forward these log events to a central log server.

Obviously, if we log events from every application and device across our infrastructure, we'll quickly be overwhelmed by a tsunami of noise, making it impossible to pick out relevant security events from all the background errors. Luckily, we've already learned how to address this with our three factors of cybersecurity model (figure 10.1). As a reminder, the three factors are three questions that force us to identify the real security threats and what we can do about them:

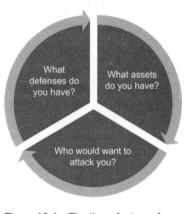

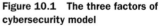

Figure 10.1   The three factors of cybersecurity model

- What assets do we have?
- Who would want to attack us?
- What defenses do we have?

We can apply the three factors to our logging problem, ensuring that only log events that are relevant to our assets, our attackers, and our defenses are being logged. Once we've done that, we need to apply our three concepts model to ensure that what we're logging, monitoring, and acting on is relevant, proportional, and sustainable (figure 10.2).

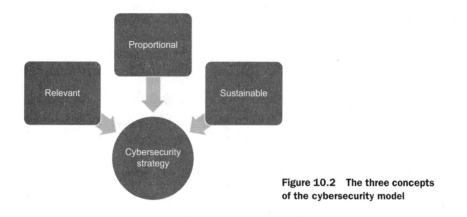

Figure 10.2 **The three concepts of the cybersecurity model**

By ensuring that what we're logging is relevant and proportional to the threats and defenses we've identified from our model, we ensure that our event logging is sustainable—the right balance of information versus noise. Later in this chapter, we'll look at an exercise to see how this works, but before that, let's look at the partner to logging: monitoring.

10.1.2 *Monitoring*

Once we've started to centrally collect log events that we think are relevant to our organization, we need to do something with them. Monitoring is where we analyze and match up (correlate) log events to identify security events we need to act on.

Manual monitoring is time-consuming and requires skilled analysts: we need to know enough about all our applications and services to be able to spot a log event, recognize it as a security issue, and then act on it. Only very small organizations or very unprepared ones carry out manual monitoring.

The default is to have a log analysis tool that can highlight and identify basic issues for us. All the major cloud service providers (CSPs), like Google, Amazon, and Microsoft, will provide a tool that does basic log event identification and correlation.

Event correlation is hugely important to SOC. By enabling us to link a suspicious event from one application to suspicious events from other applications or services, we can quickly spot an attack. Most attacks—including malware, ransomware, and automated attack tools—will leave an *indicator of compromise* (IoC). An IoC is a pattern in log events—from an application or a firewall, for example—that matches specific malware or attack tools. Most basic log analysis tools will provide a small number of simple IoC monitors, looking for the sort of attacks we covered back in chapter 4: SQLi, XSS, and malware.

A more advanced solution provides a high degree of automation around correlation and matching IoCs, and also utilizes machine learning to "train" itself by analyzing how the SOC identifies and links security events. These advanced solutions are called *security incident and event management* (SIEM), which we'll look at in more detail in section 3 of this chapter.

EXERCISE

Our company has a simple internet-facing shopping website hosted in the cloud. There are three parts to this:

- The database, which stores all our users' data and holds the inventory of widgets we are selling
- The payment gateway, a simple interface to a third party that handles collecting and processing payments and payment card data
- The web server, which presents our internet storefront to our users

This solution has a number of different logs, capturing different events:

- Web server: Successful and failed user logins
- Web server: Application errors
- Database: Successful and failed user logins
- Database: Data changes (updates, deletions, modifications)
- Payment gateway: Requests for payments and whether those were successful

You are the security person responsible for monitoring this solution by looking at entries in the logs. Which events are relevant to your security operations, and why?

- Web server?
- Database?
- Payment gateway?

All of these logs are relevant to security operations for different reasons:

- *Web server*—We need to look for failed login attempts, as they could be a sign that an attacker is trying to break in. We also need to look at the application errors to see if there is a pattern of automated attacks (e.g., SQLi or XSS).
- *Database*—Again, we need to look for failed login attempts, as they could be a sign that an attacker is trying to break in. This is easier, as only the web server and our database administrator (DBA) should be trying to directly access the database. We also want to monitor any data changes, as only the DBA should be carrying those out.
- *Payment gateway*—Although we're not directly handling credit card data or payments, we want to keep an eye on the logs. A high number of failed payments could be a sign of an attack (trying to exploit the payment gateway or fraudulent use of credit card data). A high number of payment requests that don't

match up to a high number of users on the web server could also be suspicious activity that needs further investigation; we would then need to correlate user activity across the three systems to see if an attack was happening.

Although this is a simple example, we can see how quickly the workload on our SOC could increase as our infrastructure grows and gets more complex. Later in this chapter, we'll look at some solutions to manage that. Now that we've looked at the ways the SOC can identify what's happening, the next step is to deal with the attack.

10.2 Dealing with attacks: Incident response

In this section, we'll delve into how we can respond to a security incident such as an active attack or data breach. Security events give us data points that show things are happening. The next task for the SOC is to correlate and analyze those events—to discover IoCs to decide whether there's an actual security incident taking place.

Incident response has a number of overlaps and dependencies with the vulnerability life cycle management model we looked at in chapter 9. In fact, incident response is going to struggle to be effective without understanding and using the vulnerability life cycle management approach, which, as a reminder, is a process comprised of six stages that feed into each other, providing a process of continual improvement. This is the top-level process that defines and implements vulnerability management best practices across the organization (figure 10.3):

1 *Governance*—The governance stage defines the frameworks, policies, and processes, and their ownership used throughout the process. This is not an operational stage but is a definition and management stage that is required before vulnerability scanning can be carried out.

2 *Operations*—The operations stage deals with the actual process of scanning for and then alerting and reporting on vulnerabilities.

3 *Remediation*—The remediation stage deals with addressing the found vulnerabilities, defining how automated patching and configuration take place, defining any break/fix access or processes needed, and covering all other areas of action needed to automatically remediate a vulnerability.

4 *Exceptions*—The exception stage deals with vulnerabilities that cannot be addressed automatically, requiring manual testing and approval, or even creation of a dedicated project of work. For example, patching Java may have an adverse effect on Java applications running on that host. Patching a highly available application might require a longer maintenance window. The exception stage takes input from exception management processes.

5 *Measurement*—The measurement stage deals with the performance of the previous operations, remediations, and exceptions stages, reporting on and reviewing compliance with service and business KPIs.

6 *Evaluation*—The evaluation stage reviews the entire process, verifying that KPIs, policies, and procedures are relevant and proportional, and using any lessons

Figure 10.3   The vulnerability life cycle management model from chapter 9

learned to feed back into the governance stage to improve the overall process. This is not an operational stage but is a management and review stage that is carried out after vulnerability scanning and remediation and that feeds improvements back into the governance stage.

Now that we've refreshed our memory on how vulnerability life cycle management works, let's look at a practical model for addressing incident response. The US National Institute of Standards and Technology (NIST) has the most mature model for approaching incident response, and a good SOC will follow the four stages that the NIST has outlined:

1 *Preparation*—This is not just the core stage of any incident response activity; it is the core of our entire cybersecurity strategy. Without knowing what we have,

who would want to attack us, and what defenses we have, we are completely unprepared to identify an attack, let alone respond to it. Any organization skipping the preparation stage—and many unfortunately do—is going to be headline news after a devastating breach destroys their business.

The preparation stage doesn't just map to our three factors of cybersecurity model; it also directly draws on the governance stage of the vulnerability life cycle management process we discussed in chapter 9.

2 *Detection and analysis*—The ability to detect, identify, and analyze security events to understand when they turn into security incidents (i.e., a breach) is the main goal of any security operations capability.

3 *Containment, eradication, and recovery*—This is the "Let's fix this" stage. This is where we stop the breach from spreading, remediate any vulnerabilities that led to the breach, and then recover our business services. In chapter 9, we saw the operations and remediation stages in the vulnerability life cycle management process, and this is where they enable our incident response process to actually deal with and resolve the security incident.

The specifics of what to do in this stage vary greatly and depend heavily on the type of incident. Do we need to destroy a virtual machine in the cloud and redeploy our application? Do we need our antimalware software to delete infected files and restore the originals? Or do we need to involve our ISP to help us manage a DoS attack?

4 *Post-incident activity*—Possibly the most important stage in any incident response process, this is where we review how well things went and use the lessons learned to feed into the preparation stage. This process of continuous improvement—using the data from one incident to help us get better at dealing with the next—is where many organizations fail.

Many organizations treat this process as a linear progression; the correct approach is to use this as a feedback loop to improve our organization's security maturity. What we learn from responding to one incident should be used to help us better prepare for the next one (figure 10.4).

The SANS institute, another organization dedicated to promoting cybersecurity, has a slightly more complex model, which breaks down the containment, eradication, and recovery phases into separate steps within the overall process (figure 10.5).

While this can make more sense in a more mature and capable environment, this approach can make things seem more complex when we're in the early stages of building out an SOC. Realistically, when an incident occurs, the containment, eradication, and recovery steps tend to happen at the same time, and we want to get our business back up and running as quickly as possible.

In 2021, the ransomware group LockBit announced that they had acquired 6 TB of data from Accenture, with rumors that they were holding out for a $50 million ransom to delete the data. There were a series of windows where LockBit made some of

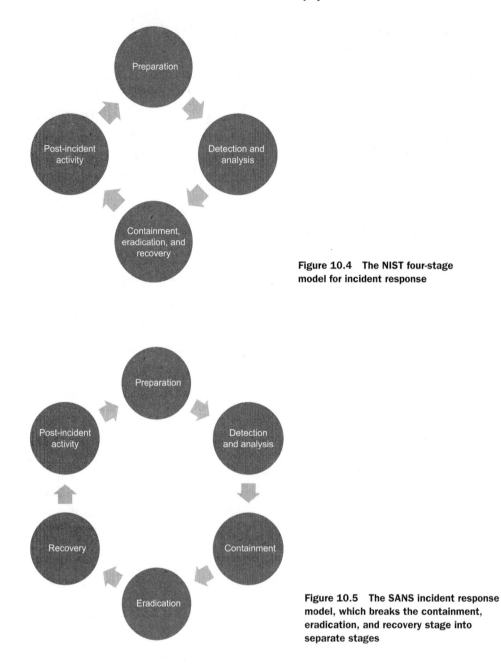

Figure 10.4   The NIST four-stage model for incident response

Figure 10.5   The SANS incident response model, which breaks the containment, eradication, and recovery stage into separate stages

the data available for download, but their servers were quickly overwhelmed and crashed. Within 48 hours, Accenture responded: their teams had restored all affected systems from their most recent backups and confirmed that no customer services were affected and no customer data had been lost.

The incident was an excellent example of good, effective incident response in action:

- *Preparation*—Accenture knew what data was held where and ensured it was regularly backed up (and that those backups could be restored).
- *Detection and analysis*—Accenture was able to quickly identify not just which systems had LockBit ransomware installed but also how the ransomware got there.
- *Containment, eradication, and recovery*—Using the knowledge of how the ransomware got installed and which systems it was installed from, Accenture was able to rebuild and reimage affected systems and restore data from backup.
- *Post-incident activity*—It wasn't just internal lessons that were learned around how the ransomware got installed, but good external communication and reputation management. Accenture's response made them look competent and in control (which is what you'd want to see from a major consultancy). LockBit's response—repeatedly trying to make snapshots of the data available, and failing—along with the assertion from Accenture that nothing of value was taken and no ransom was paid, made LockBit look ineffectual and powerless.

EXERCISE

Now that we've looked at some examples of how to detect and respond to an attack, it's your chance to see how you'd deal with an SQLi attack, which we first looked at in chapter 4.

Let's revisit our example company from the start of this chapter. Our company has a simple internet-facing shopping website, hosted in the cloud. There are three parts to this:

- The database, which stores all our users' data and also holds the inventory of widgets we are selling
- The payment gateway, a simple interface to a third party that handles collecting and processing payments and payment card data
- The web server, which presents our internet storefront to our users

The four stages of SOC should proceed as follows:

1 *Preparation*—We know what assets we have, and we captured relevant events from different logs:

  a Web server: Successful and failed user logins
  b Web server: Application errors
  c Database: Successful and failed user logins
  d Database: Data changes (updates, deletions, modifications)
  e Payment gateway: Requests for payments and whether those were successful

  As a reminder, an SQLi attack injects SQL statements into a user login form in an effort to dump data from the database.

2 *Detection and analysis*—What logs would you look at, and what events would you be looking for?

3 *Containment, eradication, and recovery*—Once you've identified an SQLi attack, what would you do to stop the attack and restore normal service?

4 *Post-incident activity*—What follow-up actions would you initiate, and how would they help incident response in the future?

There are no right or wrong answers, but let's look at some ways we could deal with this attack:

- *Detection and analysis*—SQLi attacks work by injecting SQL into a web form, such as a user login page, so we should be looking for failed user login attempts and what those failures are. Can we see SQL statements being logged as the username? Can we see a high number of login failures for a single user in a short period of time? How quickly are the login failures being logged? Does it look like a script or an automated attempt to log in?

- *Containment, eradication, and recovery*—There are a number of different ways to deal with the attack. Given the small size of the solution, the easiest method would be to disable all user logins, effectively shutting down the store so people can't log in to buy our widgets. We can then fix the user login form so that it properly checks the data being entered, stopping further SQLi attacks.

    Then, it might be a good idea to disable everyone's accounts and then send an email to all registered users, letting them know we've identified and stopped an attack and giving them instruction on how to reset their passwords.

- *Post-incident activity*—This is where we can look at improvements for the future. Some areas to look at could include these:
    - Education for developers to ensure all input is checked across the website.
    - Do we need any improvements in logging or log detail?
    - Are there more events we should capture?
    - How well did emailing our customers work?
    - How can we improve communications with customers and make it easier for them to manage and secure their accounts?

Now that we've looked at how to deal with security incidents with a relevant, proportional, and sustainable model, let's look at a more advanced way of identifying and correlating security events.

10.3 Keeping track of everything: Security and Information Event Management

We can see that any security operations capability in an organization has a tough job. There's a lot of things they need to do:

- Prepare by identifying events that need to be logged
- Detect and identify IoCs or attack patterns

- Contain any attacks or breaches, then remove any malware or attack tools, fix the causes of a breach, and recover normal service
- Review how all of this is working and implement any needed improvements

It's no wonder security teams tend to quickly become very large and very expensive. As the old joke goes, the only business cost that can grow infinitely yet still fail is security.

The big mistake many organizations make is to think that if they just throw bodies at the problem and log even more data, they will somehow spot more emerging security incidents and resolve them faster. Back in the 1930s, engineer Allen F. Morgenstern coined the phrase "Work smarter, not harder," and it's never been more appropriate than today in cybersecurity. Rather than approaching security operations as a resource problem, we need a new approach: to think of security operations and defensive cybersecurity as a data problem.

Data-driven cybersecurity takes some of the lessons and techniques from big data and machine learning disciplines and applies them to the high-volume, high-speed pattern matching that is the core of security operations at scale.

Essentially, spotting an IoC means identifying a pattern of activity within our logs that matches the way attack tools or malware works. Spotting a hacking attack is the same thing we saw back in chapter 4: data injection attacks like XSS and SQLi work in specific ways, producing a nice pattern of activity in our logs.

Security and Information Event Management (SIEM) is basically a logging and monitoring platform that has extra technology to carry out automated event correlation and pattern matching. SIEMs can vary in complexity, from the basic (if A, B, and C are observed in these logs, then raise an alert, as we have a potential SQLi attack) to very complex solutions that use machine learning algorithms and abstracted attack data analyzed in large-scale cloud environments to proactively identify suspicious events and activity.

Although they've evolved over the last 15 years or so from simple logging and alerting solutions to the complex tools we see today, current SIEM solutions all have some common functionality:

- *Open and scalable architecture*—A SIEM needs to be able to ingest data from different sources: systems across data centers, cloud environments, and even mobile, into a single instance.
- *Real-time visualization tools*—Security teams need to be able to carry out real-time trend analysis on alerts and warnings to depict incidents accurately.
- *Big data architecture*—Security teams collect a log of data. A lot. Large organizations can generate gigabytes of data a day, just in logs. Our SIEM needs to be able to handle huge data sets and also manage data that may be in different forms—even unstructured data, like feeds from social media.
- *User and entity behavior analytics (UEBA)*—All of the logs we collect give us lots of data about how our infrastructure and software is used. UEBA enables an SIEM to analyze that data and spot patterns of behavior. For example, we can expect a

flurry of login activity to our email server between 8:00 and 10:00 a.m. on a Monday morning, as everyone starts the working week. We wouldn't expect to see a huge spike in email server login activity at 2:00 a.m. on a Sunday; this is where a SIEM would identify and send an alert about this unexpected behavior.

- *Security, orchestration, and automation response (SOAR)*—Our SOC is going to be busy, especially when a large attack is taking place, so our SIEM needs to reduce their workload while helping the SOC be more effective. SOAR is a technology that automates routine, manual actions—such as locking a user's account or isolating a web server from the internet.

So, what benefits does a SIEM give our SOC? When we're at the point where the features of a SIEM are relevant and proportional to the needs of our SOC, our SIEM solution should provide the following:

- *Effective reporting*—We need to simply and concisely tell the rest of the business what is happening and what we've been doing about it. This also means a single, central SIEM with a centralized dashboard, which we can customize for our SOC needs.
- *Fewer false positive alerts*—Manual checking of logs and events always means a small number of false positives: events that looked like an attack but weren't. These can be time-consuming and disruptive to deal with, so we need our SIEM's analytic capabilities to reduce the number of false positive alerts we have to deal with.
- *Real-time visibility across the environment*—We need to respond to security events immediately, not hours or days after the different log events have been analyzed.
- *Reduced mean time to detect (MTTD) and mean time to response (MTTR)*—These are a couple of KPIs our SOC should be measured on. How long does it take the SOC to detect a security event, and how long does it take the SOC to respond? This is a key area where the automation and analytical capabilities of a SIEM should have an immediate benefit.

As SIEM solutions have evolved and matured over time, the way we can deploy them has also changed. We have three main options for how to deploy and use a SIEM:

- Some are designed to be deployed in traditional data centers and need secure communications between their different installations to provide an organization-wide view of events.
- Some are cloud-based virtual appliances that can leverage the advantages of scalability and rapid deployment of cloud services.
- Some are services that are subscribed to and need secure communications and configuration to export data from our organization to where the service is hosted.

The most advanced SIEM solutions take full advantage of machine learning algorithms and dedicated hardware. Dedicated clusters of customized hardware, designed purely for fast decision making and pattern matching, are trained to recognize "bad" and "good" events and activity; these are called *neural networks*. Some SIEM vendors use massively parallel cloud-based neural networks that have been trained on a huge variety of log events and attacks and can handle the work of identifying, alerting, responding, containing, and recovering from an attack or breach—all without human intervention.

Whichever implementation is chosen, the job of a SIEM is to do the heavy lifting for our security operations team: to identify and send alerts about potentially suspicious activity so that the human members of the team spend their time more productively analyzing the alerts rather than trying to analyze the logs and events.

The old rule of "garbage in, garbage out" still applies: we need to ensure we have the fundamentals in place and a well-defined security operations process and capability. A SIEM is a waste of money and effort for a security operations team that is just starting out but is perfect for enhancing and improving the capabilities and effectiveness of a mature, established security operations function.

EXERCISE

Let's apply what we've learned so far about logging and monitoring security events by looking at how we would map security events to different maturity levels of security for an organization. First is a quick reminder of our three concepts of cybersecurity model: our goal is to keep things *relevant, proportional,* and *sustainable.*

In the previous chapter, we carried out an exercise to look at which bug bounty programs were appropriate for three different companies. Logging and monitoring builds on finding vulnerabilities (E.g., are we detecting our bug bounty hunters? And why aren't we finding the vulnerabilities ourselves first?), so let's revisit those three companies and see what sort of security operations capability is appropriate for them:

- *A fast-growing social media start-up*—Their focus is on growth and market share, so their DevOps team is under a lot of delivery pressure and has a large backlog of work. There is only one security person in the organization, and they have their hands full just trying to ensure basic security processes are in place.
- *A global financial services company*—They've been in business for decades, with dedicated development and security teams across the world. Their business is a tempting target for attackers, so their websites and mobile applications are under constant attack.
- *An EU-based e-commerce company selling online insurance*—Their operations are limited to the EU, and they are compliant with local regulations like GDPR. With a single product (insurance), they have a single website and mobile application managed by a modest development and security team.

Which organization would benefit the most from the following three types of security operations capability?

- An enterprise SIEM, based in the cloud, which can process thousands of events a second and use advanced machine learning to correlate and map different events to generate alerts.

- A SIEM that can be installed in a data center or in the cloud and that has limited functionality; the tool essentially centralizes security events and presents a simple, web-based dashboard to allow a security team to review the findings. The tool has the capability for event correlation functionality to be added at a later date as an extra-cost option.
- A simple logging server where logs from applications and services can be centrally stored. A basic dashboard shows how often an event occurred and where it was logged from.

The first solution is probably best suited to organization 2. As a global financial services company, with multiple security teams, they will be logging thousands of events a second and will need the advanced event correlation and threat mapping capabilities of a top-end enterprise solution.

The second solution is the best fit for organization 3. They have a small security team and an infrastructure and customer base limited to one continent. They will benefit most from a tool that provides some centralization and a decent dashboard and that can have added functionality and complexity as the business grows.

The final solution is best suited to the first organization. With an infrastructure in a constant state of rapid change due to fast growth, trying to use a sophisticated SIEM would be a waste of time and money—especially with just one (already overworked) security person to manage it. Having a centralized logging solution with a simple dashboard that can be manually checked on a daily basis is the most effective solution for the organization to get some insight into security events.

Using a SIEM to log, centralize, monitor, and manage security events is a major step toward supporting a relevant, proportional, and sustainable security operations capability. But the SIEM is limited by our own infrastructure: it can only log and analyze what we can see and control. We know there are other attackers out there doing different things to other organizations. How can we get actionable data on these attacks and IoCs? This is where external intelligence data feeds can support out security operations capability.

10.4 *Gaining intelligence: Data feeds*

Our SOC can't see or know everything, no matter how great they are. While a SIEM improves the situation, this improvement is still limited to the data we have in our own organization. The effectiveness of our security operations capability depends on our three factors of cybersecurity (figure 10.6):

- *What assets do we have?* As we've seen in the previous sections, understanding our inventory of assets—and knowing what new infrastructure is being built, bought, and deployed—is key. We can't defend things if we don't know they exist.

Figure 10.6 A reminder of our three factors of cybersecurity model

- *Who would want to attack us?* Knowing how our attackers think and act, as well as what attackers (threats) are targeting other organizations, allows us to refine the risks that are relevant to our organization.
- *What defenses do we have?* Finally, knowing our defenses and how they work and ensuring that they are relevant, proportional, and sustainable to the threats we face ensure that we're effectively protecting our assets.

As we build out and mature our security operations capability, one of the biggest limitations we come across is our own knowledge. Our ability to identify, defend, and recover from attacks depends on us knowing about them. Cybersecurity is, in many ways, an arms race—with attackers and their tools growing and evolving at an ever-increasing rate. We've already looked at SIEMs and the idea of data-driven cybersecurity; now we can build on that further.

Many vendors that provide cybersecurity tools also have fantastic visibility into how effective those tools are and what sort of attacks their clients face. Cloud-based solutions, especially those that leverage machine learning, have vast data stores of anonymized attack and malware data. There are also vendors that specialize in research—not just into malware, but also attack tools, black hat hacking groups, and even investigations into state-sponsored attackers.

All of these vendors provide feeds of this data which we can import into our various security tools. Most useful is importing data into our SIEM, ensuring that we have a system that's constantly updated with the latest attack patterns and malware actions. Many SIEM vendors will do the work for us, with threat intelligence feed subscriptions included in the SIEM pricing model.

Alongside the paid-for services offered by vendors, there are a huge number of free resources (open source threat intelligence), as well as free tools and applications we can use to make the most of this data. As an example, the Awesome Threat Intelligence list (available at https://github.com/hslatman/awesome-threat-intelligence) has hundreds of free sources of threat intelligence, attack data, and tools to make effective use of the information that cybersecurity teams and researchers have gathered.

There's a downside, of course: if we start to pull in data feeds from security researchers and specialist vendors before our SOC is mature enough to handle the results, we'll be buried in alerts and warnings that we can't respond to. As always, we need to ensure that the extra data we're feeding in is relevant, proportional, and sustainable. Our three concepts of cybersecurity model is the ideal way to assess this (figure 10.7).

We can use the three concepts of cybersecurity model to ensure that adding in a data feed of threat intelligence data to our SIEM is useful:

- *Relevant*
  - If our solutions are built on Windows, do we need a data feed that lists out attacks against Linux?
  - If we use Microsoft Azure to host our cloud infrastructure, is a data feed with information on attacks against Google Cloud Platform of use?

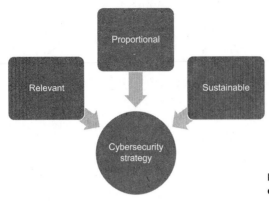

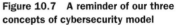

Figure 10.7   A reminder of our three concepts of cybersecurity model

- *Proportional*
  - Can our SOC cope with the current workload?
  - Do we need to expand the team?
  - Do they have the right skill set and depth of skills?
  - Do our current security tools work well? Are they effective at managing existing threats?
- *Sustainable*
  - Is the data integration with our existing tools automated?
  - Do we have to pay for a subscription, and if so, how much does it cost?
  - How can we measure the value of this?

Using the three concepts model in this way means we make sure that the external threat data we use helps—rather than hinders—our security operations capability. Enriching our SIEM with external data sources—if done correctly—can be a valuable way to increase the effectiveness and efficiency of our security operations capability.

Building an SOC doesn't mean having a science-fiction-style command center. Instead, to ensure a relevant, proportional, and sustainable security capability, we need to build out a security operations function that can support the business through effective application of the OODA loop. In chapter 11, we'll look at how we can apply all this knowledge to protect our most valuable assets: our people.

Summary

- Ensuring we log the right data and that it is properly analyzed provides our security operations capability with the actionable data needed.
- The OODA loop and the three concept models help us perform root cause analysis and quickly understand the vulnerability, the threat, and the attack, and, therefore, how to resolve the security breach successfully.
- SIEM is a logging and monitoring platform that includes technology to perform automated event correlation and pattern matching. Using a SIEM can free

up human team members to spend their time acting on alerts rather than analyzing logs and events.

- By enriching the data we gather and know about with data and analysis from external specialists, we ensure that we have the most relevant and accurate information for our security operations capabilities.

Protecting the people

This chapter covers

- Comparing different types of company cultures and learning how they impact security
- Learning how to leverage the three concepts of cybersecurity to build and enhance your own organization's security culture
- Learning how to protect against the most common form of attack: ransomware
- Providing good education and support to end users and using this to create a powerful culture of security

Computers do what we program them to do, but people are unpredictable and fallible. This makes the people in our organizations much better targets than our closely monitored and protected computers and software. But protection isn't about stopping people from doing things; it's about educating them, supporting them, and making it easier for them to be more secure when doing their everyday work. Before we go further, you'll find it helpful to have read chapter 3 (where we talk about the hacker mindset and the different types of hackers) and chapter 5 (where we looked at social engineering attacks and how these different types of hackers exploit end users).

11.1 Don't play the blame game

How many times have you heard a company say, "Our people are our best assets" or "We treat everyone like family here"? Yet security professionals will often say, "People are the weakest link" or even that it's a PEBCAK issue: problem exists between computer and keyboard. There's a grain in truth in all of these, but one of the main goals of any cyber-security team should be to inform, support, and protect people—not just fellow employees, but also end users, customers, and the wider internet community.

In chapter 2, when looking at cybersecurity strategy, we touched on how to build a culture of security. A financial services client I worked with wanted to build a "culture of security" within the company. They handled sensitive financial data, executed millions of pounds in transactions per day, and handled financial data for some of the largest global corporations. They recognized—quite rightly—that security was everyone's problem, and every employee had a role to play in keeping the company and their client's data secure.

The problem was that they kept having leaks of data. They were under constant attack, and fraud was a big problem. Financial services regulations are tough, and they were worried about fines and loss of confidence from their clients. Their security training was dull and didn't feel real to their staff, who ended up just going through the motions of paying attention so they could get that all-important yearly tick on their HR record that said their training was up to date.

Reworking their approach to user education and support helped them build a culture of security. I put in place a number of different strategies to improve the security culture:

- Ensuring that everyone knew who was on the security team—from the chief information security officer (CISO) down—and how to contact them.
- Encouraging people to report security issues, incidents, or even concerns. The maxim of "there are no stupid questions, except for the ones not asked" was adopted.
- Moving from yearly PowerPoint presentations to monthly interactive "show and tell" security sessions held during lunch break.
- Having a regular security email newsletter sent to all staff. This didn't just talk about interesting security developments or new attacks; it also reiterated how to contact all of the security team.
- Making sure that new security initiatives that impacted users didn't just happen overnight; users were kept informed of not just what was being done and when, but how it would help keep them secure.
- And the company favorite—some cool security team swag. Stickers and mugs were handed out to people who attended the security presentations, becoming coveted items within the company.

Part and parcel of the culture of security is ensuring we don't have a culture of blame. Everyone makes mistakes, no matter how hard we try not to. Given the following two scenarios, both taken from clients I worked with, which company do you think had fewer security breaches?

- *Company A*—Al reused his Exchange email login password on his blog account. His blog hosting company was hacked, and attackers made off with a copy of his credentials. The attackers were then able to log in as Al to the company email system and stole a huge trove of commercially sensitive emails—along with their attachments.

    When the security team found out what had caused the breach, Al was summoned to the office of the chief technology officer (CTO) and promptly fired. The security team then emailed all employees to let them know what happened, telling people to "not be so stupid in the future."

    The security team then implemented a policy that all passwords must be at least 15 characters long and have upper- and lower-case letters, numbers, and at least two special characters ($, %, #, etc.). These passwords were automatically expired and had to be changed every 30 days.

- *Company B*—Beth too had reused her email login password, this time on her social media account. She did so because her email password was complex (and therefore secure), and she had problems remembering two different complicated passwords.

    Her social media credentials were stolen in a social engineering attack and were then used to access the company email system. Again, attackers stole a huge trove of commercially sensitive emails and attachments.

    When the security team found out the root cause, they listened to Beth's explanation about the difficulty of remembering complex passwords. The security team installed password managers for all users and held a number of lunchtime training sessions to explain how password managers worked and how users could keep both their company and private accounts secure.

Company B was three times the size of company A, yet they had only one data breach (the one described) in three years. Company A had seven data breaches over the same time period, with a high number of qualified staff leaving during that time as well.

EXERCISE

Imagine you are the CISO at company A. You need to improve the culture of security, as well as support and educate your users. Would you feel comfortable reporting or exposing a security issue? What would you do to address this?

Company A was a particularly challenging client to work with, as the culture of blame was so embedded across the organization. However, gradually implementing a number of changes—addressing password problems and working to educate and support users—slowly turned the situation around and reduced the number of data breaches they were suffering. Let's look in more detail at specific actions we can take to support and protect our users.

11.2 MFA

Passwords suck. They have always sucked, and they will continue to suck. Passwords are a terrible way of authenticating users. Standards bodies within the cybersecurity industry are constantly coming up with rules to create more complex passwords, which only makes them more likely to be forgotten or, even worse, reused across multiple sites. Developers then make the situation worse, with websites using "password strength" meters and having random requirements on what a password should contain.

Luckily, we've got a great deal of evidence on why passwords are such rubbish and why complex rules on passwords are counterproductive:

- A survey by Google in 2019 found that 65% of people reuse the same password across multiple sites and services.
- A Dashlane study in 2015 found that even 6 years ago, the average number of passwords a person had to remember was over 90.

In 2020, *Information Security Magazine* carried out a survey that showed

- 31% of people use the same password for streaming sites as they do for other "more sensitive" accounts, such as online banking.
- 52% share their streaming site passwords.
- 45% did not consider password reuse serious.

When we look at data breaches involving huge numbers of usernames and passwords—many tied to email addresses—we can get an idea of how serious the password problem is. In 2012, attackers breached Dropbox, stealing credentials for 68 million users. In an ironic twist, the attackers were able to get access via a Dropbox employee's account: the employee had reused their password on LinkedIn, which two years earlier had a breach resulting in stolen credentials for 164 million users.

The problem caused by passwords is huge, so what do we do? There are two immediate solutions to the problem of passwords that everyone should be using:

- *Password managers*—People should just have to remember one password, and we should focus extra protection on that one account. All other passwords can be automatically generated and stored in a password manager.

  The more complex a password is, the harder it is to memorize. The harder it is to memorize, the more likely we are to use the same password across multiple accounts and to write it down on a Post-it note stuck to our monitor. Password managers get around this by securely storing and managing the usernames, passwords, and other information you need to log in to websites and online accounts. Password managers require a single, strong password to manage access, and for extra security, all the passwords, usernames, and websites they store are encrypted. Password managers like LastPass and Bitwarden are available as standalone programs for your laptop or phone, as well as browser plugins, and can synchronize data across multiple accounts. Enterprise versions are available for companies to run themselves, allowing them to centrally control and manage the passwords their employees use to access internal systems.

- *MFA*—Back in chapters 4 and 5, we first looked at MFA, as well as at why SMS is an insecure form of MFA. Security tokens like a YubiKey provide an extra layer of security when entering a username and password. YubiKeys are small devices, like a slimmed-down memory stick; they are plugged into the USB port or use NFC to talk to your phone. Pressing your finger on the device activates it, and it generates a code that is automatically entered into your web browser. Tokens like YubiKeys are ideal because you can also use them to apply MFA to your password manager, thus adding an extra layer of security. An alternative to a physical token is software "authenticators," available for free from Google, Microsoft, and other companies, and also built into password managers. They use an algorithm to generate a six-digit, time-sensitive code, which is entered along with a username and password to securely log in to an application or system.

Combining MFA and password managers gives us a number of security benefits:

- Strong, complex passwords that we don't have to remember, reducing password reuse
- Strong MFA that is virtually impossible for an attacker to duplicate
- Easier, less disruptive workflow for users when logging in to systems or applications
- Ease of implementation for an entire organization

When looking at how we can move beyond passwords for authentication, we can use a combination of something we know, something we own, and something we are. Biometric data solutions—using our fingerprints, facial, and retina scans to authenticate—are expensive and complex when done correctly. This may be relevant and proportional to secure military installations, but expecting a user to have a retinal scan before buying something on Amazon is a tad excessive.

Combining something we know (our username and password) with something we own (a hardware token or a software authenticator on our mobile) strikes the best balance between complexity, cost, and usability (see figure 11.1).

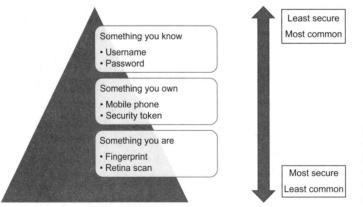

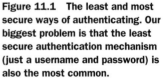

Figure 11.1 The least and most secure ways of authenticating. Our biggest problem is that the least secure authentication mechanism (just a username and password) is also the most common.

Biometric data solutions can be insecure when done cheaply, and actually dangerous if the threat isn't properly understood. Facial and fingerprint scans used to unlock mobile phones, for example, can be tricked by using photos or copies of fingerprints faked using gummy bears. The technology has improved in recent years, but a large number of mobile phones can still be unlocked with a photo printed out from Facebook.

The other problem with biometric data is that we can't change our fingerprints if they get stolen. If that asset has a high enough value, attackers and thieves will take more extreme measures. In 2005, a Malaysian businessman found this out the hard way when thieves cut off his finger to use his fingerprint to unlock his Mercedes S-Class.

EXERCISE

Our three concepts of cybersecurity model can be used to understand which forms of MFA would be most useful for us. First, let's remind ourselves of the model (figure 11.2). Our strategy for cybersecurity must be

- Relevant
- Proportional
- Sustainable

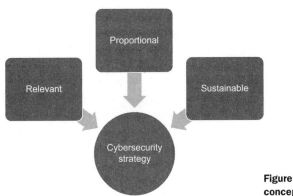

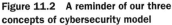

Figure 11.2 A reminder of our three concepts of cybersecurity model

Given three different types of MFA

- A security authenticator application installed on users' mobile phones
- Biometric retinal and fingerprint scanners
- YubiKey security tokens

which MFA solution would you apply to the following organizations?

- A small company of 100 employees, 80% of whom are a mobile sales force constantly traveling across the continental United States. They user their mobile phones constantly to keep in touch, talk to clients, and arrange sales meetings.

- A financial services organization of 600 employees, with a single big building in a large city. All employees have keychains with building access cards to gain entry.
- A research and development facility that carries out highly sensitive work. A small team of 20 scientists need regular access to the building. Their research is worth hundreds of millions of dollars.

These might seem like straightforward scenarios, but organization 1 was a client I worked with that was on the brink of deploying fingerprint scanners to all their sales team. Here's what we did:

- *Organization 1*—Installed security authenticator applications to everyone's mobile. The majority of the users were already constantly using their mobile phones, and this would have little disruption to their workflow while adding an extra layer of secure authentication.
- *Organization 2*—YubiKey security tokens made the most sense for this organization. Employees already had a building access card to get into the HQ, so they were used to carrying a physical token.
- *Organization 3*—With such valuable research at stake and such a small team, biometric retinal and fingerprint scanners were relevant and proportional to this organization.

Now that we've looked at how to protect users' credentials and ensure we effectively manage the problems around passwords, it's time to look at how we deal with the next biggest threat: ransomware.

11.3   *Protecting from ransomware*

Ransomware is one of the most effective—and therefore one of the most common—attacks at the moment. Every size of organization is being hit: from global consultancies like Accenture to critical national infrastructure like oil pipelines, all the way through to small companies being locked out of their office systems.

For ransomware to be effective, it needs to be installed, and to be installed, attackers leverage a number of the social engineering attacks we looked at in chapter 5. Knowing how attackers will work to trick people into installing ransomware gives us a few options to help protect people:

- *Install antimalware software.* This is the first line of defense, identifying and removing ransomware when it is copied to a machine.
- *Make it easy to install legitimate software.* We want to ensure that both business and personal users install valid copies of legitimate software, avoiding malicious copies that have been infected by attackers.
- *Install backups.* If the worst happens and we do suffer a ransomware attack, we want to minimize the impact by ensuring we have recent, clean backups of our system, applications, and data.

In most organizations, the first two rules are handled automatically by the central IT team. Even our own personal devices now default to automatically download and install the most recent operating system and application updates.

11.3.1 *Make sure everyone has antimalware software installed*

Antimalware software, sometimes called *end-point protection* (EPP), is available in both paid and free versions. Organizations should use management tools to ensure centrally managed antimalware is automatically installed on all devices.

For personal use, there's a range of trusted software, from vendors like Trend Micro, Kaspersky, Norton, McAfee, and others. Free solutions like Bitdefender and Avast are available, and built-in solutions like Microsoft Defender in Windows are perfectly adequate.

Use the app stores from the various manufacturers (Apple and Google Play app stores for mobiles, Apple and Microsoft app stores for Apple and Windows computers) to ensure that valid, security-checked versions of the software are being bought and installed.

11.3.2 *Make it easy to install legitimate software*

One of the most common routes for people to install ransomware (and other forms of malware) is installing pirated copies of software or software from a nonapproved source. A great example of this is the gaming app Pokémon GO. When it was first released, copies of the game with embedded malware were quickly shared outside the Google Play and Apple app stores. Using phishing emails or by spreading rumors of new features and unique Pokémon, attackers tricked users into downloading malicious versions of Pokémon GO. Attackers were then able to remotely control a user's mobile phone, gaining access to login credentials, personal data, and even banking applications.

One of the most pirated bits of software, Adobe Photoshop, has long been a rich target for injecting malware onto users' machines. The high cost combined with popularity of Photoshop means there has always been a large demand for illegitimate copies of the software. In 2021, a popular website for pirated software had 22 different versions of Photoshop for download; 18 of those contained ransomware or other malware.

The solutions are straightforward:

- For businesses
  - Automatically install the software your users need on their mobile phones and computers.
  - Make other software available via a central company "app store."
  - Use the tools within operating systems and mobile devices to block installation of software from other resources.
- For personal use
  - Android and Apple mobile phones all default to only allowing installation of software from the relevant companies' app stores—easy.

 – Both Microsoft and Apple have app stores for Windows and MacOS, respectively. Purchase and install software from these app stores to ensure it's been validated and security checked.

11.3.3 Backups

As Accenture found in 2021 when dealing with the LockBit ransomware attack, having up to date, regular backups makes it relatively easy to recover if the worst should happen. Large organizations like Accenture have tape backups of their systems and fileservers, with users storing their data in central locations. For small businesses or personal users, just copying our data to a cloud service like Dropbox or Google Drive isn't enough: ransomware running on our computers can access those drives and can therefore attack and encrypt our data there.

USB hard drives are cheap, portable, and easy to use. All operating systems now come with built-in backup software, and computer vendors like Lenovo and Dell bundle backup software with their machines. By disconnecting the external USB drive once a backup is complete, we ensure that if there is a ransomware infection, we can delete everything on the machine (or get a new one), reconnect the USB drive, and restore our data.

Specific guidance for ransomware is useful, but what else can we do to help protect people?

11.4 Education and support

Education and support is the make-or-break factor for any security team; it's the bar by which the long-term effectiveness of a security team is judged. At the start of this chapter, we looked at ways to build a culture of security, and user education and support was a key part of that effort. Let's look in more detail at how this could work.

11.4.1 Regular email newsletters

We've seen that cybersecurity is an arms race between attackers and defenders. The rate of change is huge, with new threats evolving on a weekly—sometimes even daily—basis. Security teams need to be informed and up to date on the latest developments, and so are perfectly placed to share that data with end users within the organization.

Our sales teams aren't going to be interested in how to reverse-engineer a power extension socket to become a listening device, but informing them of how a new phishing attack using scam calls works would definitely be of interest. Our newsletters need to be relevant and proportional if they're going to be sustainable. Simple bullet point lists or short paragraphs providing a summary are more than enough to keep people informed.

A fantastic example of a monthly security newsletter is Crypto-Gram, from security guru and cryptographer Bruce Schneier. You can subscribe and read previous issues at https://www.schneier.com/crypto-gram/. His newsletter does contain longer essays and opinion pieces, which might be a bit too much for your users, but it's a great example of how to make cybersecurity approachable and more easily understood.

11.4.2   Lunchtime talks

Some security topics are just too complex to condense into a paragraph or even an email—and many will benefit from a practical demonstration. Holding lunchtime talks on a regular basis has a number of benefits:

- Members of the security team get to show off their expertise and special areas of interest.
- Users get to learn about security in an interactive and involved way, which is much more effective than computer-based training (CBT).
- The security team gets a chance to explain a security threat in the context of the organization.

This last point is particularly valuable. A client I worked with pushed back over password security. As a small financial services consultancy, a major retailer having tens of millions of credit card numbers stolen just wasn't relevant. However, running a lunchtime session with a practical demonstration on how I could steal their credentials and the damage I could cause made the issue relevant and understood.

11.4.3   Security concierge or security champion

Having a member of the security team who is the contact point for rest of the organization can be very effective in improving an organization's culture of security. Users know they have someone they can approach with questions and for advice, and the person in the concierge role has some actionable data for the wider security team.

In many organizations, this would fall naturally to the CISO. Some places are too small to justify a full time CISO role; other companies might be so large that the CISO is too tied up at the executive and strategy level, so having a dedicated "face of security" beyond the CISO can be useful. For smaller organizations, this role can form part of someone's job description. For larger teams, it makes more sense to rotate the role through the team once a month.

This isn't just useful for educating the wider organization; it's also a great way to make the security function more visible. In too many organizations, security teams are invisible when everything is fine, and are first in the firing line when there's a breach. Having a visible security champion is a great way to address that.

11.4.4   Live exercises

In chapter 9, we looked at attack and defense exercises (red teams and blue teams) as a way of testing our security. Involving non-security people in these exercises is a great way of getting people to understand the often-hidden amounts of work that go into defending an organization. And on a purely selfish level, it's a great way to get the executive team to understand why they should be investing more in cybersecurity.

At the start of this chapter, we looked at the problem cybersecurity teams face: that people are an organization's biggest asset but at the same time are the most likely target for attackers. Implementing these different approaches to educating people within our organization—helping them become more aware of the threats they face and what can be done to mitigate them—is the most effective way to support and protect our people.

Summary

- By managing the tension between people being our most valuable asset and also our weakest security link, we can build a culture of security in our organization that protects people and encourages them to be proactive with security issues and processes.
- Passwords continue to suck. But MFA enables us to provide another level of authentication and security to basic passwords. Using physical MFA security tokens, we help our end users become more secure and more proactive about their security.
- We can provide relevant, proportional, and sustainable protection against ransomware attacks by ensuring our users have up-to-date antimalware software, by making it easy for them to install legitimate software, and by ensuring that we not only make regular data backups, but that we also check them, too.
- We can directly support our users by providing them with regular email newsletters and lunchtime talks and demos.
- Security champions and getting users involved in live security exercises are more proactive ways to get our users involved with, and learning from, the work that security teams often take for granted.

After the hack

12

This chapter covers

- Working through real-life breaches to understand how events unfold
- Who we can turn to for help during a security incident and how to derive the information we need to capture and share
- Using critical thinking skills and root-cause analysis
- Applying agile techniques to a security breach
- Distilling key actionable data that can be used to improve and enhance our security strategy

As mentioned in previous chapters, we will all get hacked. What's important is how we prepare for that, how we mitigate the risks we face, and—most important of all—how we recover after a successful attack. In this final chapter, we look at how to prepare to fail. Because we know that we will eventually face a security breach, we can use this "failure" to improve our organization's security.

Failing (i.e., having a security breach) should be a good thing. If approached in the right way, this failure can have big benefits. Let's see how.

12.1   *Responding to a breach*

So, the hackers have finally gotten in. Our security operations team has responded to the security incident and has recovered our systems and applications. Does that mean it's all over? What do we do next?

First, let's revisit a model we first looked at back in chapter 1: the OODA loop (figure 12.1). The OODA loop has four stages:

1 *Observe*—What is happening?
2 *Orient*—Based on what I know, analyze the situation.
3 *Decide*—What happens if I do this thing?
4 *Act*—Let's do that thing.

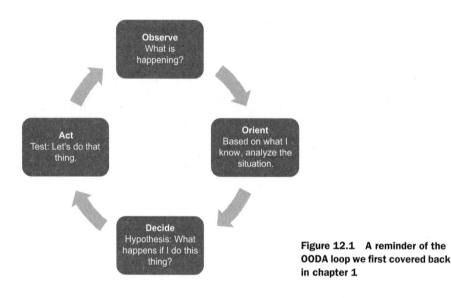

Figure 12.1   **A reminder of the OODA loop we first covered back in chapter 1**

The OODA loop is a powerful model to apply when dealing with the aftermath of a security breach. Later in this chapter, we'll look at how we can use the OODA loop to aid our root-cause analysis. For the moment, let's compare how the OODA loop and the US four-stage model for incident response complement each other (figure 12.2):

- *Observe* in the OODA loop complements the *preparation* stage in the NIST model.
- *Orient* covers the same actions as the *detection and analysis* stage.
- *Decide*, in this context, addresses the *containment, eradication, and recovery* stage: the decision is made for us (we must address the security breach), but the approach (how do we actually do that?) is where we can *decide* on the most appropriate way forward.
- *Act*, in this context, isn't about fixing the actual security breach; this maps to *post-incident activity*. The output of the feedback loop is to act to improve our cybersecurity and feed back into the observe/preparation stages.

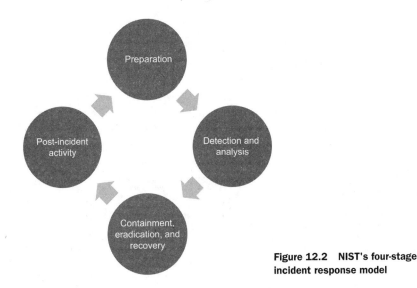

Figure 12.2 NIST's four-stage incident response model

We first looked at the NIST Incident Response model in chapter 10, but it remains relevant and useful even after a security breach has been addressed.

For dealing with post-incident issues—after the hack—the two most important parts of this model are as follows:

- *Preparation*—This may feel counterintuitive—how does preparation for incident response help with the aftermath?—but putting in the work up front to deal with a security breach is one of the most effective ways to address any post-incident work.
- *Post-incident activity*—This is where our preparation pays off. We need to understand who is responsible for which systems and software, how to restore data, and who we should alert.

So what does preparation need to involve? From the following list of items, which ones do you think should be covered in the preparation stage?

- Asset ownership business continuity process
- Data/system restore
- Public relations (PR)/media communications
- Internal notification/communication groups
- Customer communications policy
- Cyber insurance policies
- Legal team involvement/advice
- Law enforcement engagement policy
- Country-specific data controller communications

The correct answer is that all of these should be covered by the preparation stage. Let's dig into more detail on each one and see why they're so important.

12.1.1 Asset ownership

If we don't know who is responsible for an asset—who the business owner is—then how can we understand the business impact of a security incident? And if we don't understand the business impact, how can we recover our business services? Lots of organizations have a configuration management database (CMDB) where they store asset information. However, very few organizations have accurate and consistent information in their CMDB about who is responsible for these assets—who the business owner is. For an incident response process (and our security team!) to be effective, accurate asset ownership information is critical.

12.1.2 Business continuity process

Many organizations are stuck with the old-fashioned mind-set that technology (IT and security) is somehow separate from the rest of the business. The reality is that the whole point of IT and security functions is to support and maintain business services. Business continuity is about having a process, a plan, for how IT and security will work to restore the services our organization needs to function. A mistake many organizations make is to assume this means we can rebuild a web server or restore data from backup.

What business continuity processes should actually address is how we go from "this system has been restored" to "our customers are using our business services normally." Business continuity needs to involve not just the technology part, but also the communications policies that are covered later.

12.1.3 Data/system restore

Part of any business continuity process needs to cover how we restore systems, applications, and their associated data. More than just having backups, we need to know that those backups can actually be restored—or that our systems or applications can be rebuilt and redeployed. This means having a regular test run, where we try to restore/ rebuild our systems in a non-production environment. Only in this way can we prove that we could recover from a security incident.

12.1.4 PR/media communications

No matter how secretive we try to be, information on our security breach will be made public. That might be from irate customers complaining in headlines across major media, and could even be competitors bad-mouthing us. Many regulatory frameworks— like the EU's General Data Protection Regulation (GDPR)—not only require companies to report security breaches when involving personal data, but also impose strict timeframes in which the report must be made. This also includes informing customers.

Involving either our internal marketing team or, preferably, an external PR consultancy (with experience in crisis management) will help manage the sharing of information and ensure that the right things are communicated. I worked with a manufacturing organization who had an external group carry out a penetration test on an older product without their knowledge. The external group found serious flaws in the product, but even worse was that their communications to the manufacturing client asking for their feedback were somehow missed. The end result was that the external security group published their findings in the press.

The leadership team from the manufacturing client was outraged and wanted to immediately publish a full and detailed technical rebuttal of the findings. This would have been a terrible move because it would have not only fueled the story in the media, but it would also have made it about the external security group's findings and not about the ways that the manufacturing client had addressed the security flaws.

Luckily, the manufacturing client had engaged an external PR firm that specialized in this sort of situation. Following the PR firm's advice, the manufacturing client released a small statement and provided a detailed technical rebuttal as well as product roadmaps to the clients and partners. What could have been headline news—security flaw in a global manufacturer's main product—instead became a minor item on a handful of small websites. Customers and partners were pleased with the more direct and detailed information they got, and this in turn helped build more client loyalty and future product sales.

12.1.5 *Internal notification/communication groups*

Regular communications internally, throughout the life cycle of dealing with a security breach, means that key stakeholders across our organization are kept up to date on root cause, incident developments, and business impact. Having a prebuilt series of mailing lists, with backup details like home and mobile phone numbers, second points of contact, and whom can be delegated to, will save everyone time and effort when trying to keep the rest of the organization informed during and after a breach.

12.1.6 *Customer communications policy*

Organizations exist to provide customers (in whatever form that may be) with a service. If that service is disrupted, a clear, well-understood process for not only how to communicate with customers, but what to tell them, is needed. For example, if we need to involve law enforcement agencies, that might impact the level of detail we can initially share with customers about a security breach. It's equally important not to jump the gun and share details with customers before we have finished our investigation. Equifax found this out the hard way in 2017: with each public communication about the data breach, the numbers involved, the severity of the attack, and the data stolen continued to change. Eventually, despite initially saying no sensitive personal information had been stolen, Equifax admitted that data on 148 million people had been stolen, including credit card data and social security numbers.

12.1.7 *Cyber insurance policies*

Many organizations are turning to cybersecurity insurance policies to cover the costs of lost business, recovery, and reputational damage from a security breach. These are very different from standard business insurance policies, which now will explicitly exclude any cybersecurity-related claims. Working closely with our insurance provider is key to ensuring that we have a cybersecurity insurance policy that meets the needs of our business and provides the right level of coverage.

Many insurers are now also adding requirements and exclusions to their policies. Being able to demonstrate that our organization has a tested business continuity/recovery plan, for example, or external business certifications like ISO27001 or Cyber Essentials Plus, shows the organization has provable, tested, and audited security measures in place.

12.1.8 Legal team involvement/advice

There will always be legal repercussions from a security breach. Whether that's someone losing their job, the organization facing lawsuits from angry clients or partners, or the organization needing to sue a supplier or a partner, the legal team will always need to be involved. Whether we have in-house counsel or use an external law firm, we need to know who to contact and how to contact them.

12.1.9 Law enforcement engagement policy

A security breach, by its very nature, is a criminal act. But which law enforcement agency can prosecute it? And how do we engage with them? This is a complex area that varies significantly between countries, causing a headache for a multinational organization. Planning ahead for who to contact and how we should be engaging with law enforcement means that we will be in the best position to help them with a prosecution.

12.1.10 Country-specific data controller communications

The EU's General Data Protection Regulation (GDPR) defines responsibilities around the management and security of personal data being processed by an organization. Similar legislation, like the California Consumer Privacy Act (CCPA), exists outside the EU, while countries like Turkey, Mauritius, Chile, Japan, Brazil, South Korea, South Africa, Argentina, and Kenya have used the GDPR as a blueprint on which to base their own privacy legislation. All these regulations have specific requirements on how to report data breaches and whom to report them to.

Those last four are probably the most important, not least because they will be external third parties who need to be involved in our internal post-incident activity. In the next section, let's look at how we should work with them in more detail.

12.2   Where to get help?

Let's look in more detail at those four key groups we will need to work closely with after a security breach.

12.2.1 Cyber insurance providers

The costs and complexity of dealing with security breaches have soared: a report by IBM and the Ponemon Institute found that the average cost of dealing with a data breach in 2021 was \$4.24 million—a 10% increase from the average cost in 2019. Out of that, the post-breach response accounted for 27%—an average of \$1.14 million.

Insurance providers have moved on from covering cybersecurity attacks in normal business insurance and now have specialist cybersecurity insurance policies. These now have further exclusions: in 2021, Lloyd's of London carved out specific exclusions in their cybersecurity insurance policies for "acts of cyber-war" or state actors' retaliation attacks.

After suffering a devastating attack from NotPetya malware in 2017, Mondelez International sued their insurance provider, Zurich, for \$100 million in damages, after Zurich classified the malware as an "act of war" and said it was excluded from Mondelez's cyber insurance policy. Three years in and the case remains undecided, but it's clear that any organization that just "buys some cyber insurance" is going to be in trouble.

So, how can we ensure that our cyber insurance actually helps us rather than gives us a false sense of comfort? How can we use our security processes and models to ensure our cyber insurance is effective and our insurance provider can support us when cleaning up a security breach?

This is where the preparation stage of our incident response model helps. Specifically, we need to look at two key models we first covered back in chapter 2: the three factors of cybersecurity and the three concepts of a cybersecurity strategy (figure 12.3).

Figure 12.3   The three factors of cybersecurity model. It's time to apply it in a slightly different way: to our cyber insurance policy.

Preparation, like the wider approach to cybersecurity, needs to start with the basics:

- What assets do we have?
- Who would want to attack us?
- What defenses do we have?

Applying this model to the preparation stage sets us up to ensure that our cyber insurance policy meets the cybersecurity strategy three concepts (figure 12.4)—that the policy is

- *Relevant*—Does the cyber insurance policy cover the threats we face and the type of assets we have? There is no point in having a clause that covers assembly lines if our business writes software.
- *Proportional*—Does the policy provide the right amount of coverage? Does it provide coverage for the sort of attacks we face? For example, if our organization operates critical national infrastructure (CNI), we would expect to be attacked by state-sponsored or nation-state attackers. An insurance policy that doesn't cover those sorts of attacks wouldn't be proportional to our threats.
- *Sustainable*—How much do the policy premiums cost? What compliance activities does our organization have to carry out?

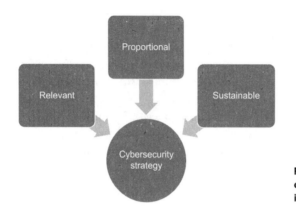

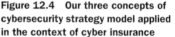
Figure 12.4   Our three concepts of cybersecurity strategy model applied in the context of cyber insurance

By applying these two models when considering a cyber insurance policy, we can achieve two main outcomes:

- We have a cyber insurance policy that is fit for our organization: one that's relevant, proportional, and sustainable.
- Our cyber insurance provider has a much better idea of the type of organization we are:
  - The assets we have
  - The threats we face
  - What our defenses are

This means they are in a much better position to support us if the worst happens and we need to make a claim. On top of this, specialist cyber insurance providers can connect us with relevant law enforcement teams, specialized legal advisors, and even specialized post-breach cybersecurity teams.

A few years ago, I worked with a specialist insurance provider in the UK on building exactly this sort of service. It makes no sense to have highly skilled and expensive digital forensics experts within our security operations teams: if the rest of us are doing our jobs correctly, the digital forensics people will spend 99% of their time sitting around with no work to do.

As part of the cyber insurance package, the insurance provider had a range of dedicated cybersecurity teams who could immediately go on site to an affected customer and carry out audits, security reviews, digital forensics, and even recovery operations, as well as provide help on a revised security strategy.

Having the correct cyber insurance provider, with policies that are relevant, proportional, and sustainable, can help with much more than simply covering the financial cost of cleaning up after a security breach.

12.2.2 Legal teams

In many ways, the legal team is the natural partner to the security team: their job is to protect the company. It is essential that the legal team be involved in not just the preparation stage but is also kept involved and informed at each stage and new development when responding to an incident.

Whether internal or an external third party, legal specialists can advise on how to manage and structure communications with clients, partners, and law enforcement. They will also be able to advise, post-incident, on whether any action can—or should—be taken against suppliers, partners, or other third parties who may have been involved in a security breach.

Supply chain attacks are becoming increasingly common. The largest occurred in 2020, when technology firm SolarWinds was breached. Attackers breached SolarWinds' internal systems and added malicious code to their product. This then allowed the attackers to compromise customer installations of that product: SolarWinds estimated some 18,000 customers were affected. Victims included the US Departments of Commerce, Defense, Energy, Homeland Security, State, the Treasury, and Health, as well as private firms, including Microsoft, Intel, Cisco, Nvidia, VMware, and Belkin.

Having our legal team involved at every stage is vitally important, as they can advise and support at all stages of a breach—from ensuring a supplier contract contains security clauses covering breaches, compromised code, and business continuity to understanding whether a supplier of compromised tools could be sued to recover some of the breach costs.

12.2.3 Law enforcement agencies

This can be a complicated area, where local knowledge of the geographic areas that our organization operates in is important. At a high level

- Identify which agency in the country our organization is based in deals with cybercrime.
- If our organization operates in more than one location, identify the agency responsible within each location.
- Nominate a named individual in each geographic location to liaise with local law enforcement as needed.

  Sometimes this can be the CISO, the data protection officer (DPO), or someone from the legal team.

- Document the process for contacting and engaging law enforcement to report and escalate a security breach.
- Regularly review this information (at least twice a year) to ensure it is accurate and up to date.

In the UK, the main agency to contact is the National Cyber Security Center (NCSC). In the US, it's the Federal Bureau of Investigation (FBI). Within the EU, our first point of contact should be Europol, which can then direct us to the relevant agency in our local Member State. Other countries will have similar agencies.

The method of reporting and engaging with law enforcement is the same:

- Always ensure that the action has been discussed with the leadership team (CISO, CTO, and CEO, at a minimum) and that our organization's legal team is fully involved.
- Ensure we have clear records of who, what, how, and which systems or applications have been impacted.
- Be clear on the goal:
  - Do we need to engage law enforcement as part of our cyber insurance policy requirements?
  - Does regulatory compliance require us to report the breach to law enforcement?
  - Does our organization operate CNI? (E.g., is our organization a telecoms company, electricity supplier, transport network, or hosting provider?)
- What is the outcome?
  - Do we need help from law enforcement to resolve the breach?
  - Do we want to prosecute the attackers?
  - Do we just need to report the breach to comply with our insurance policy requirements?

One thing we need to be prepared for is to hand over evidence to law enforcement. To do this effectively—in other words, so that law enforcement has evidence they could submit in court—we need to comply with something called the *chain of custody*.

Chain of custody refers to the logical steps that record the sequence of custody, control, transfer, analysis, and disposition of evidence so that it's suitable for submission as evidence in a court case. Breaching the chain of custody means that the evidence supplied could be ruled inadmissible.

Just like criminal investigations use forensic evidence (popularized by US shows like *CSI*), within cybersecurity we use digital forensics to collect and manage digital evidence. The chain of custody process involves four main steps (figure 12.5):

1 *Data collection*—This is where the chain of custody process starts. In this stage, we need to collect, identify, label, and record all relevant information while preserving the integrity of the data and evidence.

Figure 12.5 The chain of custody four-stage process

2 *Examination*—In this stage, we examine the collected data, detailing how we carry out the examination, making sure to document the tasks we carry out and any evidence that's uncovered.

3 *Analysis*—Here, we review the collected evidence from the previous stage, pulling out any information and resulting evidence that could help a prosecution.

4 *Reporting*—This is the final stage, which produces the final report. At a minimum, this report should include the following:

   – A statement regarding chain of custody
   – An explanation of the various tools used
   – A description of the analysis of various data sources
   – Issues identified
   – Vulnerabilities identified
   – Recommendations for additional forensic measures that can be taken

Accompanying all of this should be the chain of custody form. The exact contents vary depending on geographic location and the depth of analysis that's taking place, but it should at least cover the following:

- What is the evidence?
- How did you get it?
- When was it collected?
- Who has handled it?
- Why did that person handle it?
- Where was it stored?
- How was it transported?
- How was it tracked?
- How was it stored?
- Who has access to the evidence?

For many organizations, only the data collection stage is relevant, as this information is then handed off to law enforcement for the examination, analysis, and reporting phases. The basics of the data collection process should ensure that we

- Save the original material
- Take photos of the physical evidence
- Take screenshots of the digital evidence
- Document the date, time, and any other information on the receipt of the evidence

As we can see, things can quickly get complex—and that's before we involve multiple law enforcement agencies across different countries. Good practice is to ensure that at the preparation stage of any incident response planning, the relevant law enforcement agencies are identified and their guidance is sought on exactly how they require incidents to be reported and escalated, as well as their preferred approach for data collection.

12.2.4 *Country-specific data controller organizations*

Good planning and a solid understanding of the data protection regulations are also very important. As we've already discussed, there are a number of different data privacy regulations across the globe. However, as most are either based on, or use concepts of, the EU's GDPR, we'll look at that as an example. Article 33 (https://gdpr -info.eu/art-33-gdpr/) of the GDPR lays out an organization's responsibilities when it comes to a security breach involving personal data:

- The data breach must be reported to the supervising authority of the relevant EU Member State.
- This must be reported within 72 hours after becoming aware of the breach.

So, what is personal data? To summarize the GDPR definition, personal data includes information that relates to a natural person, such as their name, contact details, financial information, or health records, as opposed to intellectual property or company details.

To manage our compliance, our organization should have a nominated DPO who is an expert on the GDPR and data privacy regulations. The DPO has their hands full; they need to

- Monitor the organization's compliance with data privacy and protection regulations
- Inform and advise on our data protection obligations
- Provide advice regarding data protection impact assessments (DPIAs)
- Act as a contact point for data subjects (e.g., for fielding subject access requests)
- Act as the contact point for the relevant supervising authority (e.g., in the UK this would be the Information Commissioner's Office [ICO])

The moment we discover that our security breach involves personal information, our security team needs to involve our DPO, who then has to manage reporting the breach and ongoing communications and status updates with the relevant supervisory authority.

The GDPR is viewed as the strictest data privacy legislation—one of the reasons it's been used as the basis for so many other data privacy and protection laws across the globe. Whichever data privacy legislation our organization needs to deal with, it's important for security teams to work closely with their legal team and DPO to plan out and test the processes for managing post-incident communications.

12.2.5 *Hosting providers*

Often forgotten, CSPs and hosting providers running our data centers should be one of the external organizations we work most closely with. Not only are they hosting our infrastructure—giving them potentially much greater visibility into an attack—but they will also have specialist security tools, dedicated security teams, and existing relationships with law enforcement agencies. Hosting contracts should have clauses that address responding to and escalating security issues, with information on dedicated contacts and the reporting and escalation process.

Obviously, the preparation stage of our incident response planning should also include a contract review of all hosting contracts to ensure that security incidents and reporting are properly addressed.

EXERCISE

Chain of custody issues can be complex, even for security people who are trained in digital forensics. In this quick quiz, see if you can identify the correct approach for ensuring the chain of custody in each situation:

1 A virtual machine (VM) has been breached using some custom malware. You need to send a sample of the malware to law enforcement. How should you capture it?

    a Log on to the VM and try to find the malware to copy it to a USB drive.

    b Shut down the VM and make a backup to tape.

    c Take a live snapshot of the VM and send the copy to law enforcement.

2 Customer credit card data was copied from our database server via an XSS attack. We need to send the database server log files to law enforcement. How should we do that?

    a Export the log files from our SIEM system along with a chain of custody document detailing how the logs were captured and exported.

    b Write a script that connects to the database server, archives all the log files, and then copies them to another, non-production server. We can then send the log file archive and the script we used.

    c Log in to the database server and manually copy all log files to a USB stick, and then send that to law enforcement.

3 How could we further ensure the integrity of the log files (extra credit)?

    a We could use software to create a secure checksum of each file and document the process and tool used. During the examination stage, law enforcement could follow this document to reproduce an identical hash value, confirming the logs haven't been altered.

    b We could encrypt the log files and securely send law enforcement the encryption keys so they can decrypt the log files.

    c No further action is needed; we have documented how and where we captured the log files, and that satisfies our chain of custody requirements.

ANSWERS

1 **c** is the correct answer here. Taking a live snapshot of the VM means we maintain all of the state of the virtual machine: the memory contents, programs being executed, and all data. Any other actions could modify or even overwrite critical log files or remove malicious applications that might be running in memory.

2 **a** is the correct answer. Our chain of custody document would detail the technical measures we used to securely transmit and store log files on our SIEM, as well as how we used the SIEM's tools to securely export the relevant logs.

3   a would be the right approach here. Using checksum calculations ensures that the law enforcement team can prove that the files haven't been modified.

Now that we've looked at our different options for getting some extra help, let's look at what we do next.

12.3   *What to do next?*

This section builds on what we learned in chapter 10 when looking at security operations. Our goal is to not only successfully restore business service (recover from the security breach) but to also ensure that breach doesn't happen again.

Many organizations make the mistake of thinking that this means we apply some patches, addressing the security vulnerability that was the root cause of the breach. These same organizations end up dealing with breach after breach, while playing a game of technology whack-a-mole, constantly trying to deploy patches.

Our security operations team and security breach response will have gathered a mass of actionable data and can then use that to improve our security. If this sounds familiar, it's because this fits into our OODA loop model we first looked at in chapter 1 and have used throughout the book.

Let's quickly revisit what the OODA loop is and then see how we can use this to minimize the chance of another security breach. When we apply the OODA loop model (figure 12.6) to our post-breach activity, the actions in each of the four stages have a slightly different focus:

- *Observe*—What happened before, during, and after the security breach?
- *Orient*—After analyzing all the data we gathered, what was the root cause?
- *Decide*—How will we address the root cause to not only stop similar breaches occurring but also improve our overall security posture?
- *Act*—Implement our changes and test their impact.

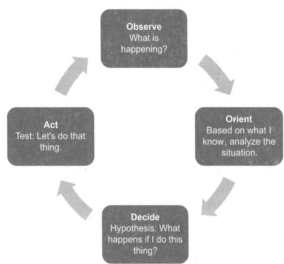

Figure 12.6   The OODA loop model. Here, we'll use it to aid us in root-cause analysis of our security breach.

Essentially, we're using the OODA loop to carry out root-cause analysis, avoiding looking only at the symptoms of the security breach ("Our customer data was copied from our database!") and instead looking at where the problem really lies ("We didn't monitor this web server for XSS attack attempts, and we didn't check out code for XSS issues"). This root-cause analysis is what makes a security operations team—and their associated incident response actions—effective. Many organizations waste millions of dollars on huge teams of security people who do nothing but scan for software vulnerabilities and then apply security patches. Not only is this a Sisyphean task—something that's impossible to complete—but it also diverts resources away from thinking strategically about security. These organizations are stuck in a mode of being reactive to security issues when they badly need to be proactive.

12.4 Lessons learned

Agile software development has the concept of a *retrospective*: a session where the team reviews how things have been going and how they can be improved. Lots of security processes and models—like the vulnerability life cycle management model we looked at in chapter 10—have this concept of working through "lessons learned" in dealing with a security incident.

The Agile model of a retrospective is a much more effective way of reviewing incident response activities. A retrospective encourages both technical and non-technical teams to have an open, honest, and blame-free discussion of how the response to the security incident went. By encouraging participation from all involved—not just the security teams—we can gather valuable actionable data that would otherwise be missed from a traditional "lessons learned" session with the security and IT teams.

Getting actionable data this way isn't just valuable when looking at how we responded to a security breach; we can also feed this back into our overall security strategy. Let's quickly remind ourselves of the security strategy model we first looked at in chapter 2 (figure 12.7).

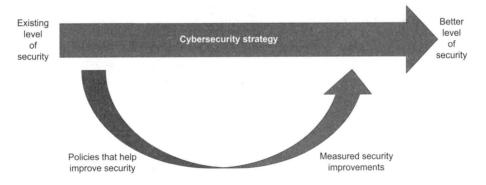

Figure 12.7 A reminder of how a good cybersecurity strategy (one that is relevant, proportional, and sustainable) improves our level of security

The goal of any cybersecurity strategy is to take us from our existing level of security to a better level of security. We can achieve this by formulating security policies that help improve security while measuring the security actions we implement to ensure they are improving our overall security.

It's clear that gathering actionable data from a post-security breach retrospective can be very valuable for our overall cybersecurity strategy. But how does an agile retrospective apply to a security breach?

Before we get started, we need to ensure the right people are involved. Obviously, the security team involved in dealing with the security breach should be there, but we should also involve

- Business service and asset owners who were affected by the breach
- Stakeholders from the leadership team
- Product owners, where the breach affected/was caused by our own products
- Stakeholders from the customer service and/or sales teams—people who deal with customers face to face
- Someone from the legal and marketing/PR teams

All these people are traditionally not involved in a purely technical "lessons learned" review of a security breach, but as we've seen, they all play key roles in managing and resolving a security breach, and that means they will have valuable insight into how to improve our response.

Let's look at the four key questions we have to address in a security retrospective:

- *What went well?* We should always start by identifying and acknowledging success. By identifying what went well—and why—we can then use these parts as blueprints for other security activities.
- *What could have gone better?* Nothing is ever perfect. Without assigning blame, what needed improvement?
- *What do we need more of?* Now that we know what went well, how can we use that information to improve things?
- *What do we need less of?* Now that we know what could have gone better, how can we use that information to improve things?

A good retrospective should give us a well-rounded list of technical and nontechnical items that we can feed back into our security strategy, as well as our vulnerability management and incident management processes, helping us refine and improve their effectiveness.

EXERCISE

Building on what we've learned so far, let's work through an exercise looking at how we can apply the concept of an agile retrospective to a security breach and how we can use this to feed actionable data back into our security strategy.

SCENARIO

Our organization suffered a security breach—a team of hackers from eastern Europe used an XSS attack to extract customer credit card data from our main database. This information was then sold on the Dark Web, and a number of our customers suffered identity fraud and financial loss.

The project was scheduled to add the web server logs to the security operations team's SIEM system but was delayed as the business owner of the web server couldn't be identified. The database logs were already added to the SIEM, which was how the security operations team identified the breach.

Once the breach was identified, the security team worked with development, and a version of the website code, with the XSS issue fixed, was deployed to production four hours after the incident was first identified.

The revised code not only fixed the XSS issue that led to the breach, but the developers also found and fixed two other XSS issues.

For the incident retrospective, what would you say

- Went well?
- Could have gone better?
- We need more of?
- We need less of?

There are no hard and fast answers here, but a retrospective should have covered:

- What went well?
  - The fast deployment of the security patch.
  - That the developers found and fixed two other XSS issues in the code.
- What could have gone better?
  - Not having the web server logs in the SIEM would have delayed and made more difficult the initial detection and identification of the breach.
  - Not knowing who the business owner of the web server asset was.
- What do we need more of?
  - The proactive work of the developers in spotting the extra XSS issues. Could there be security tools we could give them—as part of their development workflow—to help automate this process?
- What do we need less of?
  - Less inaccurate asset and configuration information. Work should be started to quickly identify which assets don't have a business owner and to work out who is responsible for those assets.

Summary

- The most effective way to respond to a security breach is by preparing to fail. Applying the NIST incident response model enables us to effectively plan for and review our incident response.

- When responding to a breach, we need to understand who is responsible for which systems and software, how to restore data, and who we should be alerting.
- We need to effectively communicate with and get help and support from external third parties: the insurance providers, legal teams, law enforcement groups, and data-protection authorities.
- Improving our response: by applying Agile retrospective principles to our review process, we can gather valuable actionable data we can use to improve our overall security posture.

index